FINDING MY GROOVE

Enjoy!

Life, Love, & Lyrics

LARRY AMSTUTZ

FriesenPress

One Printers Way
Altona, MB R0G 0B0
Canada

www.friesenpress.com

First Edition — 2022

ISBN
978-1-03-913408-9 (Hardcover)
978-1-03-913407-2 (Paperback)
978-1-03-913409-6 (eBook)

1. BIOGRAPHY & AUTOBIOGRAPHY, PERSONAL MEMOIRS

Distributed to the trade by The Ingram Book Company

This book is dedicated to my brother Davey,
who will be with me every moment of my life.
February 18, 1957 – October 11, 2021
I love you, Bro.

Introduction

Lyrics have been the poetry of my life. Take Gordon Lightfoot writing, "…the sidewalk is a shoulder for her tears," or John Denver expressing mystery: "He was born in the summer of his 27th year / Coming home to a place he'd never been before," or Van Morrison: "I can hear her heartbeat for a thousand miles." Music has always touched my soul.

Voices as pure and powerful as k.d. lang's, as expressive as Ray Charles's, and as universally loved as Bob Marley's have stirred my emotions, and I have been blown away by Stevie Ray Vaughan's guitar wizardry.

Each chapter of my life has been marked by different songs and artists. Hopefully my "album cuts" will remind you of a moment in your life when you were moved to smile, to dance, or to reflect. If a cut is unfamiliar, I encourage you to take a listen.

When I was a child, my mother read stories to us, and when we were able to read, we read them back to her; since then, books have always been in my hands. Although she had a formal education up to only grade eight, she would order books through the mail to read, and I would read everything that came to her. My mother's impact on my life through books and music can never be overstated.

I have changed the names of all characters in the book to protect their privacy and have chosen in some instances to alter names of companies or towns for the same reason.

Rock on!

Contents

Island Boy

<u>Album Cut</u>:
"Into the Mystic"
Van Morrison
***Moondance*, released 1970**

TO THIS DAY I DEFINE myself as an "Island boy," although I have now lived more years away from Vancouver Island than on it. My earliest imprint was a lasting one. Vancouver Island is beautiful, wild, rugged, pastoral, forested, and cosmopolitan—four hundred and sixty kilometres long, from Cape Scott's windswept beaches and rugged headlands at the northern tip to Victoria, the placid capital city of British Columbia at the southern end, with Tofino, Long Beach, and Ucluelet on the world-renowned West Coast. I have always thought of the shape of the Island as like a long potato, running parallel along the British Columbia Mainland, more or less from north to south. My soul has always pulled me back toward the Island. I was born there and have lived, worked, and played in every corner.

I have always considered myself a regular guy, although my mom gave me the uncommon name Larry. It was not her first choice; she'd wanted to call me Ronald and my twin brother

Donald. My dad had a problem with having a "Ronnie and Donnie" running around the house and put the brakes on her choice. While my twin brother kept Donald, it continues to be a family mystery as to why Mom came up with my name. Funny I never thought to ask my parents while I had the opportunity.

Everyone has their own mysteries, and their own individual questions; but *everyone* also asks the Universal Question, "What if?" For instance, "What if I had not gone into broadcasting?" Asking myself this question proves how tricky the "what if" question can become. First, I need to look back at how I made the decision in the first place. I got the idea of being a radio DJ (or deejay, both short for disc jockey) by riding a school bus in my teens, listening to AM Top 40 radio stations in Vancouver; CFUN and CKLG were the big two, with Fred Latremouille, "Doc" Harris, Tom Lucas, the "Real" Roy Hennessy, and even "The Raccoon." It struck me that the best job in the world would be to listen to music all day and be famous like my heroes. But what if I had never ridden the school bus? What if the bus driver had refused to put the radio on for the forty-five-minute ride each way? What if my parents had not moved to the logging camp forty-five minutes from school in the first place, forcing us to ride the school bus? What if my dad never had immigrated to Canada? Would I have ever dreamt of becoming a radio star?

Following the multitude of possible threads makes my head spin. It becomes apparent very quickly that other people and their actions, intertwining with your own, expand the possibilities endlessly. As a big science fiction fan from a kid, I have always been intrigued by the idea of endless dimensions and timelines. I realize that even if I could have controlled my actions better or had made different decisions throughout my life, there is nothing I could have done about the infinite number of interactions with others along the way.

As we get older, we begin to ponder more of the "big" questions:

- How did my parents meet?
- Why did my dad leave his family behind in Europe to come to Canada?
- Why does no one talk to Uncle Phil?

Paul and May

<u>Album Cut</u>:
"When I'm Sixty-Four"
The Beatles
***Sgt. Pepper's Lonely Hearts Club Band*, released 1967**

LIKE MOST PEOPLE, I LEARNED my earliest life lessons (some much more painful than others) from my parents. Because these lessons happened too early for me to remember, my parents took pleasure in telling me about them much later: "Larry, one day when you were a baby in your highchair, you reached over to Don's highchair to get something to eat off his tray, and you fell out and cracked your skull." My mom May never filled in too many blanks when she relayed this story; it is entirely possible that I did not reach over for my twin brother's food out of greed (the first thing people think). Perhaps instead Mom simply mixed us up and thought she had fed me already and I was just hungry. I mean, she told me that she would sometimes give Don my medicine or punish him, thinking it was me.

My mom was a farm girl from Spirit River in northern Alberta, with sixteen siblings and three half-siblings. Apart from working hard on the farm, she had a love of softball from a girl, playing with her family in the summer evenings after the chores were complete. Later in her thirties, she played on a women's softball team in Lake Cowichan; we had moved there when I was about five years old. My parents had moved to Vancouver Island, I had been born in Campbell River in February 1957, and we lived in Cumberland while my dad was a civilian cook at the air force base in Comox. I have very few memories of my life in Cumberland. Today it is still a sleepy community synonymous with hippies, pot, and quaint shops.

My earliest memories came from when I was about four years old living at Mahatta River, a tiny logging camp accessible only by float plane. We lived in one of a grouping of float-houses secured to the shoreline by cables with a walkway to shore. I am not sure if Mom was ever anxious about having four youngsters from two to four years old living on the ocean in a floating house.

Bingo was popular in every small community. It was easy to set up and operate, anyone could play it, it was fun, and there was always the possibility of winning a jackpot. Mom loved bingo. In Mahatta River, bingo night was Wednesday, and Mom left my dad Paul in charge so she could get a break from her four children and to enjoy adult company. One Wednesday she came home and found me extremely sick, vomiting, and restless. She instantly took care of me and thought nothing of it. However, the next Wednesday after bingo she came home to find me sick again. She asked Dad if he knew why I was sick two weeks in a row. His answer did not go over well: "Larry likes to sit up with me and smoke cigarettes when you are gone." Mom quickly established new rules; neither Dad nor I came away unscathed. Although both my parents were smokers for the majority of their lives, I never did smoke. Maybe Dad had something in his strategy.

Lake Cowichan also had a men's senior softball team, and the whole community would turn out to the ball field in the summer. One warm, sunny, summer day, our whole family was in the bleachers enjoying a game. I would have been about ten years old. There was the usual activity in the bleachers: people talking, eating hot dogs, and booing the umpire for his calls. I made the mistake of following suit and yelled as loudly as I could to the opposing pitcher, "What's the matter, Pitcher, you sick or something?" My dad reacted instantly, taking me from my seat in the bleachers with the family to sit in the car and reflect on how to behave. He left me there to sit for the remainder of the game by myself. I have never forgotten that moment or the lesson; talk about tough love!

My parents were kind and loving, each having their own role. For segments of our life, Dad worked away from home. He would leave, while the family was sleeping, on Monday morning at about three o'clock and come home for a late dinner on a Wednesday evening, and then leave the next morning at about three o'clock to return home for dinner on Friday. This was our life from when I was five until I was twelve years old.

It is funny how the simplest of life's activities can bring back memories, isn't it? Washing my face with icy water from my bathroom sink the other day instantly brought me back to summer when I was ten years old. Dad brought me to camp with him one Monday morning during summer break from school. He woke me up at 2:45 in the morning, ushered me to the bathroom, and told me to wash my face with icy water so that I would wake up. I obediently turned on the tap and was awake in an instant, with water running off my nose. Mom had packed clothes for me the night before, and I quietly left the house with Dad so as to not wake up any of our family, who were slumbering and oblivious to our departure. Once on the gravel logging road, the car's headlights brought to life every dip in the road and every pothole. Dad told me to keep my eyes open for deer, bears, or even cougar. It was a wonderfully effective way for me to stay awake during the forty-five-minute drive.

Once at camp, Dad took me to his bunkhouse room to drop our bags. The room had two single beds end to end with the headboards on opposing walls. The footboards were tall enough to make a barrier between the beds so two men sharing the room would have more privacy. The toilet, sink, and shower were situated through a door on the wall across from the beds. A similar door opened into the bathroom from the next room down the hall, as four men shared the bathroom when the bunkhouse was full. As my dad was the cook, he never had to share a room, making it possible to bring me along.

It was a wonderful experience. I went with Dad into the cookhouse and watched him start up all of the stoves and ovens and begin preparing breakfast for the loggers. At the same time, he also began his daily baking, particularly bread doughs that needed to rise. I was able to enjoy every morsel of Dad's lofty and fluffy pancakes with syrup and crispy bacon for breakfast, washed down with hot chocolate. After breakfast, while Dad was working, I had the freedom to roam up and down the bunkhouse and go see Steve, who was the bullcook who lived at the opposite end of the building. Steve was a bachelor and always had Pepe and Chico, his two Pomeranians, under his coat jacket anywhere he went. He also had a room to himself, and loggers would gravitate to his room after work, as he had a small fridge and would sell cold pop and chips to the loggers, making his room a happy hub of activity and stories. Dad also took me over to play with kids from one of the families who lived in camp, who in turn fed me lunch and took me to the lake to swim. Dad collected me after his afternoon break, and we returned to the cookhouse in time for dinner. I was able to choose anything I wanted from what Dad had prepared. There were always three entrée selections to choose from. It might be roast beef, spaghetti with meat sauce, and fried chicken to choose from. After dinner and the ensuing cleanup, Dad would head back to the bunkhouse, remove his white uniform, have a shower, and put on his regular clothes. Dad always wore slacks. I never saw my dad in blue jeans. On days when dad would come home from work, my dad always had a familiar and welcoming smell of the cookhouse, combined with his sweat and the remnants of the Old Spice aftershave he always wore. After dinner on Wednesday evening, we packed up and drove home to Mom, my adventure complete.

My dad was a baker by trade, having come to Canada in 1951 at the age of twenty-one. He had apprenticed in Switzerland, later working at a bakeshop in Bern. He had left his mother, father, two brothers, and three sisters behind in Altkirch, France. My great-great-grandparents originated from Sigriswil, Switzerland, and Dad always identified as Swiss, even though he was born in the tiny French village of Bettendorf.

I am unclear why he decided to leave his family; perhaps living through the Nazi occupation of France as a teenager compelled him. Perhaps it was to make it easier for his family with one less mouth to feed. Perhaps he did not want to do his obligatory annual stint in the Swiss army after turning eighteen, which he did at least once and did not enjoy. Perhaps he simply wanted adventure.

His original plan was to travel to an Italian seaport with two Hungarian friends—no small feat in those days following the Second World War. His two friends had tickets on a ship heading to Australia and offered to smuggle him aboard as a stowaway. When they arrived at their destination in Italy, they engaged a dock worker to row my dad out to the ship in the middle of the night. However, when the night arrived, there were too many soldiers with machine guns patrolling the docks, and it became too risky to chance taking him out. So, the unfolding events forced Dad's hand; he turned around with the little money he had left, his friends and dreams of Australia behind him, and found his way back home alone.

A family friend in Switzerland, Miss Launer, had provided him room and board when he was about seventeen and apprenticing as a baker. After completing his apprenticeship and working at a bakeshop in Bern, he made his way back home to France. After his failed attempt to reach Australia, he turned to her, and she generously offered to pay his way to leave Europe, but stipulated he had to go to Canada. Thus, he arrived in November 1951 at a dock in Quebec City after suffering a gruelling, seven-day crossing of the North Atlantic, seasick for a good portion of the way. He made his way to Montreal and got a job at a hotel as a baker. He had a small room to stay in, with little heat, one blanket, and ice frosting the windows. Fortunately, he was able to secure a better accommodation once he was able to save part of his pay.

Dad stayed in Montreal for nearly a year and a half, and while there he met a group of other Swiss emigrants—"six guys and one girl," as he described them (when Dad told this story to me decades later, he could not remember their names, except his friend Kurt). They made the mutual decision to hitchhike their way across Canada to get to Vancouver. Each day they picked an end point, and one of them would hitchhike with "the girl," who was always able to secure a ride from passing motorists quickly. The two of them would arrive at the destination and wait for the others to catch up. The next day, someone else would hitchhike with "the girl." Once they eventually made their way to Vancouver, one of the guys and "the girl" ended up getting married, while Kurt became Dad's best friend.

Kurt was a nice man whose hometown was St. Gallen, Switzerland, and when my parents were married, Kurt was my dad's best man. I loved it when we were kids and Kurt or one of Dad's other Swiss friends would visit, as they always brought candy for us, and Dad would spend hours speaking with them in Swiss German. I could never understand any of what they said but was fascinated that my dad knew more than one language. Decades later, when Kurt passed away and my dad was too unwell to travel to Vancouver, I stood at his graveside and said goodbye to Dad's longtime friend on behalf of our family.

When Dad arrived in Canada, he spoke virtually no English and limited French, as his family spoke Swiss German at home. I can understand now how much these visits with Kurt and other Swiss friends meant to him, including the opportunity to speak his native language. With little money and no friends or family, he started his new life with tremendous uncertainty. His courage and strength I greatly admire; I have never been adventurous and know in my heart that I would not have done what he had done. I might have left home to help the family but would have found work in my own country. I am immensely proud of him and extremely glad he immigrated to Canada.

Just think of all the "what if" questions, the big one being: What if he had made it onto that boat in Italy and ended up in Australia? (Perhaps the Aussies would have sent him back, and he might still have found his way to Canada.)

Saturday nights were family nights in front of the TV. At four p.m. was the *Bugs Bunny/Road Runner Hour* (I loved that "wascally wabbit") and then *Hockey Night in Canada*. Dad was a Montreal Canadiens fan, as was my younger brother Peter. At ten years old in 1967, I watched Dave Keon, Normie Ullmann, George Armstrong, and the Toronto Maple Leafs win the Stanley Cup. Dave Keon was my favourite, and the Leafs became my favourite team. From that moment on, I became one of the millions of long-suffering fans who took grief wherever they went. But most importantly, it meant noisy, exuberant Saturday nights in our living room watching the Leafs vs. les Canadiens on our black-and-white television. As a professional speaker decades later, I would joke that the biggest failing I had as a parent was that my son David became an enormous Canadiens fan. His grandpa would have had a good laugh.

My first memory of my dad's work was in Cumberland on Vancouver Island, when he cooked at the Royal Canadian Air Force base in nearby Comox. An early memory from then: I remember Dad coming into the bedroom after work with three of the paper hats they had to wear in the cookhouse (in the style you see air force cadets wearing)—one each for me and my brothers. I was about four years old at the time. I remember picking up the hat and putting it on sideways; I thought it was a nurse's cap and cried that it was not for me. Dad kindly put it properly on his head and showed me how to wear it. I was embarrassed but then happily wore it until it fell apart.

From Cumberland, I remember us moving to Lake Cowichan, as Dad got a job as the cook/baker at the Crown Zellerbach Camp 3 logging camp. It was at the north end of Cowichan Lake at a company-owned community called Nitinat. Further down the logging roads was the Ditidaht First Nation community on Nitinat Lake, now world-famous as a kiteboarding destination. When we moved to Lake Cowichan, ten years since his landing at the dock in Quebec City, Dad was thirty-one. Lake Cowichan was and still is a small community of about thirty-five hundred people. When we were young, it was booming with primary industry—sawmills at Mesachie Lake and Honeymoon Bay, and the biggest at Youbou surrounding Cowichan Lake. At the top end sat two logging communities, Nitinat and Caycuse. Countless logging, lumber, and chip trucks would roll by our window day and night when I was a kid. Trucks still rumble through town today, partially supporting the local economy, but the camps and sawmills are ghosts of the past. Recreational development around the lake has now brought in seniors, and wealthier people from the Mainland, looking for lakefront getaways.

Over the years, and especially later as an adult, I pieced together an idea of what work Dad did in between his landing at the dock in Quebec and arriving at Lake Cowichan. Although trained as a professional baker in Switzerland, once he arrived in Vancouver he had to start at the bottom as a "flunky," doing basic kitchen help. He worked in the far north on the DEW (Distant Early

Warning) Line as a cook—surviving a crash landing in a DC-3 and a fire that burned down the cookhouse after someone filled the cookstove with airplane fuel rather than regular diesel. He also worked at construction camps at the smelter in Kitimat and at the Lajoie Dam.

Years later he met my mother, and they were married on December 15, 1956, with my twin brother Don and I born a couple of months later in February 1957. We were followed by my sister Eve less than a year later in January 1958. After my dad was unable to find work for months following Eve's birth, the family moved to be close to my mother's family in Spirit River in the Peace River Country of northern Alberta. Hearing of Dad's struggles, his friend Kurt called him and encouraged him to go with him to work for an American oil company in Iran; he told him that it would be good money and give Dad a chance to support his family. So, with no other options and with three kids and one on the way, Dad left on an eighteen-month contract. After nine months, he could not bear being away longer; with a bit of a financial stake, he left Iran and journeyed back to Spirit River, meeting my youngest brother Peter (who had been born while he was away) for the first time in January 1959.

Much later, when he was in his seventies, my dad told me how guilty he still felt all those years later for abandoning the family and going to Iran. With two sons of my own, I had experienced my own challenges and been away from them for work (fortunately, for only days at a time). His words and his pain gave me considerable pause. It was unfair for him to feel guilty, when the reality was that he was a loving dad and we never felt we had missed out on anything. I cannot speak for how my mother felt; I expect that she loved him and knew he had tried his best. I went home and pondered our conversation, and then I wrote him a three-page letter telling him how much I loved him, what a great dad he had been to us, and that it was okay; I understood that he did what he thought had to be done at the time, and that it was a huge sacrifice for him too.

My dad was a man of very few words, especially when we were talking long-distance on the phone (which was expensive back then). About a week after I had mailed him the letter, I got a phone call from Dad. For a couple of minutes, we simply talked about his health and the weather, and then he paused and said, "That letter . . . it was nice." Sadly, Dad had carried this guilt with him silently throughout his life, and yet any of us would have reassured him, if only he had shared his angst with us sooner. I hope my letter eased his burden somewhat.

My mother was born in her family's farmhouse on New Year's Day 1935. She was the second daughter and the fifth child in her family. Her parents and grandparents had fled poverty in County Donegal in Ireland in 1912 to make a life homesteading in northern Alberta. She had auburn hair, laughed readily, loved to dance, and enjoyed getting dressed up and going to parties. She met Dad in either Edmonton or Vancouver; none of our remaining family is certain. At twenty-one she was married, and at twenty-two the mother of twin boys. Like Canadian farm children of her generation, she had only an elementary school education, having left school in about grade eight to help my grandmother at home on the farm, taking care of her brothers and sisters. Without a good education, she spent her life waitressing; once we moved to the logging camp, she served meals at the cookhouse (not always easy having your spouse as your boss!).

Mom did the best she could, and never once gave me the sense that our family was disadvantaged or poor. To get by between paydays, she would sometimes have to buy groceries "on credit." In those days prior to credit cards, local merchants were kind enough to extend credit on their own. We shopped at the thrift store for clothes, and Mom mended our jeans to make them last. Her rule was that patched jeans were okay as long as they were clean.

Dad would bring home leftovers from the cookhouse on Wednesday nights and again on Friday. There was always a cardboard box loaded with aromatic food (hamburgers in gravy was one I can still evoke). It would have been much tougher for our family to feed five kids without this support. Dad told us the food he brought home would not be servable to the loggers in camp after the weekend, so we all felt good about eating it.

Saturday mornings were amazing, as Dad would pack a big, brown, paper bag full to the top with cake, cookies, Danish pastries, brownies, and other sweets for us and tuck it away in that wonderful cardboard box. Imagine five kids in their pyjamas in front of the TV on a Saturday morning, watching cartoons, with pastries for breakfast! To tell the truth, I am a sucker for bakeries to this day. I cannot walk past one without at least going in and taking a look. Most often, I taste a pastry and it is quite good, but it can never be as good as Dad's. I have an eye to bakeries and restaurants, growing up helping Dad all those years ago and working in kitchens myself. I can be fussy about how they look and operate. At the same time, I do take the time to offer praise to the staff or owner when I find one that impresses me.

Mom always encouraged us to play outside and would join us and the neighbourhood kids to play softball in the backyard until the sun went down and we could not see the ball. Often our games were interrupted as everyone searched through the bushes surrounding the yard for a lost softball, as we could afford only one. We learned to catch fly balls bare-handed, as we had only enough gloves for the infielders. She patched up scraped knees, removed slivers from fingers, and made sure we got to school every day. She was proud of our accomplishments and clipped every article out of the local paper when our names appeared (and continued doing so as we became adults). She enjoyed knitting, and we always got new slippers, toques, and scarves each Christmas. In the summers she would sit for hours watching us swim in the lake (although she never learned to swim herself). I can remember standing on a diving board and yelling to Mom on shore to watch me make my dive. When I would resurface, I would immediately look to her and find her looking in another direction or talking to another mother. I always had faith that she had watched me dive and only diverted her attention once I was below the surface.

The highlight of her week was going out to bingo at the local Legion or Elks Club. It was one of the only times she could have a break from five kids and have other adult companionship. We would ask her the next morning if she won anything and were always excited when she said she had. With the little extra money she had in her purse, she would occasionally take us downtown to Ernie's Five & Dime Store, sit us at the counter on bar stools, and buy us an orange pop. It was such a rare treat that I treasured the experience, and you really made that pop last as long as possible. Quite different from the Slurpees my sons would enjoy as kids.

One day while living in Nitinat when I was fifteen, I remember my dad answering the phone and passing it to my mom. Another memory I will never forget—her family calling to let her know her youngest brother, my Uncle Doug, at twenty-four years of age had been involved in a farm accident when a tractor he was driving home from their fields had flipped over and crushed him to death instantly. It was even more tragic to know that his brothers, who went looking for him, found his pinned body. Her shock and grief were so profound that almost fifty years later I can still see her standing in our living room with the wall phone in her hand. I can imagine how difficult it was for Mom when we would get hurt or be sick.

In grade twelve I got work for a week with my friend Brad at the sawmill in Honeymoon Bay. It was near graduation, and the manager at the mill had called the high school and asked the principal if he could get two students to work for one week. Having good grades, I was one of the two he asked. At the job site on

Monday morning, the foreman explained our job and showed us piles of scrap lumber, which he instructed us to use to cover the tops of the lumber stacks scattered around the mill yard. There was fear of a labour strike that summer, and the company wanted to protect the valuable wood on the tops of the stacks from the elements. He told us that when we ran out of scrap wood, he would arrange for more to be dropped off, and then he left with no other instructions. Brad and I looked at each other and decided that one of us would climb to the top of the stack and the other would pass him the scrap lumber to cover the top. We agreed to take turns climbing the stacks, as that was the hardest and trickiest part of the task. At first, we were lucky, and things progressed well. It was close to lunch break, with my turn to climb the stacks, when disaster happened. Although we were covering stacks comprising different sizes of lumber, at that moment it was my turn to climb a stack of four-by-fours—very heavy stuff. I extended my arms far above my head to reach the top of the pile, put one foot on a cross support that extended slightly from the pile, and put all my weight onto my arms to lift myself. I remember the sensations that the top of the stack was coming loose beneath my hands and my body was falling backwards. The next thing I knew, I was on my hands and knees, my hard hat and glasses scattered near me. I shook my head to try and recover my senses. I reached up and rubbed my face, and my hand came back covered in blood. I got up on my feet and started staggering away as Brad and the first aid attendant came running to help. I was lucky. I had instinctively thrown my arm up to protect myself, my hard hat had taken the brunt of the blow, and the stack had only partially collapsed on top of me. I suffered only a mouthful of chipped teeth, a bruised nose, a cut on my left cheekbone, and a mild concussion. After I'd been bandaged, Brad and I went back to the scene of the accident, sat on the ground, and ate our lunches. I must have scared Brad something awful. He said he saw the stack collapse and me lying still on my face on the ground and bolted for the first aid attendant. Near the end of our half-hour lunch break, the foreman showed up to see how we were doing. He was shocked to see me bandaged and bruised and quickly surveyed the collapsed lumber stack. We told him we refused to go back to work unless he got us a ladder to use to climb the stacks, which he readily agreed to. How he thought we were to do the job in the first place I still do not understand. At eighteen, we did not want to look stupid, so we did not ask for a ladder, or even the simple question, "How are we to get on top of the stacks?" There was a slogan on a workers' compensation poster at the logging camp mechanical shop that I read every day I went in to work, but that obviously did not sink in before my accident: "It is better to ask a dumb question than to make a stupid mistake."

I can still see the look on my mom's face when I got home that night, bandaged and bruised. Worse, years later she received a phone call from the logging camp first aid attendant, who said my brother Peter had been hurt in a logging accident and was on his way out of the woods in an ambulance, and she had no idea of how gravely injured he was (this happened more than once). When he was twenty-five, his surgeon called my parents from Vancouver General Hospital and told them that he had about thirty minutes before they knew if he would pull through lymphoma surgery. It is impossible to explain how grateful I have been every day since that he pulled through. Years later he would be injured in another workplace accident, severely burned by heated toxic chemicals used in the pulp making process when pipes came apart that he was working on at a pulp mill on Vancouver Island. He suffered first-, second-, and third-degree burns on his arms and legs and went through a hellish recovery. He can take more credit than I can for my mother's grey hair!

I was twelve when the family moved from Lake Cowichan to the logging camp at Nitinat to be with Dad. We went from village to logging camp, from thirty-three hundred residents to thirty-five families. Although this meant uprooting us from our friends and leaving behind "civilization," it was the best possible solution for our family. Mom and Dad were together every day, we had our dad home all the time, and we had a secure house to live in. It meant a forty-five-minute drive (half over gravel logging roads) to get to school, grocery stores, gas stations, restaurants, movie theatres, and Walt's Diner, the favourite haunt of students looking for a burger or fries at lunchtime. Financially, it was a benefit for my parents too, as small-town logging camps and sawmill towns offered subsidized housing to lucky workers; you had to put your name on a list and wait to get a home, sometimes for months or years. Having a home in camp meant that my parents were able to put a little aside for the future.

Mom and Dad bought their only home years later when they moved back to Lake Cowichan, the year after I graduated from high school. Prior to moving to Nitinat they could only afford to rent. This meant that we bounced from house to house; in fact, we lived in about twelve different houses in Lake Cowichan between when I was five and twelve years old. My two brothers and I would always share the same bedroom, and my two sisters shared one as well. Sometimes property owners would ask us to leave because they had family they wanted to accommodate, sometimes we moved because the landlord would raise the rent and we could not afford to stay, and sometimes the house and yard were not ideal and Mom insisted on something a bit better. She always asked the property owner for paint, and she would freshen up whatever house we moved into. I remember helping Dad clean up messy yards, removing garbage and assorted junk, cutting the grass, and trimming bushes so we had a place to play and run around. Although they had little, my parents had a quiet pride and soft dignity. Poor or not, they always held their heads high and raised us to have humility and an appreciation for what we had—never jealousy over what we did not and could not have.

My best friend from back in grade one went on to build a multi-million-dollar business, becoming the largest employer in Lake Cowichan. I was proud of Barry and glad for his success. To me he is still my "brother from another mother," as we say. Today I live a modest retirement and have friends far wealthier than me. Their wealth does not impede our deep friendships; it is an affirmation that worth as a person is based on more than the amount of money in your jeans. My parents did their absolute best with the little they had, and in turn I am deeply grateful for what I have today, with a profound understanding of my good fortune compared to millions around the world. My dad had always wanted us to do "better than he did," which he would equate with income and opportunity.

Not to say that my parents did not have their own demons and struggles. There would be nights that I would lie awake in my bed and hear them arguing through the adjoining bedroom wall. Mom would cry, and I knew she was really upset. At the time I did not understand what they were fighting about. Later I would come to understood that my mother had a problem with alcohol, and Dad with gambling. Years later, after attending a family reunion in Alberta, my mom just stopped drinking. I am not sure if something specific happened, or if a family member spoke to her, but the outcome was positive for the balance of her life.

Western Mines

Album Cut:
"Sixteen Tons"
Tennessee Ernie Ford
***Sixteen Tons*, released 1955**

AT SIXTEEN, I EXPERIENCED ONE of the most significant events of my young life. We had just finished school for the year and had the summer ahead of us: swimming, softball, camping on the West Coast, berry picking, and picnics. My twin brother and I happened to be with Dad at the cookhouse one afternoon. He took us out the back door of the cookhouse and told us there was a summer job available with his company (Cal-Van Canus Catering) at Western Mines near Campbell River. It would mean work for the whole summer living away far from home, but with the opportunity to make big money; of course, we both wanted the job. For fifty dollars, Dad had bought from a cousin a beat-up 1950 Pontiac panel van that he used to commute back and forth to work and that we learned to drive on. Dad took out a deck of cards and dealt a single hand of poker for Don and me on the hood of the panel van. No draws. No wild cards. That one single hand of poker changed my life. After winning the hand, I left home for the first time and headed off to work for the summer at Western Mines.

Although I was excited to have a full-time job over the summer, I was also incredibly nervous about being away from home for the first time. I had taken the bus to Campbell River and ordered a taxi to take me the one-hour drive out to the mine site. I jumped into the front passenger seat beside the driver because I get motion sick riding in the backs of cars. It was a hot, sunny day, and the taxi did not have air conditioning, so I rolled down my window and stuck my arm out. Good thing that I had sat in the front, as it became quickly apparent that the road was very winding, following a path around Buttle Lake. The driver drove too quickly, in my opinion, and when we careened around a corner on the lake edge, I asked him to slow down, fearing for my life. Instead, he made a comment that I should bring my arm inside the window so that I would not get skin cancer. I thought to myself that if I did not survive the ride into the mine site, it would be a moot point.

When I arrived at the mine site an hour later, I went straight to the cookhouse and reported to the chef, Gabe. He greeted me and showed me to my room, told me to unpack and come back for dinner, and said I would start in the morning. I liked Gabe straight away: a dark-haired Hungarian, very much a professional like my dad. He ran a good operation and treated people fairly. That first summer Cal-Van Canus Catering hired me as a bull-cook, which meant my job was to clean bunkhouses and rooms for eighty miners. Every day I would work room by room, making beds, emptying garbage, sweeping and washing floors, and cleaning communal washrooms: sinks, toilets, and communal showers. Weekly I would also replace bedding. I had to hustle to get my work done each day.

On my first day after lunch Gabe asked me to come with him to his room. He showed me his bed and told me directly that I had not made it to his satisfaction. He surmised that if his bed did not meet his standards, then he could only assume that the rest were substandard as well; in other words, he set me straight on his standards immediately. In truth, my work was up to standard overall, but how was he to know? My bad luck was that Gabe's bed was flush against a wall on one side, he was a tall man, and he must have tossed and turned when he slept because his bed was always a mess. I understood that I had to take extra time with his to make it perfect every day.

I proved my worth to Gabe that summer, and he called me back to work for each of two more summers—the second year as a pot washer and the last summer as a dishwasher. Each of the jobs had its own pros and cons, but what was common to all three summers was that as August started to wind down, I started crossing off days on my wall calendar, counting the days until I could go home again.

It was quite an education at the mine. I was a sixteen-year-old kid working with over two hundred adults from all over the world, including Hungarians, Czechs, Italians, French, Germans, Greeks, and Turks. Not everyone got along, but the camp rule was that if you had a fight on the mine site, the company would fire both combatants instantly—which kept things at bay, for the most part. But booze was everywhere around camp, and when guys got drunk, things got exciting. One day a German electrician drank too much, and after a disagreement with a French miner, chased him to his room and stuck a knife into his door.

Tempers flared throughout the summer of 1974 as the World Cup of Soccer produced national rivalries. Although there was no television at the mine site, everyone on site listened to the radio. I was not a soccer fan but could not help being interested in the outcome. West Germany beat the Netherlands 2–1 in the final on July 7 to win the cup.

We had a Greek person working on the cookhouse staff in the summer of 1973 during my second year at the mine. Nick was a nice guy, very handsome, but with limited English. Gabe assigned him to be the "sandwich man." In the cookhouse there were the chef, the first, second, and third cooks, the "salad man," the "sandwich man," and a couple of bakers. Nick's job was to make lunches every night for all of the two hundred miners so they could pick them up on their way out of the cookhouse after breakfast. The miners would put lunch requests on small slips of paper. For example, one might see under SANDWICH: "ham and cheese with butter and mustard"; "peanut butter and jam"; under FRUIT: "one apple"; "one banana"; under DESSERTS: "a piece of apple pie." There could be two hundred different slips with two hundred different combinations. The first day after he started, the miners revolted against him. Nick with his limited English had misunderstood how to do his job, and when the hungry miners stopped work at noon and opened their lunch bags, they found unpalatable surprises. For example, one of the miners had requested one ham and cheese sandwich with mustard, and a second sandwich with peanut butter and jam. Nick misunderstood, and the miner ended up with a single sandwich with all the ingredients combined. Nick did not make the same mistake the next day.

When I returned for my final summer in 1974, Nick was there again. I was glad to see him and found that he had gone to school in the interim and was now a baker hired to make bread for the camp. I was happy for him. But in July 1974, Turkey invaded Cyprus, starting a war between Greece and Turkey. As I mentioned earlier, we had both Turks and Greeks working at the mine site, so tensions ran high. Nick insisted that he was going to return to Greece to fight. I encouraged him to stay; I liked him and did not want him killed in combat. I left the mine site at the end of August to return to start grade twelve, and I never saw Nick again. I hope that, whatever he did, he survived.

There was a beer strike in BC during the summer of 1973. Observant people saw the strike coming and stockpiled cases of beer to pull them through. At the mine, no one had fridges in their room. At best they would keep beer in cold tap water in buckets. The rooms were not air conditioned, so in the extreme heat beer would be warm at best. I had an advantage that kept me in beer for the summer; I had a key to the cookhouse. I started saving one-gallon cans, filling them with water, and storing them away in corners of our big walk-in freezer in the cookhouse. I would trade these cans of solid ice for beer, so I never went dry that summer (a story I never told my parents, as I was underage in each of the three summers I worked at the mine). Entertainment at the camp consisted of two pool tables and movie nights twice a week at the commissary. The commissary manager, Marie, would typically bring in B movies, mostly westerns and action movies, and occasionally movies like *The Texas Chainsaw Massacre*. She knew her audience.

Jobs at the mine were dangerous, and accidents happened. At the beginning of my first summer at Western Mines, a rock falling from the ceiling underground struck and killed John while he sat eating his lunch underground. During my second year, a worker had returned from a work-related accident the year before, and he related his story to me. His job was to "walk the tailings line." Tailings are the residue from extracting minerals from the ore. Western Mines stored the tailings in ponds—a combination of residue, toxic chemicals used in the processing of the ore, and water. He would spend about four hours walking in one direction on an elevated walkway around the perimeter of the pond and finish his shift by returning the same way. Early in his shift one day, he slipped, fell over the railing on the walkway, and landed about thirty feet below into a creek, breaking his back. He remained in the creek for hours until someone noticed he had not returned from his shift. After his accident, mine management introduced new protocols whereby the worker walking the tailings line reported periodically during their shift at checkpoints to avoid someone being undiscovered for hours. I have never forgotten his story.

But it was a card game at the mining camp my first summer in 1972 that gave me an insight into my dad's challenge with gambling. When we were kids, our parents taught us a variety of card games: Fish, Crazy Eights, Rummy, Cribbage, and Kings in the Corner were our favourites. Mom loved playing cards, and friends came over often to sit around the kitchen table, with food and drinks at hand, to play games with her and Dad. Dad always wanted there to be something at stake, so when playing as kids we always had something to compete over. The winner got a candy, or the winner did not have to do dishes that day, or when we were a bit older, we might play for a nickel. We did not think much of it as kids; it became normal to us. In truth, it was fun to win, and I hated losing. It made me (us) competitive.

Early during my first summer at Western Mines, I noticed a side room in the commissary where a card game was going on. When they saw me watching them, one of the players invited me to sit in on a poker game with the four of them. I had about fifteen dollars in my wallet, which then was a fair amount of money. I sat down, and within a blink of an eye it was gone. I remember clearly standing up to leave, and they asked me where I was going. I said I had no more money with me, and they suggested that I "go get some more money and come back." I declined and left. I mentally made the connection between how hard I had to work to earn that money and that I had given it away in a flash. I also came to understand that these men were prepared to lose entire paycheques in card games. I learned my lesson early at sixteen, and yet it staggers me to this day; it was and is still incomprehensible to me how anyone could gamble away their hard-earned wages.

I was relating this story to my dad years later, and he got a funny look in his eye. I asked him if he had known anyone who had lost an entire two weeks' worth of earnings in a single card game. Shockingly, he told me he had lost his paycheque in card games "more than once." I imagined him coming home to Mom telling her that there was no money to buy groceries for two weeks for a family of five children. No wonder they argued nights and I heard Mom crying through my bedroom wall.

After Mom had passed on, I had to go on a trip to Nanaimo and asked Dad if he wanted to come along for a ride. He said yes, and off we went. We came into Nanaimo from the south on the Island Highway, and I found that developers had converted the old Sears store into a casino. Dad suggested we pop in, and I obliged him, pulling into the parking lot. With money in hand, Dad headed off to play slot machines. As I was there, I gambled with ten dollars and was lucky enough to make about twenty-five dollars extra and decided to stop and check on how Dad was doing. Dad had won over a hundred dollars! His gambling plan was to put his winnings in one pocket and spend only the money he came in with; once that was gone, he would leave, hopefully to the positive, with more money in his winnings pocket than what he had spent. As we had other things to do, I suggested we pack up and go. However, Dad insisted on staying. Once his starting money was gone, he wanted to keep going and dipped into his "winnings pocket." I encouraged him to leave while he was ahead. Unfortunately, I watched him then lose all his winnings. When I again said we should leave, he asked me if I could go back to the truck and get some more money he had there. I declined, saying I had business to do, and off we went. I now understood that my dad had a deep problem, a gambling addiction. He was okay if the opportunity did not present itself to him, and later in life satisfied his need by simply spending a portion of his retirement income on "scratch" lottery tickets.

I had a particularly good friend whom I also found to be a compulsive gambler. The pattern was identical: while winning and ahead, they refused to stop. When they lost, they wanted to keep going to "win it back." The disease is costly. In my friend's case, he did not play cards, roll dice, or go to Vegas. He never considered that he had a problem. His gambling was on the stock market. Over my thirty years knowing him, I would hear that he was "way ahead"; he had made "over a million dollars in the market"; it was "how his family was able to go on big holidays." Then the next time I met him, he would have had a downturn in the market and had lost almost all of it. The cycle would repeat over the years—highs and lows. Working for more than twenty-five years in the financial planning industry, I counselled him to put aside at least ten percent into safer investments and then "play with the rest," knowing he would not change his pattern wholly. As he got closer to retirement, I also coached him to secure a substantial amount of life insurance in case his portfolio had bottomed out when he died. Otherwise, his wife would have very little for herself in retirement. You see, he never let her know what was going on with their money. He always told her things were okay, knowing that she would never let him take these risks with their future financial security. He would get up each morning with his coffee and watch the stock reports on the TV and contact his broker to make changes for him. Then he would go about his day. I never did get him to change, and because we drifted apart, to this day I do not know how it played out for them. I hope for his wife that when he eventually passes, it will be on an "up market." I do have empathy for my dad and my friend, knowing that gambling is an addiction, while at the same time I struggle with reconciling the hard truths that a family can go hungry and that a spouse can be left with no roof over their head.

Camp Life

Album Cut:
"Small Town"
John Mellencamp
***Scarecrow*, released 1985**

PERHAPS IT WAS BECAUSE WE had moved so many times up until I was twelve that I do not remember any particulars about our move to Nitinat in 1969. It was noteworthy that once in camp, over the next six years of my life, we only moved once more, across the street to a little larger house once the family who lived there moved away. Today I am philosophical about the decision and have a deep understanding of the importance this transition was for Mom and the family—not that it did not come without sacrifices and painful experiences.

For Mom, it brought her and Dad back together daily after seven years. It gave her parenting support for her family of five kids: Don and me now twelve, Eve eleven, Peter ten, and Rose four. At that young age, it was probably the least traumatic for Rose. For the rest of us, we left school friends behind and the familiarity of town. We found ourselves essentially in the forest, about forty-five minutes up the road from town in a logging community of thirty-five families and another one hundred twenty men living in bunkhouses that my dad cooked for.

About one kilometre down a gravel logging road from the northern tip of Cowichan Lake, and Heather Provincial Campground, you found yourself on a section of pavement that ran through camp. In summer, dust from vehicle traffic over the parched gravel road would coat the trees, bushes, and ferns in a layer of thick, fine, dust, turning everything a dull grey. For the balance of the year it seemed to rain incessantly; in fact, it could rain for a month straight, and then everything would transform from muted grey into myriad shades of green. Sometimes you could blast along the gravel roads at high speed, especially when the company had sent the graders out to smooth the road and fill in the potholes. Otherwise, it was like driving through a minefield, trying to miss large potholes that could force you to come to a full stop and then slowly inch through them. I mentioned that my dad had bought an old 1950 Pontiac panel van so he could commute around camp and get to work (although on nice days it was only about a five-minute walk from our home). It was a sun-faded, blueish-green colour, with two doors at the front and a single large door at the back that swung open to the left. It had a single leather bench seat in front, with a push-button starter and a column shifter ("three on the tree"). The back compartment was empty, and to keep it clean, Dad put a sheet of plywood on the floor so we could sweep it out easily. Dad found a battered sofa and placed it in the back for us kids to sit on. Apart from the consequential hand of poker Dad played on the hood for Don and me, it was also the vehicle that the four oldest of us learned to drive on, and the one that we would stack camping gear into, including an eight-by-ten canvas tent and five kids to go camping at Pachena Bay on Vancouver Island's famous West Coast. When the battery got weak and we could not get it to start, three of us would get out and push the van from behind, with the driver pushing from their spot at the driver's side door until there was enough momentum and the driver would quickly jump in and pop the clutch to start the motor. Once the motor caught, we would usually drive down the road a short way and stop to rev the motor and let the other kids jump back in, gasping for breath, and then off we would go. This seemed to happen more frequently the longer we had it.

Although Mom was outgoing, loved company, and loved to visit, in camp she found the closeness of the community a bit too much at times. Literally everybody knew everybody. Nothing happened in camp that did not spread like wildfire. Mom found that there were alliances, and even in a community of only thirty-five families there was politics. Fortunately, she found a best friend in Linda, who lived across the street. My friends' parents were mechanics, truck drivers, machine operators, loggers, office workers, surveyors, teachers, and foremen.

The camp manager had the nicest house, situated on a slight rise overlooking Kissinger Lake. This tiny lake was the centre of activity in the summer. It had an almost immediate drop-off close to shore, and then you swam out about fifty feet to a large rectangular dock. There was a lower diving board facing into the rectangle with a higher diving board facing out into the lake. We would spend hours each day taking swimming lessons, playing on the dock, and having fun on inflated tire tubes supplied by the camp. The lake was plentiful with trout, and I learned to fish with my friend Tim as he had an aluminum boat and invited me out with him one day. A couple of years later Dad bought the family a two-person, inflatable rubber raft. In the spring, summer, and into the early fall, I would get up before sunrise on Saturday mornings and quietly sneak out of the house and take the raft, my fishing rod, and a can of earthworms for bait and go fishing by myself. The lake was always placid and serene. Mist rising from the lake would hide from view deer, bears, and other forest creatures coming down for a drink. As I rowed slowly around the lake, there was almost perfect silence except for an occasional rustle in the bushes, or the sound of a duck flapping its wings as it took off from the surface of the lake. I loved the peace and solitude, and I would row for a couple of hours, occasionally bringing home one or two trout, which Dad particularly enjoyed. The odd winter the lake would also freeze over, and we learned to skate on the uneven lake surface and play hockey. At night, the camp would set up a pickup truck with large bright lights mounted on top to see by, so we could extend our fun and so the adults who worked during the day could also get out on the ice.

We had moved to Nitinat when I was twelve, and in December 1970 an ice arena and curling rink opened in Lake Cowichan, just prior to my fourteenth birthday. Apart from the occasional opportunity to skate on Kissinger Lake, Dad drove us to town for public skating as often as he could, and I got pretty good at skating in one direction. My friends in town all joined hockey teams and with coaching and practices became good hockey players. If I could go back in time and change anything, I would find a way to have joined a team with them. When I did start playing on a hockey team, I was fifteen. The mechanical shop foreman asked me one day if I wanted to join the men's hockey team, and I was beyond ecstatic! Dad and Mom gave me permission even though games started at 11:00 p.m. on Sunday evenings and finished after midnight, with school the next morning. I bought a bag with used hockey equipment from one of the families in camp and went to Lake Cowichan to buy a new hockey stick, not knowing really what to look for. I was not a strong skater and wisely decided to buy myself brand-new skates. I splurged and bought a pair of CCM Tacks and spent more money on the skates than on the bag full of gear. My first game I sat in the dressing room full of grown men drinking beer, who showed me how to put on each piece of equipment. I played with the Nitinat Flyers for three years and got better by getting out and playing (and falling down). I played hockey intermittently until I was about forty years old and loved every single moment. There was nothing better than to be the first one to step onto a fresh sheet of ice and glide over the frozen surface.

At camp there was a one-room schoolhouse for kids from grades one through five that Eve, Peter, and Rose attended. Because Don and I were starting grade six when we moved into camp, we never went to the camp school; instead we travelled by school bus to the British Columbia Forest Products (BCFP) logging camp about twenty minutes down the road at Caycuse on the west side of Cowichan Lake. Then the next year we went all the way back to Lake Cowichan and our friends for grade seven onward.

Camp had a large community hall that hosted Halloween parties with costume contests, hot dogs, and an enormous bonfire each year made from old railroad ties. There was a Christmas party with Santa and presents for every child. The dances were epic, with adults and teens mingling, plentiful alcohol, and great music, and occasionally Dad would prepare a late dinner of chicken and fries. When Mom and Dad went out to dances, we saw them transformed. Mom would put on her best dress and lipstick, and Dad would look handsome in dress pants and a sports jacket with the familiar smell of Old Spice about him. One dance when I was about seventeen, my friend John Weld and I stepped out of the hall for fresh air and found one of the dads sprawled on the ground, at the base of the half-dozen steps leading into the community hall. He was moaning, "I broke my legs, I broke my legs." We checked him out and determined he was simply too drunk to know where he was. We got him to his feet and carried him up the stairs and back into the hall, killing ourselves laughing all the way.

Each house had its own telephone, but the whole camp was on a "party line" system, which meant that you could pick up the receiver to make a call and find someone else having a conversation going on. You would simply wait and try again. If it were urgent, or an emergency, you would alert the other party that you needed to cut in. An absolutely terrible situation if you were a teenager. In grade twelve I was dating Catherine, who lived in Youbou about half an hour away. Because I was madly in love with her, I wanted to talk with her every night, but with a house full of siblings I wanted privacy. The only option was to walk down to the camp office buildings to use the lone phone booth. The booth allowed the loggers living in the bunkhouses a facility to do business and reach out to loved ones, distant from camp. I remember one evening trying to talk with Catherine and one of the dads in camp trying to make a call out while I was on the phone. After lifting the receiver about three times and finding me still gabbing, he asked me to please get off the line. I reluctantly said goodbye to Catherine and hung up, hanging around the phone booth for about ten minutes, not wanting to go home yet. Lifting the receiver again, I found the line empty and redialled Catherine's number, picking up our conversation where we had left off. No sooner had we continued our conversation than the same neighbour picked up the line again and heard my voice on the line. He started swearing, and I had to tell him I had hung up when he had asked and had waited patiently for ten minutes before using the phone again. Caveman days compared to today's miracles of communication.

The Cookhouse

<u>Album Cut</u>:
"The Hockey Song"
Stompin' Tom Connors
***Stompin' Tom and the Hockey Song*, released 1972**

ONCE WE MOVED TO CAMP, we also started helping Dad out at the cookhouse. Dad would go in on Sunday afternoons for a couple of hours to prep for Monday morning and would drag one or two of us with him. I like to think now that I volunteered more often than Dad had to compel me, as it has become a fond memory for me. Many of these Sunday afternoons as we worked, we would listen to NHL hockey play-by-play, on a 1940s-era radio, to games from Maple Leaf Gardens in Toronto, Madison Square Garden in New York City, and the Forum in Montreal.

Crown Zellerbach abandoned and completely demolished the buildings on their exit, years after I graduated from high school. Yet they could not obliterate my memories. I can literally see every square inch of the cookhouse in my mind's eye. It was essentially two long, rectangular buildings connected with a short walkway between them at the centre, shaped like a letter "H." The left side comprised the bakeshop and a small office area for my dad at the top of the "H," with a small doorway leading into the kitchen area housing three stacking wall ovens, an enormous flat-top oil cookstove with a multitude of ovens below, and fronted by a huge stainless-steel countertop to prepare food on and from which to distribute the prepared meals. Cal-Van Canus Catering ran the kitchen as "family style," meaning that Dad would artfully distribute all of the food he had prepared into large serving bowls and onto platters. Servers would then deliver the meal to each of the dozen long tables in the dining hall. Etta was a grandmother, the wife of the school bus driver, and was a constant on the cookhouse staff; Dad also hired my mom when necessary. Etta was amazing. With jet-black hair, she was sturdy and quick, she could carry three large, hot serving bowls or platters on her left arm and carry another in her right. She could move quickly and never drop a thing. She had to hustle too, with one hundred twenty loggers watching the food coming out of the kitchen, and with Dad wanting to get it out while it was hot.

Past the cookstove were double deep fryers for making fish and chips, and most importantly doughnuts. "Doughnut day" was generally a Thursday, and it was the best day in camp. All the managers and office workers would drop by for morning coffee and fresh glazed doughnuts. When we were on summer break, we would help Dad make doughnuts. He would make a huge amount of dough in his commercial floor mixer and dump it onto his baking shop counter. In batches he would roll out the soft, fragrant dough, and we would cut the doughnut holes by hand with a special cutter. Dad would cover all the prepared doughnuts with clean cloths and leave them to rest on rectangular baking sheets to proof. Once they had doubled in size, Dad carried the trays to the preheated deep fryers, and he showed us how to carefully submerge each doughnut into the hot oil. We could get about six in each side of the deep fryer at a time. We would use two wooden spoons with very long handles, holding the spoon ends in our hands and using the points to flip the doughnuts over. Once the doughnuts had cooked evenly on both sides, we cautiously removed them from the hot oil and gently set them onto trays, which were moved to the stainless-steel countertop to cool. Dad would make a large pot of glaze, and while the doughnuts were still hot, we picked one up with our hand and quickly dipped the doughnut into the glaze and set it down onto racks to cool. We repeated this process over and over again until the dozens of doughnuts were finished and begging to be eaten. Not only were we now staring at dozens of delicious doughnuts, but the warm sweet fragrance was almost overpowering. Our reward was to joyfully sample one or two doughnuts while they were still warm and delicious. They were soft, fresh, and tasted better than anyone could imagine. To this day I have only found a couple of bakeries after all these decades that made doughnuts to match the quality of Dad's.

Down the wall a short way past the deep fryers were large, stainless-steel wash sinks and racks holding all the cups, saucers, bowls, and plates. On the other side of the room was a small, wooden table with a couple of chairs. When we were younger and helped Dad, we would sit at this table and have dinner with him rather than going into the dining hall with the loggers. When we were older, we would wait until there were only a handful of men left sitting in the dining hall, and then we would join them to enjoy our meal. Alongside the table was a large chest freezer, and then, to navigate to the bottom of the "H," we went through swinging doors into a long, narrow hallway with rooms to the right. The first room was a stockroom with shelves loaded with canned goods, and the next housed a large cutting block with Dad's butcher knives and a stainless-steel sink with a meat-slicing machine on the counter. There was also a large walk-in fridge and a walk-in freezer. Across the hall was a delivery door where the bread truck, the milk truck, and large freight trucks deposited sides of beef and hundred-pound sacks of potatoes, carrots, onions, flour, and sugar. There were also fifty-pound boxes of shortening, candied fruit, and chocolate chips for the bakeshop, all offloaded by Dad (with help from us as we got bigger and stronger). Until we moved to camp and started helping Dad, I had no idea of how hard the job was and how physically demanding. He did not just stir pots and taste gravy. He was a professional baker primarily, who was proud to later earn his chef's ticket.

Days would start incredibly early for him at about 4:00 a.m., with a nap break midday and then a return to work in the afternoon until about 6:00 p.m., after he got through dinner and cleanup. Whenever I mentioned that I would like to be a baker, he would always discourage me, telling me it meant "lousy hours" and demanding work. My dad always wanted us to do something better than what he did, which in part also meant getting a better-paying job. As an unintentional reinforcement of his warning, I remember him being off work following back surgery for months when he was about fourty-years old, and I know he also suffered with ulcers.

Dad was a wonderful work role model and set exacting standards, with no shortcuts and no second-best. I distinctly remember one afternoon making pies with him. Fruit pies were mostly apple, cherry, blueberry, and sometimes peach, which he made along with cream pies—banana, coconut, or chocolate. He had a long-handled, wooden paddle to put pies into the big wall oven, and he also used the paddle to remove them when they were fully baked. You could get three pies on the widest part of the paddle, and if you were exceptionally good you could get a fourth pie balanced on the narrow part of the handle. He was quick and efficient in all his movements; he had to be, to complete everything on time. When we were learning we would be too afraid to put more than one pie on the paddle at a time, but this would mess up the baking time when you had so many pies to bake simultaneously, so Dad would encourage us to try more. As I got more confident it became two pies, then three, and finally four. However, one day I remember having three pies on the paddle heading into the oven to bake, and as I moved too quickly, I dropped all three upsides down onto the floor. Dad did not blink an eye. He simply cleaned up the mess, and in a couple of minutes he had whipped together three replacement pies. His patience and guidance at the cookhouse guided me for the rest of my working life.

Once a year the logging company would hold a huge "Pin Dinner," awarding employees with lapel pins in honour of their years of service; for instance, five-year pins or ten-year pins were given. This was really a big deal. Crown Zellerbach would send big shots from head office, and Dad would have help from other chefs who came over from Vancouver to help prepare canapés and shrimp cocktails. Dinner would be T-bone steaks and all the trimmings, and there would be a variety of fancy desserts. I will never forget working one of these Pin Dinners when I was about sixteen. As part of the team, I wore the same white uniform as all the chefs and worked side by side with them; to be perfectly clear, I was nervous much of the evening.

Near the end of the serving of dinner, Dad asked me to come with him into the bakeshop and showed me how to put the finishing touches on all the strawberry shortcakes. He had made a huge amount of fresh whipped cream and showed me how to put it into a large piping bag and use the piping bag to decorate each cake; and then he left me to my task and headed back to the kitchen. Although I know my work was not anywhere near Dad's level of expertise, I appreciated his confidence in me, and I decorated each shortcake to the best of my ability. All the guests enjoyed the cakes, and I did feel proud of myself at the end of the night. To this day I still embrace these memories of my dad and the other chefs and how they worked together so well and so cooperatively and professionally. Now I watch cooking shows on TV, with chefs swearing and throwing things around, yelling and insulting their staff, and it is hard to watch. I wonder who would ever want to put up with that abuse? It makes me even more proud of my dad, and so grateful for how he mentored and showed me a better way to work and get along with people.

He also forced me out of my comfort zone. He produced the idea that Don and I should be "milkmen" for camp, delivering milk and dairy products to the families there. Every week the dairy truck would come into camp, and Dad decided one day that Don and I could buy milk, ice cream, cheese, and other dairy products from his supplier and then resell them to the families around camp. Remember, we lived isolated from grocery stores; the closest major grocer was in Lake Cowichan forty-five minutes away. So, we would walk around camp knocking on doors and taking individual family orders for the following week and then put the order in with the dairy supplier. When the order arrived the following week on the truck, we would deliver product around camp and collect payment. This was very entrepreneurial: it involved order taking, managing inventory, home delivery, and collections (families who would say they did not have the money when you delivered their order forced us to come around and collect later, eventually dropping them if they were delinquent for too long).

Dad extended his idea and pushed my comfort zone even further the next summer. He decided we could load cooler chests with dry ice into the panel van and drive a kilometre out of camp to Heather Campsite on the northern tip of Cowichan Lake and sell ice cream, pop, and potato chips to the campers there. After camping for a couple of days the kids would be driving their parents crazy, and we sold out of our treats quickly. All of this experience was invaluable later in life when I started careers in different business ventures.

The Glass "Half Full"

Album Cut:
"Small Towns and Big Dreams"
Paul Brandt
***Small Town and Big Dreams*, released 2001**

I HAD EXPERIENCES AND OPPORTUNITIES living in camp that my friends did not have living in town, most of them positive (that's easier to say now than it was back then). We learned to drive in our early teens long before our friends did, on private logging roads where driver licences and insurance were unnecessary. For my brothers and me, our first jobs as teens (apart from babysitting) were well-paid union jobs rather than paper routes. Art, who lived next door, and his cousin Andy both got work washing the company vehicles on weekends—a job prized by the rest of us. They would hold that job until they graduated from school and would tie it up for years. Fortunately, I got what I felt was a better job. At fifteen, the shop foreman offered me a job to fuel all the pickup trucks every night after school. This was about two hours a night at union wages, five days a week. After I'd been doing this for months, Dave asked me to move into the mechanical shop to do oil changes on all the trucks, and my brother Don took over the fuelling. Not naturally gifted with my hands, through different life experiences I became at least handy along the way. By doing the oil changes I gained another skill set, and I also became better known by the shop foreman and the mechanics and welders. One evening, Dave, the night shift foreman, walked me over to a logging truck sitting in the shop yard and told me to climb in. He explained how the air brake system worked and how to start it up. He then had me drive it over to the fuel pumps to fill up. It was an amazing experience to drive such an impressive vehicle. On successive evenings Dave also showed me how to drive a grader, the camp fire truck, and a large bus. As I became more confident at doing oil changes, Dave also had me assist the mechanics from time to time. This largely meant going into the woods to fix machinery, where my job would be to pass them tools, hold a flashlight, and observe. It was also a safety measure, as I would be able to get help if they injured themselves on the job, as we could be dozens of kilometres from camp in remote, barely accessible spots. I really enjoyed the camaraderie and having something different to experience. That's not to say that I did not make costly mistakes along the way.

Doing an oil change on pickup trucks meant also checking the axle's rear-end fluid level. This meant standing in a pit under the vehicle and taking out a plug in the "rear end" and inserting your pinky finger in to see if you could feel the fluid; by this method you could tell if it needed topping up or not. Once I had completed this task, I screwed the plug back into the hole and tightened it with a wrench to make it snug. One night working on one of the older pickups, I kept turning the plug with the wrench, and it did not seem to get tight. The next thing I knew, the plug fell into the axle reservoir; by its doing this, the truck became undriveable, and mechanics now had to replace the rear axle, which was a costly affair. Dave, like the majority of the bosses I had over my lifetime, was generous and fair. Dave never seemed to be an excitable person; he never yelled or gave me hell for such a rookie mistake. Instead, he simply had the truck towed off the pit, and mechanics repaired it the next day. I continued on, having learned from my mistake. I can never understand people who think it necessary to yell, swear, stomp, and belittle people who make mistakes (whether on the job or at home). I internalized my mistakes and tried to not make the same one twice.

On Monday to Thursday nights as I was going to school, I had to quit work by 11:00 p.m.; however, on Friday nights I worked to the end of the night shift, which was at about 1:00 a.m. One Friday that I remember clearly to this day, everyone wanted to finish and leave early because it was a long weekend. Everything was going well until near the very end of the shift when the foreman came over to give me one last job. A mechanic had driven a small excavator over the pit, and the foreman took me over to where it sat and explained that the operator had been complaining that the cab had been filling with water when it rained and that his feet were getting wet. The foreman instructed I get a drill and make holes in different spots into the floor of the cab to let the water escape. I had my friend John Weld, who was also working there and who later became a heavy-duty mechanic, get into the pit and try to watch where I was drilling to avoid me hitting any gas or brake lines. It went well until the very last hole, when by accident I drilled through the steering cylinder of the excavator. This was at midnight. On the Friday of a long weekend. When everyone wanted to leave early! Now everyone had to stay until the excavator was operational again. A mechanic had to remove the cylinder, a welder had to repair the hole I had drilled, and the mechanic then had to put it back in place on the machine. No one yelled at me. No one gave me a tough time (I felt bad enough). However, the next week I had to bring a bottle of Canadian Club whisky to work. I neglected to mention that it was a normal ritual on regular Friday nights, at the end of their shift, for the shop crew to sit and have a couple of beers, chasing down swigs of Canadian Club from the bottle. The crew worked in camp, so we could walk home at the end of the shift.

During my time at the shop, I learned different skills and priceless lessons. One of the most memorable lessons started innocently enough. Lars, one of the mechanics, was bringing a logging truck, with its trailer behind it, over the pit to do repairs. The shop foreman had asked me to stand at the front of the pit facing Lars and provide hand signals to him so he could bring it safely over, without the wheels dropping into the pit. The foreman was at the large doors where the truck was coming in, talking to someone else, both ignoring what was going on. Right beside them was a regular door for everyone to come through, without having to walk through the huge shop doors. Watching the front wheels of the logging truck as it inched forward, with occasional upward glances at Lars, completely absorbed my attention. With the cab of the logging truck completely over the pit and the trailer following, I heard an enormous crash and saw the foreman and his companion leap out of the way. What I could not see from my vantage point was that the back bunk of the logging truck trailer had caught onto the back of the foreman's parked pickup truck and slammed it through the small door where the foreman had been standing a second earlier. There was considerable damage to the building and to the pickup truck. Dave never reprimanded me, in part I believe because he had been standing at the rear of the vehicle the entire time and should have noticed what was about to happen. Later on in my life, I spent decades in business, in a variety of leadership roles. From this mishap with Lars, I became aware of the necessity of having short- and long-term vision and the need to take in all aspects of any task or objective.

Sadly, with one hundred twenty single loggers living in the bunkhouses, the job opportunities for my sisters or any of their friends were scarce. All the parents were vigilant in keeping the loggers from interacting with their daughters. Even serving in the cookhouse was not an option. For my sister Eve it was "spark watching," which entailed driving around the logging roads in a pickup truck keeping an eye out for possible forest fires.

Close Encounters

<u>Album Cut</u>:
"Ole Slew Foot"
Johnny Horton
***Honky Tonk Man*, released 1956**

I MENTIONED THAT NITINAT WAS situated in a rainforest on Vancouver Island, so naturally there was an abundance of wildlife that traversed through camp. Most common were deer (except during hunting season, when they made themselves scarce) and bears. There were hunters among our neighbours, and as he became older my younger brother Peter became one too, mostly going after deer and grouse. As Dad was not a hunter, the only wild game that came to our table were gifts from neighbours. As far as I knew, the only weapons my dad ever fired were during his stint in the Swiss army. I really did not enjoy venison; the only way I remember it being edible was when Mom canned deer meat in jars and we heated it up later, making a stew with gravy.

As Dad was a meat cutter by trade, occasionally one of the hunters would ask him to dress their deer, and he would get a portion of it in return along with a bottle of booze or a case of beer. The barter system was big in camp. When Dad would need a mechanical repair on his car, he would get one of the mechanics to do it in return for dressing his deer. The accountant might help someone with taxes in return for painting his fence, and so it went. In the happiest example of the barter system, we got our dog "Tippy," so named because she was black with a white tip at the end of her tail. She was a "case of beer dog" of nondescript breed, small in stature and big in heart. We loved her, and she was a constant companion of the family, going on our camping adventures, with seven people and one dog in the eight-by-ten canvas tent.

Black bears were always wandering around camp. They were especially fond of the cookhouse garbage, which Dad locked in a shed across the road from the cookhouse. There was no garbage pickup for families in camp. Everyone drove their vehicles a couple of kilometres outside of camp to the dump. You would drive your car to the turnaround, back it close to the edge, and then throw your garbage out and over the bank. When we first arrived in camp Dad would drive the panel van to the dump, and when we had finished disposing of our garbage, he would back about one hundred feet down the road and shut the motor off and wait. Within about five minutes the bears would wander out of the bush to scavenge. I remember an instance one spring when a mother black bear with two cubs came out of the woods, and she guided them to the trash. After a while one of the cubs decided to climb a nearby tree. It either did not or could not come back down, and mother bear stood on her back legs and leaned against the tree and bawled at her baby to come down. After persistence on her part, the cub did drop to the ground, and they all disappeared back into the woods, and the day's entertainment was over for us.

Sadly, when a bear became too comfortable and started wandering through camp where families lived, residents would worry about the threat to kids and pets, and one of the dads would shoot and kill the bear. I have had countless encounters in the wild with bears both at Nitinat and later at Western Mines near Campbell River.

One day when I was eighteen, I was driving down one of the logging roads outside of camp with my girlfriend Catherine, and we saw two large black bears wander slowly across the road in front of us and down and over the bank on the passenger side. I drove for about fifty feet up the road, stopped, and got out with my camera to take a picture (Catherine wisely stayed in the truck). I slowly walked back down the road to about where I thought the bears had gone over the side, and with camera in hand I went to the edge and leaned over to see if I could spot them. Looking directly back at me was one of the bears, who had climbed back up the bank to see if we had gone, and for an instant we looked into each other's eyes! I instinctively turned and ran back to the truck, opened the door, and jumped in as quickly as possible. I was shaking with excitement, panting for air, and Catherine was laughing her head off. Apparently, we had each startled the other, simultaneously turning and bolting. There had been no attempt to chase me down the road.

Western Mines was also located in the forest, situated in Strathcona Provincial Park in the Myra Valley approximately ninety kilometres southwest of the coastal town of Campbell River. The mine produced zinc, copper, gold, and silver. My first summer there it operated both open-pit and underground mining operations, and later only underground mining. Being in the middle of a provincial park where the government prohibited hunting, raccoons, deer, and bear wandered freely around the mine site and were also frequent visitors to the cookhouse, looking for a meal in the garbage containers. The garbage bins were large, reinforced metal containers, with a heavy piece of angle iron secured across the top to stop the bears from getting inside. However, the larger black bears were strong enough to bend the metal lid up from the container and get inside.

Cookhouse staff came and went with high frequency; generally, alcoholism would get them fired. One day a new worker arrived in camp just prior to noon. I only saw him once, a thin, dark-haired man who seemed anxious. The chef took him to his designated bunkhouse room and told him when he had finished unpacking to come over to the cookhouse for lunch and afterwards start his first shift. The problem was he never returned! After lunch, the chef went looking for him and found him drunk in his room—he had one suitcase full of clothes and the other full of booze. He departed hours later when a cab returned to take him away. I did not even get his name. Then there was Ed. Ed was also employed there for a brief time. One day Ed had gone into Campbell River on his days off and come back drunk. After going through his pockets, he found a receipt for the purchase of an expensive motorboat that he had no recollection of purchasing, and to my good fortune he had bought a new pair of work shoes that were too small for him and that fit me perfectly. About a week later, I met Ed coming down the steps from the cookhouse one evening after his shift. He stopped to talk and to my surprise unbuckled his belt and dropped his pants to show me his leg. He had nasty red gashes along his inner thigh on his left leg. He told me that he had attempted to come into the cookhouse the night before and found a bear inside the foyer; Ed, drunk at the time, made the unwise decision to try and throw the bear out. Clearly the bear had won.

Each bunkhouse was a long, rectangular building and could hold about forty men: ten doors lined each side of the hallway with one or two workers to a room. In the centre of the building would be a communal washroom with showers, sinks, and toilets. In the summer it could get extremely hot, and because there was no air conditioning miners would leave the doors at each end of the building open through the night. I awoke one morning at about 5:00 a.m. At first, I could not figure out what had woken me so early, but then I heard a thumping noise that progressively became louder and closer to my room. As my head cleared, it slowly dawned on me that a bear had gotten into the building. As the sound got closer and closer, I started to panic. I realized that my door to the hallway was my only escape route, as the window was too small to escape through. My greater fear was knowing that my door did not latch properly, and that if the bear bumped against it, the door would open easily. I lay on my back in bed, trying desperately to not make a sound, and hardly breathed. I heard the bear stop outside my door, and then with a crash heard him enter the room directly across from mine and trash it. He destroyed the room, while I waited for him to turn and come into mine. Fortunately, the ruckus had woken other occupants of the bunkhouse, who wisely closed off one end of the building and made enough noise to draw the bear out of the room and out the only remaining exit door. It was one of the scariest encounters of my life, but not the last.

Working as a dishwasher one of the three summers I worked at Western Mines meant I had a split shift. I would start early in the morning to do both the breakfast and lunch rushes and then would have a two-hour break at midday, returning later to work for the dinner shift. This break in the afternoon I generally used to read or simply relax. However, someone introduced me to Myra Falls, which was a short walk through the forest from the mine site. You could fish for trout at the base of the falls, so I purchased gear at the commissary, and then began spending some of my downtime fishing.

One day, with my fishing pole on my shoulder and a tackle box in my hand, I was wandering down the path to the falls. As I turned a corner, blocking my path about ten feet from me, was a large black bear. We had startled each other, and again I acted instinctively. I stepped sideways to my right into the bush, off of the path. Instantly I realized that I had made an error. By stepping off the path, I now had no idea where the bear had gone. So, I stepped back onto the path and found it empty; the bear had vanished. My dilemma now was whether to turn and go back home to the mine site or continue to the falls. I had no idea which way the bear had gone. Deciding there was risk either way, I decided to continue to the falls. My last close encounter with a black bear ended abruptly—and, mercifully, safely.

I had only one experience with a lion—in this case, a mountain lion, or, as we called them, cougars. We rarely saw cougars, unlike bears. Their unpredictability frightened me much more than did bears—my experience with black bears demonstrated that they would leave you alone if you in turn left them alone, and especially if you did not get between them and their cubs. I met with a high school friend one day travelling on a business trip to Nelson, BC. I had not seen Wally since school days and accepted his gracious offer to dinner and met his wife and family. In conversation, I found out that Wally was a hunter, and we started sharing stories. He told me a story about a terrifying encounter he'd experienced one day when he was out deer hunting. He described lying on his stomach on a ledge overlooking a clearing, aiming at a deer standing below him, his finger on the trigger, when all the hairs on the back of his neck stood up on end and he had this terrible premonition of danger. He spun around and found a cougar had leaped off a higher ledge above him, attempting to pounce on him. Luckily, Wally had his rifle cocked and ready and was able to shoot the cougar while it was in mid-air, saving his life. My cougar encounter was not life-threatening, as Wally's had been, but dramatic and spectacular in its own right.

My dad was a great lover of nature and the outdoors, which I am sure came from his youth in France and Switzerland. We watched all the nature and animal shows on TV: *The Undersea World of Jacques Cousteau*, *Mutual of Omaha's Wild Kingdom*, and every Natural Geographic special that came on television. So, we used to go for drives for fun around the logging roads to spot deer and elk, and always with hopes of spotting a black bear.

The terrain around camp was mountainous, and the majority of logging was done on rugged, steep hillsides, but kilometres out of camp there was a low-lying plain with a creek running through it where elk herds could always be spotted. One afternoon, Dad decided we would go for a drive in our old panel van to look at the elk. When we got to the spot, we saw that there were a couple of other vehicles parked on the roadside, so we pulled in behind them and got out to see what was happening. On the other side of the creek on the plain, a group of men and dogs were standing under a grouping of large evergreens. The dogs were in a frenzy and baying loudly, and men with rifles were standing under the trees. Dad decided we would wade across the creek and see what was happening. So, we did. Over the bank, wading through the rocky creek bed, we found ourselves on the other side with the group of men standing under the tree. To my dismay, they were hunting cougars and had treed a mother cougar in one of the evergreens that we were standing directly under.

The dogs had had a rough time. A couple of them had tangled with the cougar prior to it escaping to a high bough in the tree, and the cougar's claws had cut their snouts badly. One of the men, intent on ending the stalemate, or perhaps from sadistic pleasure to torment the cougar, picked up a large branch and started beating on the tree. The cougar was spectacular, perched above us. Snarling and twitching, its muscles flexing, it was magnificent and breathtaking to be so close to it. The blows on the tree trunk caused vibrations up the tree, and the cougar became increasingly agitated and snarled and cried out more wildly. When it finally sprang from its perch to a second tree about six feet away to escape the torment, its claws did not hold. The moss-wrapped tree gave the cougar no purchase, and instead of securing itself, the cougar dropped about fifteen feet to the ground, landing among us only a couple of feet from me! As soon as its feet hit the ground the cougar instantaneously was gone, running so fast you could not follow its motion, with the dogs chasing behind, baying as they ran, and with us standing there, mouths agape and hearts pounding.

My dad decided it was enough excitement for the day, so we waded back across the creek, climbed the bank, and went home with an adventure I have never forgotten. Later, we learned that the hunters had treed the cougar a second time a short distance away on the same plain. This time, however, they also discovered a den among fallen trees, with a couple of cubs inside. Realizing the cougar was a mother protecting her young, they left the cougar and went home. Although it was the right thing to do, in my eyes it did not excuse their "sport"; I was told that the primary hunter in the group was renowned in the local area as a "cougar hunter" and sought them out to kill for sport and their hides. I have a deep, heartfelt disgust over killing animals—or any creature, for that matter—for "sport." I do not like antlers hanging on walls or even seeing mounted fish. I understand the necessity of hunting for food and embrace the Indigenous practice of thanking the creatures they kill out of respect for the life taken for their use.

The "Stinking Yellow Bus"

Album Cut:
"Yellow Submarine"
The Beatles
***Revolver*, released 1966**

HOW TO START?

Power dynamics, hierarchy, bullying, or simple transportation?

I mentioned living in camp meant taking a school bus to Lake Cowichan for all kids living in both Nitinat and Caycuse beyond grade six. Going into grade six the year we moved to Nitinat, however, meant a short bus ride to Caycuse and a two-room school. Grades one, two, and three were in one room, while grades four, five, and six were on the other side. It was a relatively unremarkable year with limited trauma, and I did gain a great friend, Bren, whose dad was a heavy-duty mechanic. Brady is a great guy, and Bren's mom Dorie is a real sweetheart, both now in their eighties and still living in the same house decades later. The ride to Caycuse was thankfully only about twenty minutes long.

Heading to Lake Cowichan the next year and entering grade seven was a different matter. The bus ride was about forty-five minutes long, with a stop in Caycuse to pick up kids there and passing through two sawmill towns along the way, Honeymoon Bay and Mesachie Lake, and ending in Lake Cowichan.

Quickly the students made the bus hierarchy clear. The oldest kids sat at the back of the bus and the youngest at the front, nearest the driver. Each year that passed as the grade twelve students disappeared, everyone moved back a row or two, advancing in the ecosystem of the bus. Like any community, most kids just rode along minding their own business, sleeping, eating, talking with friends, or reading. There were also rowdies, kids yelling to the bus driver to turn up the radio. Then there were the bullies, male and female. There was a tough element to the kids who came from homes headed by crusty loggers, alcoholics, and abusers. They in turn became tormentors and bullies.

In 1966 the rock group The Beatles put out their seventh album, *Revolver*, which included one of my favourite songs, "Eleanor Rigby." It also included an innocuous song with Ringo Starr on lead vocals, "Yellow Submarine." Kids around the world loved this charming tune, but kids on our bus in 1969 commandeered it as their protest song. Bored, tired of riding the bus, angry at the driver for not allowing horseplay or another slight, the protestors began singing, "We all ride on a stinking yellow bus / A stinking yellow bus," rather than The Beatles' "We all live in a yellow submarine / A yellow submarine." Quite a shame, as I have never enjoyed that song to this day.

If you happened to be late leaving school at the end of the day, you got on the bus when it was mostly full. Seat options became tricky. You would climb up the steps and scan the entire bus, front to back, as quickly as possible, looking for a suitable seat, not wanting to take too much time. Generally, kids made room for others to sit down willingly, but not always. One afternoon when I was in grade nine, I was late boarding the bus. Stopping at the top of the stairs, I scanned the bus front to back. Facing me on my left were rows of seats for two and on my right rows of seats for three. The most immediate spot was about six rows back on the left, where I saw Brian Reynolds sitting. Brian's dad was one of the foremen in camp, and he was a wiry, cocky kid who had a lovely older sister. As I approached the seat and indicated I wanted to sit with him, he blocked the seat with his body and shook his head "no." This put me in a tough spot. Everyone on the bus quickly saw and understood the dynamic. I could move away and attempt to find another spot on an already-crowded bus, but I would have looked weak. It was clear that I needed to forcefully sit myself down beside him. As I started to sit on the seat next to Brian, he grabbed onto the seat handle in front of him and wedged his body in an attempt to block me. The next thing I knew was that I was sitting beside him, and Brian had a bloody nose. It was a scary moment for me, as I did not even remember hitting him. I had lost my temper, and in the moment, everything had gone black.

Mom, without thinking of consequences or bus dynamics, one morning gave bullies a green light to attack me for months. I am not sure that she ever understood the ramifications of her demand of me. The school bus driver parked the bus two houses up the street from our home, and directly across from his home. Normally he would be up early and have the bus running and warming up for us in the morning, as he did his pre-trip inspection. In the winter he needed extra time to defrost all of the frozen windows and mirrors. All kids in camp would walk over to the bus and line up to get in if we got there before him. One frosty winter morning we walked to the bus and found it sitting empty; the driver was not there yet. We waited for about ten minutes, stamping our feet to keep warm and constantly adjusting our toques and scarves for maximum benefit. Finally, someone suggested we should all go home, hoping that we would get a day off school. Mom had no such plans. She told me to go over to the driver's home and knock on his door and wake him up. I knew instantly that would be a terrible idea, and I asked her to please phone him instead. I do not know if she did not have his phone number (with only thirty-five families, I doubt that) or thought it was easier for me to go to his house. What I did know was that I could not argue with Mom.

The kids were still standing outside the bus waiting when I reluctantly walked to the driver's house. They saw me knock on the door. He was obviously awake because he came to the door fully dressed and told me that he was on the way. That did not matter to the bullies; my knocking on his door precipitated a campaign of "revenge" for making them go to school that day. Word spread quickly through the bus when we picked up the kids in Caycuse. Similar to society in general, the majority had expected and wanted to go to school, and with them, my action caused not a ripple. The bullies seized on this moment, though, and I became a target.

One of my school friends was Ben, a nice kid, giant in stature and heart. His older brother John was shorter and wiry. Another afternoon, almost at home this time, John made his play. I had been sitting beside him the whole way from school, and just as we were entering camp, minutes from our homes, he reached to the floor of the bus and scooped mud in his hand and rubbed it across my face. I reacted quickly, again knowing everyone left on the bus was aware of what was going down. I reached up to my face and used my fingers to wipe off the mud and smeared it back on his face. Fists followed. The bus driver pulled over when he heard the ruckus, gave us both hell, and dropped John and Ben off at their house, next on the route, and I continued home with heart racing.

Down the road was the Benson family. Lenny the dad, the camp fire warden and a tough old bird to boot, had a single arm, having lost one as a youth after falling onto a picket fence. His wife was a nice lady, and they had a lovely daughter, Mary. The sons were big and mean. The older and larger was Bob. He was one or two grades ahead, and Jake was close to my age. Both hunted, fished, rode dirt bikes, cussed, and fought. The rumour I heard later was that Lenny would beat them. Coming home on the bus as seats emptied, the kids in the back would gradually move closer to the front to get off more quickly. One day, about two stops from home, I was moving to change seats with Jake directly in front of me. Without warning, he lunged backward, throwing me off balance backwards, almost knocking me to the floor of the bus. There was no time to think. I saw red and swung with my right fist as hard as I could, landing a blow in the middle of his back. He spun around and growled, "Wait 'til we get off the bus." Anticipating a fight, when I got to the last stop, I manoeuvred myself off the bus first. As soon as I touched the ground, I dropped my books, put up my fists, and spun around to face him as he stepped off the bus. When he saw me stand ready for him, he unleashed a flurry of curses and turned away. As with all the other bullies who had forced me into a confrontation, once I stood my ground, they never bothered me again.

Boxing, Baseball, and Trouble with "Ls"

<u>Album Cut</u>:
"Centerfield"
John Fogerty
***Centerfield*, released 1985**

THE SCHOOL BULLYING HAD STARTED in grade five, prior to us moving to camp, by our teacher, Mr. Waters. He was a charismatic man, with dark, curly hair, a muscular physique, and an engaging personality. He would occasionally bring his guitar and play, and the class would sing songs. In the summer before school ended, he arranged for a big summer party outdoors with the whole class. He was also on the senior men's fastball team in town, a wicked pitcher. His was not the profile of a bully, and for the most part, I thought he was fun; and then he started with the nicknames.

Jenny was a cute girl, and innocently enough he called her "Jellybean," but then kids started being nicknamed as defined by their personal appearance. Mary was diminutive, and he called her "Mouse"; another girl who was very thin he called "Twiggy" after the then-famous model; and my twin brother and me he called "Porkers." You can guess that we were chubby (still hard to say fat, more than five decades later) and had been for years at that time. As a result, kids taunted us for months afterwards with this horrible nickname. One day I had been relating to my classmates that my baby sister, who was learning to talk, was having trouble saying "Ls," which meant that trying to say "Larry" came out more like "Warry." Minutes later I asked permission to leave the room, and as I passed through the door into the hallway, I could hear Mr. Waters say to the class, "Warry waddles," and my classmates laughing along. I was completely embarrassed.

I spoke with Don a couple of weeks ago now about grade five and Mr. Waters and his recollections of that year. His experiences had deeply scarred him, causing him to be obsessed with his weight since, with the sad irony that he became almost unhealthily thin at one point. I went in a slightly different direction. By about grade eight I started losing weight, and by grades eleven and twelve looked like my friends (although in my mind's eye I never saw myself this way) and started demanding to be treated equally.

Mr. Waters also precipitated an event in grade five that deeply scarred me, and for which I have apologized to Don as an adult. My memory is that during a phys. ed. class that year, he selected Don and me to box against each other. I had never worn boxing gloves, did not like to fight, and had never hit my twin brother before. And I did not want to fight him now. But in those days, you blindly followed authority figures, and so Don and I had boxing gloves tied on, and we exchanged blows; to my dismay, I gave him a bloody nose. That mercifully ended our bout in the moment, but I have agonized over it ever since. Don has a slightly different memory, in that he remembers that Mr. Waters put on this boxing display as entertainment for himself during lunchtime, not as part of our phys. ed. class. Either way, we were both traumatized in our own way at the time and have carried it with us to this day.

Being chubby meant phys. ed. was one of my least favourite classes. I enjoyed the break from academics, but it was not always fun. I particularly hated gymnastics and track and field. One of the worst parts was playing floor hockey or indoor soccer, as the teacher would choose teams and instruct one group to be Skins and the other Shirts. The Skins had to remove their sweatshirts and play naked from the waist up. This was not easy for non-athletic-looking kids, whether too skinny or too fat. I always kept my fingers crossed that the teacher would assign me to be on the Shirts team. It also meant always playing the position that the athletic kids did not want to play. That meant playing the goalie in soccer and floor hockey and outfielder when playing softball. You never got to play as a forward and get a chance to score a goal, and you never got to play first base or pitcher. When the other kids picked who they wanted on their team, they always picked us last. By grade eleven I was in decent shape and insisted on playing up front, refusing to play goal any longer. I started having fun, finding that I had good athletic abilities and reflexes.

As an adult I played recreational floor hockey, softball, and ice hockey and loved every minute. It was a shame that in 1975, community coaches and phys. ed. teachers were not better equipped to make it a more inclusive experience.

I got the chance to play part of a season of Little League baseball in Lake Cowichan prior to moving to Nitinat. It felt good to wear a uniform and become a Pirate. Although I played lots of softball in the backyard with my family and friends and in phys. ed., I had never played hardball with overhand pitching and a smaller ball. My friends had played baseball for two or three years, so I needed to catch up with them. However, Little League coaches were fixated on team standings and winning championships, so I spent my time sitting on the bench during games. When the coach finally told me to grab my glove and get into the game, it was in the outfield standing around waiting for a ball to come my way and hoping at the same time that it would not. The fate of the fat kid.

The coach even put me into the outfield during practices, and when one of the kids hit the ball out of the park (an automatic home run), the coach instructed us to climb over the top of the outfield fence, retrieve the ball, and climb back over with it. This was not an easy feat for kids like me. So, of course, fate meant that I was in the outfield in an actual game against an opposing team with the stands filled with parents and siblings, when a ball driven in my direction sailed over the outfield fence. Not knowing any different, I climbed over the fence to get the ball, only recognizing my mistake when I could hear laughter from the field and the stands! To compound my misery, when I climbed back over the fence, I realized I had left my ball glove on the other side, and one of the coaches from the opposing team brought it to me. It was one of the most humiliating experiences of my life. It was the only time I played Little League.

I have two sons, and when they became old enough to play baseball, we lived in Penticton, BC, and I took a coaching course and earned a certificate so that I could volunteer as a coach. I wanted my sons and other kids to have a more positive experience than I had. As coach I pledged that every single kid, girls and boys, would have a chance to play each position: on base, in the field, at catcher, and as pitcher. I kept meticulous records for every game so that I knew that all kids got an equal amount of playing time during games. If we had too many players, everyone, even the best players, had to sit out an inning during a game. When infrequently a parent would complain to me that their child had not been playing enough, I would reassure them by bringing out my book and showing them the record of every game, including the positions and the number of innings that their child had played.

I coached for three years and volunteered as a director of the Penticton Minor Baseball Association for one year. Although my older son David stopped playing when he became too old, he volunteered to help coach his little brother's team with me, Josh being five years younger. In contrast to my baseball trauma, the biggest disappointment my sons had was when Dairy Queen was announced to be their sponsor (giving them visions of free ice cream after every game) and at the last minute a local travel company became their sponsor instead.

We Are Not Rabble

Album Cut:
"Signs"
Five Man Electrical Band
***Good-byes and Butterflies*, released 1970**

A WHILE AGO MY WIFE called me a "faux" hippie. Although I occasionally talk about the "sex, drugs, and rock 'n' roll" of the 1960s and 1970s, it was only the rock 'n' roll I can claim any real affinity with. Music is part of my soul, and I would argue that those decades produced arguably the best artists and music ever. As far as drugs, well, I only puffed on a joint once walking home with my friend Carol, without even inhaling; and sex, well, let us leave that where it is for the time being. Saying all of that, I did have the long hair and sideburns and a peace-loving, rebel spirit.

Although I did not make my mark in the school through athletics, I was successful academically and socially. I loved history and literature and struggled with science and math, making me more suited for broadcasting than pharmacy.

By the time I had reached grade twelve, our school no longer had an active students council. I meant to change that. In the spirit of the times and in protest to Americanism (having lived through a period of history watching their race riots and the Vietnam War fiasco on the evening news), I decided to rebrand the new group the "students committee." Students and faculty supported our new mandate and students ran the election. When election results came in, I was happy to become the new students committee chair, and a grade eleven student, Jane Peters, became the vice-chair.

The students really made it a fun year. The local movie theatre had closed, so with permission from the principal, we rented movies and sold tickets in the community, and the school auditorium became the ad hoc theatre. On Halloween we organized a costume contest for students and faculty and had full participation. The administration also provided an office space for us so that we could meet with students at lunchtime, to answer their questions and help with problems. It was a truly rewarding experience.

Then one afternoon near the end of the year, we called a meeting of all students to meet in the auditorium to declare that we were walking out in a protest march to the school board office downtown. Our graduating year in 1975 also marked the retirement of the school principal, Al McCloy, and his wife Sharon, the high school librarian. Both were much-loved and respected in the community for their decades of service. The natural replacement was to be Lew Joseph, who was the current vice-principal. Mr. Joseph was a tough guy, lean with a demanding voice, but well-respected and loved by students and faculty. He had just earned his master's degree and had been an educator for eighteen years with the last six as our vice-principal. However, we had gotten wind of news that the school board had instead approved a less-experienced educator from another school district.

Once informed, I helped rally a group of senior students, and in a matter of hours we had organized ourselves. By noon when we had our auditorium gathering, almost all the three-hundred-plus students had become aware of the situation. In between I had called the local RCMP detachment, making them aware of our protest march, and gotten support and agreement to march down one lane only, to allow vehicle traffic through the heart of town. I had a half-dozen of the bigger and more mature grade twelves to function as perimeter guards to ensure there was no excess or vandalism. I contacted newspaper outlets in larger communities such as Duncan and Victoria, as well as television stations to cover the event. I then went in and talked to both Mr. McCloy and Mr. Joseph and told them what we were about to do. They obviously could not publicly sanction a walkout of students, but knew it was about to happen and did not stand in our way at my assurance of steps taken to protect the school's reputation and the students. As it was a voluntary walkout, not every student went, and we respected that. Afterwards there were parents who voiced their displeasure with me, including those who declared they "hated me."

We had great media coverage, both print and radio. I imagine the incoming principal also saw the coverage and got a glimpse of the situation, and I am sure that it could not have been fun for him. The march through town to the school board office took about thirty minutes. Arriving with placards and banners, we stood outside chanting for someone to come out and talk with us. After about ten minutes, I entered the building to find a board member to engage with. The only one in the office turned out to be Kirk Tanner, the treasurer. I calmly explained why we were there, and our position on the unfairness of the board's passing over Mr. Joseph for principal. I requested he come back out with me to accept a signed petition in front of the students, and we would then simply return to school. He did what elected officials in his situation would do; he dug in. In no way would he come out in front of a bunch of "rabble," he said, and told me it would be in our best interest to turn around and go back to school. I said that was out of the question and assured him the "rabble" were decent students who were peacefully exercising their rights and expressing their displeasure. I went back outside, consulted with my group of senior students, and with their agreement went back in to speak with Mr. Tanner again. I assured him the students were committed to staying as long as it took and would not leave until he came out and accepted our petition. He dug in further, saying that he had called the principal to come down and get us to go back. He was concerned students would not have returned by the end of the school day, and he did not want bus drivers on overtime. So, I left a second time and went out of the office, down the stairs into the crowd, and spoke with the team. Then, making a stand on the steps of the building, I told them that the treasurer had declared them "rabble" and that the school board was instructing us to go back to school. I asked them to instead continue to support our position and urged them to stay as long as necessary. To loud cheers we solidified our position as Mr. McCloy arrived. He sought me out and told me that the school board had asked him to come down and send us away. I told him respectfully that we were staying until the school board representative came out and accepted our petition, and it was no reflection on his authority or our respect for him. With great dignity and courtesy, he left and went back to his office, and the standoff continued.

I am not sure whether it was a call from Mr. McCloy to Kirk Tanner to tell him the students were committed to the protest, or whether conversations with other board members understanding the downside of negative media coverage swayed him, or if I finally convinced him on our third face-to-face meeting that the best move was to come out and accept our petition, but Kirk Tanner finally agreed to accept our petition. We came out of the board office together, and I finally was able to present him with the petition. Amid loud cheering, with banners and placards waving, we triumphantly returned to school. Buses were waiting, drivers and staff were on overtime, and we were enormously proud. My final moment before leaving that day came in Al McCloy's office with only him, Mr. Joseph, and myself present. It was a moment that was incredibly emotional and transformative. In that moment, in that room, I felt equal in stature to these two men. Privately they thanked me and the students for our support and caring; they were both very emotional. We also understood this moment would always only be between the three of us. We shook hands, and I closed the door behind me.

Although the union, faculty, and members of the community wrote letters to the board, attended board meetings, and wrote editorials and letters to the editor in the local newspaper, the board stood firm. Mr. Joseph stayed on as vice-principal for the next year, but shortly afterwards accepted a principalship in the Interior of BC, hundreds of kilometres away. He died years later while still young from lung disease. I was fortunate, about nine years after graduating, to meet Mr. McCloy at a local coffee shop for a reunion of sorts. Now, nearly seventy-five years old, he was well and happy. The community had gotten him a golf cart when he retired, and he spent much of his time on the links. I told him of how things had fared for me, including my stint in broadcasting and the career changes in between. I was also married and a dad. To my dismay, his wife was having health challenges and could not join us. A short while later, ten years after our graduation and protest, Mr. McCloy died. I sent Mrs. McCloy a card expressing how much they had both meant to me as a student and as a person, and I got a lovely note in return just prior to her passing. I also wrote a letter to the editor expressing my gratitude to both of them and my grief at their loss. I also recapped the course of events of the protest march, now more than a decade past, including my private meeting with the principal and vice-principal. My experience as students committee chair gave me a rare opportunity to forge a lifelong respect and admiration for them all. Love and peace . . . always.

Falling from the Sky

<u>Album Cut</u>:
"Free Fallin'"
Tom Petty and the Heartbreakers
***Full Moon Fever*, released 1980**

I HAVE DONE DUMB THINGS, stupid things, dangerous things, and survived. Thankfully, fewer as I get older. Sometimes I took risks I should not have, I lacked experience and judgment, I took foolish chances, and other times I followed other people's prodding rather than my gut instinct; and yet my gut or instinct has rarely failed. Your gut feeling is really the essence of yourself; your moral centre, your conscience, your inner voice (often the voice of your parents).

I am not by any stretch an adventurer, although I have travelled around the world. I am definitely not a risk taker, although I have almost died making poor decisions driving vehicles; and for reasons I still do not understand today, I "jumped out of a perfectly good airplane" as my friend Scott has often said, on September 21, 1975.

I was only in my first couple of weeks at the British Columbia Institute of Technology (BCIT) when I spotted a poster advertising a meeting of the BCIT Skydiving Club. To this day I do not know what compelled me to attend the meeting that Wednesday afternoon, particularly because I am not even comfortable with getting on a high ladder. By Saturday I was at a small airfield in Abbotsford, BC, with a group of other BCIT students, taking instruction prior to boarding a tiny plane to become airborne and then purposefully plunge out the door at 2,800 feet. The leader of our group was in his second year at BCIT, the president of the BCIT Skydiving Club and a veteran skydiver of over three hundred jumps. So, while we took our instruction, he decided to do a jump. It seemed that hardly any time had passed, and we saw him returning from his jump, walking back toward us around the end of the building. As he got closer, we all stopped dead in what we were doing. Blood covered his jumpsuit and his face! It was horrifying to see this veteran coming back bloodied. His explanation was moderately reassuring. It seems that as he jumped from the plane, a current of wind had thrown his arm back striking himself in the face and causing a bloody nose. So, we continued on.

By mid-afternoon we were ready to board our plane and "fall from the sky." The plane held the pilot, a jump master, and five of us ready for our first jump. In those days it was a solo event; you were not jumping in tandem. It meant that the pilot would take us in a circle to come over the target (jump site), then would signal the jump master, who would then yell at us to jump from the plane. Once out the door, the pilot would circle around to the jump site, and the process kept repeating until we had all exited the plane. I was the last to jump, giving me the unique advantage of watching everyone else go first; but it also cursed me with more time to fret. Of the five of us that day, only one person still stands out to me. Remember, we were all strangers having only met on Wednesday at BCIT, and again on the day of our jump. But I will never forget her. She was petite, blond, cute, and paralyzed by fear. To leave the plane, we first had to sit on the floor and wriggle our bottoms slowly forward to the open doorway and swing our legs out into space. Buffeted by wind, we placed our left hand onto the side of the door frame, and our right held tightly on the edge of the open door at the floor. We sat precariously balanced on the edge, ready to spring out the door on command. On the first pass over the jump site, the jump master yelled, "Go," and she did not move; she sat in place with her blue eyes opened wide. As the pilot circled around a second time, he asked her if she really wanted to do this, and that it would be okay for her to change her mind. She shook her head and said she wanted to try again. The second pass was a repeat of the first one; she froze in place when he yelled, "Go," and the pilot in turn had to make another circle. He told her they would make only one more attempt if she wished, but again suggested she could change her mind. She chose to try a third time. When over the jump site the third time, with her balancing on the precipice, he screamed, "Go!" at her with incredible force, and she finally fell out of the plane. After two more had jumped, it was my turn. The "last man sitting," in this case.

My reaction was indicative of someone conditioned to act in the moment without thinking. When the jump master yelled, "Go," I propelled myself from that tiny plane, 2,800 feet above Earth, out into space on command. The actual free fall seemed instantaneous, lasting for only three seconds until the attached rip cord automatically opened my chute. Our instructor had trained us to look up instantly after leaving the plane to make sure our chute had opened properly; if not, there would be only a moment to try and fix it. The only alternative was to discard the defective parachute and open the emergency chute on my chest. Looking up above my head, my heart skipped a beat when I discovered that the lines of my chute were tangled. To my great relief, I was able to reach up and separate and free the lines quickly. Only at this time was I able to take account of my parachute drop.

It was a beautiful day, all blue sky and sunshine. By pulling my chute directional chords on my left or right, I could turn myself around in the sky, scanning 360 degrees to admire the scenery. I discovered that I experienced no sense of downward movement, and the air was silent around me. It occurred to me to check if I was over the landing area (there was an actual dot placed on the ground to see from the air). I panicked when I could not see it after rotating 360 degrees until it occurred to me to look straight down below my feet, and there was the landing spot almost directly below me. As I approached Earth, it seemed finally that I was plummeting downward at a frightening speed. I bent and relaxed my knees as instructed and got ready to execute a somersault upon touching the ground, which was the method taught in 1975. Once on my feet, standing on solid ground, with my parachute stretched out on the ground beside me, I whooped with joy. I could not wait to go back up and do it again. Adrenalin and exhilaration ruled over common sense; however, we were at the end of the afternoon, and there was no time for second jumps. Not all of my fellow jumpers had fared as well as me, and some certainly did not feel exhilarated. I found that one guy had landed in an irrigation ditch; another had landed among a herd of cows and had struck one with his two feet, knocking the cow over and the wind out of his own body. Sadly, the petite jumper, who had made her exit on the third attempt, panicked as the ground rushed at her, and instead of relaxing her legs, she froze, landing rigidly, and broke one of her ankles. When September 21 rolls around each year I remember my falling out of the sky with wonder and pride.

The only thing I have done more dangerous than jumping out of the sky is to drive or ride as a passenger in a car.

Returning from a family camping trip to Pachena Bay in our old panel van with my brother Don driving was one of those moments. The thought crossed our minds that we were all going to die. We had spent three days over a weekend camping, and on the last day my dad decided we should take the long hike to the Pachena Point lighthouse and back. Originally named Beghadoss

Point after a shipwrecked vessel in 1879, the BC government changed the name to Pachena Point, an anglicized version of the Ditidaht name meaning "foam on the rocks" and in recognition of the Pacheedaht First Nation. Built in 1907 following one of Canada's worst maritime disasters—the sinking of the passenger vessel *Valencia*, taking with it 133 souls—the lighthouse projected its beacon out fourteen nautical miles from the rugged coastline on Vancouver Island's West Coast. The trail wound through the forest for about eight kilometres, a moderate hike that all ages could do that also included steep inclines and rocky sections.

The next morning, with everyone stiff and sore from our hike the day before, we packed up camp—tent, kids, dog, and all the gear—and into the panel van we went. As much as I loved camping, getting home to a hot shower and a meal without twigs and bugs was starting to be very appealing. We had travelled about two-thirds of the way home with about twenty kilometres left to go along the back gravel logging roads, when we started feeling a thump, thumping, from the back of the van, forcing Dad and all of us out to see what the matter was. We were disappointed to find that the rear passenger side tire had gone flat. We all pitched in and removed every bit of gear to allow Dad to retrieve the spare tire placed under the plywood flooring of the van. Dad, being a practised hand, had the tire replaced and us all loaded back in fairly quickly, and off down the road toward home we continued. We had not driven more than a couple of kilometres more when to all of our dismay the spare also went flat; in hindsight, a spare tire that came with a fifty-dollar panel van was never destined to support seven people, a dog, an eight-by-ten-foot canvas tent, and about five pounds of beach sand, especially pounding over potholes on a bumpy, gravel logging road.

But now we were stuck. No more spare tires. Tantalizingly close to home. After waiting about an hour, hoping someone would come along and help us out, Dad set out on foot toward camp to get our family car and a new spare tire to rescue the family. His hope was that along the way someone would pick him up and offer him a ride, which unfortunately for him never happened. There were no logging operations on weekends, and no company vehicles were about. So, we sat and waited for Dad, getting thirsty and hungry, and I imagine probably getting on Mom's nerves fairly quickly. When Dad arrived hours later with the family car and a spare tire for the panel van, we were elated. He looked exhausted. After the previous day's hike to and from the Pachena Bay Lighthouse, he had just completed a twenty-kilometre trek on rocky, uneven roads. What he did not know until he arrived back was that there was one last hurdle to overcome. In the spirit of being helpful I had jacked up the van and tried to take the flat tire off, so it would be easier and quicker for Dad when he got back with the spare. Unfortunately, I was not entirely successful; having removed four of the five lug nuts holding the wheel on the car, I had stripped the final nut in trying to get it off. So, although we now had a fully inflated spare ready to be put on the panel van, we could not get the flat tire off first. Dad was really upset but did not rant or yell because he knew I had acted with good intentions. Fortunately, with effort, a hammer, and a battered screwdriver, he managed to pound the nut enough to free it up, so the tire was finally replaced. The final hurdle was driving two vehicles back the final twenty kilometres to camp. Dad decided he would drive Mom and my two sisters in the family car, a 1965 navy blue Pontiac Laurentian bought the year that Rose was born, and that Don would drive the panel van with myself and our younger brother Peter.

Don and I were only fifteen, and although a competent driver, he had little experience at that time. He cautiously pulled away with Dad following behind in case any other disaster befell us, and off we went. After a time, Don became more confident, and with our urging (remember we were hungry, thirsty, and wanting hot showers) he gradually picked up his speed. He found himself accelerating up a long, steep hill, and when hitting the crest, the car rocketed forward on the level ground. The next thing we knew we were approaching a sharp turn to the right and Don found himself going too fast to make the corner, and we felt the whole van sliding sideways toward a cliff on the left side of the road. Peter was certain we were going over the cliff and that we would all die, so he grabbed the door handle and started opening the door to jump out the passenger side. Instinctively, I reached over and grabbed the back of his shirt collar and pulled him back into the van just as Don regained control at the edge of the cliff, sliding safely to a halt on the gravel. With dust swirling in the air, Peter hurled himself out of his door and ran sobbing to the family car. With Mom consoling him, Dad came over to check Don and me out. He told Don to relinquish his spot, and I became the driver for the final part of the journey. Funny, after decades I can still picture Peter bailing out the door and me hauling him back in. He would have been safer jumping from 2,800 feet with a parachute than taking his chances bailing out of a speeding panel van into a gravel roadway or a boulder-strewn ditch.

Years later I was fulfilling my dream. I had graduated from BCIT and was an on-air announcer at radio station CJLD in Kamloops, BC. I was fortunate that they played syndicated programming during the 1:00 a.m. to 5:00 a.m. slot, as students began their broadcasting careers on the midnight shift at their respective stations. Of the twenty of us who had started the program, only eleven of us had completed the Broadcast Communications diploma, and only six got jobs on air. I had secured my job in Kamloops in part because I had worked the earlier summer at their satellite station in Princeton, BC, CKLD Radio. I had done well enough there that the station manager Rob had recommended me for the Kamloops spot. After a month at the station, I started to settle into my new life and decided to drive two hours back to Princeton one day to visit Rob and his wife Eden. Eden loved me and would always feed me, so it was a joy to see them. The day started off sunny and bright, and my trip went smoothly. As usual, Rob was grumpy and Eden sweet, and their kids—Ellie, two, and Jude, four—climbed all over me.

After lunch, with the weather starting to turn and a two-hour drive ahead of me, I decided I should head back to Kamloops as I was also on air at 8:00 p.m. Hugging the kids and Eden, and with a "See you later, Boss" to Rob, I left town, choosing to take the old highway between Princeton and Merritt before linking up on the main highway to Kamloops. My drive would be slightly longer, but it was more fun; winding roads, old churches, and sometimes herds of cattle crossing your path. I was about halfway to Merritt when the sky darkened rapidly and it began to pour. Rain pounded on the pavement so hard it bounced inches off the roadway into the air. My windshield wipers could hardly keep up, and yet I continued at my same speed, hurrying on my way. That is, until I faced an unexpected, sharp right-hand turn rushing up at me. Shades of Don on that gravel logging road on the way back from Pachena a long while ago, except I totally lost control with my little fastback, spinning one and a half times in the roadway until I came to a stop facing the direction I had just come from, with my driver's side tires resting in a ditch. It was the first and only time I experienced an "out of body" vision. While spinning in circles on the wet pavement I saw myself sitting behind the steering wheel, clutching it tightly with white knuckles, wearing my denim jacket. Seconds later I found myself stuck in a ditch on the side of the highway. I was angry at my situation and my carelessness. I slammed my right hand on the steering wheel; but apart from the bruise I would have later, I was unscathed. I opened my car door and cautiously stepped out and walked around my vehicle to survey any damage. The car appeared as well off as I was, so then I took stock of my situation. The rain had eased up by this time, and I stepped into the roadway and looked both ways, finding no cars or people in either direction. It was then that I decided to walk across the road and see what the other side looked like, as it occurred to me that my car could have spun the other way around and my fate would have been whatever I found there. The road had been rising for kilometres, and when I crashed, my car ended up in the ditch next to a high rock face. What I found on the other side was very disturbing; a cliff of hundreds of feet stared back at me. My whole body began to tremble, partially from shock, but also from the realization that if my car had spun in the opposite direction, I would have plummeted to my death at twenty years of age.

I staggered back over to my car and leaned against it, not caring that it was wet. Time passed, how much I cannot remember, but eventually another vehicle came by and, seeing my predicament, gave me a ride to Merritt to get a tow truck. Even if there had been cellular phones in those days, the region is mountainous, and there would have been no signal, so people were more inclined to pick you up. After a tow truck had hauled me into Merritt, the mechanic who inspected my car assured me there was no damage; however, he pointed out that my tires were in poor condition—almost bare, in fact. So, in spite of the downpour and my excessive speed, I might have avoided this near-death experience if I had had better tires on my car. Before I left the garage, I had all four tires replaced with the little money I had saved in my account (my pay was a meagre seven hundred dollars per month). To this day I am fastidious about my tires.

There was an episode with my dad about six years later when my older son David was about two years old. I was visiting my parents back in Lake Cowichan, and Dad wanted to take David for a ride in his truck to get ice cream. I went out and checked his tires, and they were in very much the same condition my fastback's tires had been years before when I had almost lost my life on the Merritt highway. So, I told Dad that I was sorry, but I did not feel his vehicle was safe, and before David could go riding with him, I would like him to get new tires. The next morning everyone got up expecting Dad's famous pancake breakfast, but we could not find him anywhere in the house. Looking out the kitchen window to the driveway, I noticed his truck was gone. To his credit, and because of his love for his grandson and me, he had gotten up early and gone over to a local tire shop and had four new tires installed on his truck. I was happy and proud of him for understanding how important this was to me. After pancakes, he took David for a ride in his truck.

Danger in the City

<u>Album Cut</u>:
"Mack the Knife"
Bobby Darin
***That's All*, released 1959**

COMING TO THE "BIG CITY" was exciting and scary at the same time. Having lived my first eighteen years in communities as small as thirty-five families, or thirty-three hundred residents, meant trips to Nanaimo and Victoria were highlights. I remember the first time I drove into Victoria with my dad I was so nervous I was shaking, and when we got there, I was as relieved as I was happy. After moving to Ontario, I had a similar experience. I drove an hour in morning rush hour traffic from where I lived in Ajax to downtown Toronto. I drove an eleven-passenger commuter van to work, and when everyone had left, I sat for a moment to collect myself before getting out because my legs were shaking so badly. In the decades since then I have driven around a good part of Europe, across the United States, and much of Canada, and now take driving in stride.

My first experience off the Island and in a large city was Vancouver in 1975 when I was eighteen, heading into the broadcast program at BCIT. I remember the Pacific Coach Lines bus stopping at the corner of Georgia and Granville Streets, and out my window was a group of Hare Krishna devotees in orange robes with shaved heads, banging tambourines. I remember the bustle of people, buses, and cars and the noise. The constant thrum of traffic and every few minutes a siren, if not a police siren, then it would be an ambulance on its way to an accident scene or rushing back to St. Paul's Hospital.

It took time to figure my way around the city, but I soon became proficient with using the bus system to get around. Without my own vehicle I walked or took a bus. My best friend Barry, Dal, and Christine all went to the University of British Columbia (UBC), which was about an hour trip by bus from Burnaby where I now lived. On weekends I would head out there to visit and party. We had only been in Vancouver for about one month when I arrived one Saturday night at UBC with a smile on my face looking forward to time with my friends. Everyone was sitting in Barry's room, and no one was in a party mood. Word had come from Lake Cowichan that one of our friends from elementary school had driven off the road and died in a car crash. Eighteen years old, the world ahead of him, and his car had careened off the road late one night, killing him instantly. It was hard to comprehend. We sat and talked sombrely for a time and then, without any fanfare, we simply got quietly up, and we all went home. Russ had sat behind me in homeroom for years. The reality of life is that we never forget our friends, and the passing of time does not seem to age them. I will always picture Russ in my mind as he was at eighteen.

Transit buses would stop running out of UBC at about 1:00 a.m., so I would have to leave shortly after midnight, whether the party was going strong or not. Students at the university who lived in dorms had keys and picture ID to get in and out of their residences. One night I got stuck; I had met a girl at a party who brought me back to her dorm, but after talking for a while she disappointedly sent me off. I was stranded, as the buses had stopped running. I had nowhere to go, was tired, and only mildly inebriated. Not sure what to do, I went to an administration building and told the guard there that I lived on campus, had been out partying, and had left my key and ID in my dorm by accident. I told him my name was Barry and gave him my friend's dorm and room number. He probably heard a similar story from drunk students every weekend, but he looked up my friend's information and gave me a key to the building. Barry had left me much earlier when I had gone off with the girl, expecting not to see me again that night. I got inside his dorm building and banged on his door, waking him and his roommate. He laughed and cursed me for waking him up but threw me a blanket. I slept on the cold, linoleum floor, with a thin blanket covering me and no pillow. Not the best sleep I ever had, but I was grateful not to have found myself stranded in the cold outside.

So, I made sure I left earlier from UBC from that time on. Not knowing the city well enough to know which areas were sketchy also became a problem. Coming home after midnight after visiting Barry one night, I made the mistake of getting off at a stop in a bad part of the city. My trip between UBC and home meant a couple of transfers, and on this night, I got off at the intersection of Hastings and Abbott Streets. Still a very rough area of the east end of Vancouver today, then it was less populated and more poorly lit. After the bus left, I realized I was in an area I felt nervous about. There was a group of three guys standing near the stop, and a couple of other people waiting for the next bus, which to my dismay I found would be another half an hour away. I had not stood there exceptionally long when I heard a woman in distress yelling for help. No one moved. I looked around and saw a long dark entry into one of the buildings and figured out that was where the ruckus was coming from. With my heart pounding, I walked a dozen steps into the darkness of the entryway and could see a huge man with his back to me and a woman pinned against the door facing me with her pants partially down. She was still calling out, so I loudly asked, "Can I help . . . Do you need help?"

She said, "No," so I happily went back out onto the street. I looked around and noticed not a soul had moved; everyone was minding their own business. I had barely emerged when I heard her yelling for help even more loudly than the first time. So again, I went into the darkened entryway and saw the exact same situation; a woman in distress with an exceptionally large and drunk man forcing himself on her. This time, when I asked if she needed help, she said, "Yes."

Without thinking, and not appreciating the full danger I was putting myself into, I reached up and grabbed him from behind by his right shoulder and spun him around to face me while she stood up, pulling her pants back up to her waist. Before any fists flew, a bright spotlight shone into the doorway, and a voice over a loudspeaker commanded everyone to leave the entryway. To my great good luck, at the exact moment that I had spun the drunk around to face me, a Vancouver police paddy wagon had happened by and interceded. I let the woman walk out first, followed by the drunk, with me close behind. We all walked toward the paddy wagon. There was a cop standing close to his vehicle waiting and one sitting behind the driver's seat. As the woman was within about six feet of the paddy wagon, the drunk suddenly sprang forward and shoved her violently against the side of the vehicle and turned and ran up Hastings Street heading west. The cop in the driver's seat sprang out of the vehicle, and both cops quickly chased him up the street, catching him, knocking him to the ground, handcuffing him, and throwing him roughly into the back of the paddy wagon. They then came back and asked me what had happened, and I explained the story and that I had only responded to cries of help, and that all I wanted was to get home to Burnaby. They told the woman and me to get on the next bus and to go home. Moments later the bus arrived, and she boarded the bus, and I followed steps behind. She sat across from me, and I really saw her for the first time. She was also drunk. She never said a word to me; she never said thank you or acknowledged that I had stopped her rape.

After my adrenalin slowed down, I began to freak out. I realized the risk I had placed myself in. The drunken man in the doorway had been much bigger, well over six feet tall and hefty, and could have had a knife or even a gun. If the paddy wagon had not passed by at exactly the right moment, at the very least I would have been in a fist fight. I wondered if any of the others who had stood silently on the street would have stepped in to help me. It also occurred to me that the drunk and the woman were not strangers. The fact that she turned me away the first time suggested to me later that they likely knew each other. I was sweating, my body began shaking, and I was truly frightened. When I finally got home, I phoned my brother Don and woke him up to tell him my story; I needed to hear his voice and have a familiar touchstone.

I realized that, put in the same situation, I would have done the same thing again; I would not have been able to stand by and ignore calls of distress. My parents had brought me up differently. Injury or death might have been my fate in those early morning hours. Dead at eighteen years old because I had interceded between two drunks in a sketchy neighbourhood in the east end of Vancouver. I cannot imagine my parents getting that news. So, I smartened up quickly. Soon afterwards I figured out the layout of the city, and how the bus routes worked, and from that point on I transferred buses only on busy, well-lit streets. When I walked the city at night, I would cross over when I saw groups of young guys, to be as far away as possible from them.

The largest city I worked in was Toronto, between 1987 and 1991. Boy, was that different from Vancouver! Not only in size and noise, but in vibrancy. Everyone was in a hurry; no one looked at each other on the street or said hello. People grabbed coffees on the run, and doughnut shops were on every corner. People ate lunches quickly at counters or on park benches, and then they scurried quickly back to their cubicles. My transfer from Nanaimo, BC to the head office of Sears Canada in downtown Toronto came in the spring of 1987. The single worst decision I have made in my life. After four years living there, my marriage was on the rocks; I had had more than enough of Ontario and just wanted to head back to BC with my family. After accepting a severance package, I was destined to leave on Boxing Day, December 26, 1990. With only one week left working for Sears, I found myself at 8:00 a.m. on a Tuesday morning at the corner of Front and Bay Streets with dozens of others waiting for a walk signal. Being at the front of the pack and in a hurry, as soon as the walk signal came on, I sprang from the curb, rushing to get across. As I got to the centre of the intersection, a large pickup truck, going against the light, turned left directly in my path, nearly striking me. I instinctively banged my gloved hand on his tailgate as he went by, as if to say, "Hey, buddy, watch out, will ya." As I was in a rush to get to my office and to work, I just kept walking briskly on. About halfway up the next block I felt a tap on my shoulder. I stopped, turned, and found an angry, aggressive guy nose to nose with me, yelling and swearing in my face. I took a step backwards, confused at first at what was going on. Then I realized this maniac was the driver of the pickup that had nearly run me down in the intersection moments earlier. He had parked his truck on one of Toronto's busiest streets in morning rush hour traffic, with hundreds of commuters rushing to work, to come and attack me. My first experience with road rage. Fortunately, a group of four other commuters stopped and stood around us, as backup for me. They had seen the attack from behind. After screaming in my face for minutes he threatened me physically, telling me he was going to punch me out and challenging me to fight him right there on the street. To this next level of aggression, one of my supporters challenged him by telling him if he attacked me, he would be committing assault. His response was telling: "I don't care; I just got out of jail anyway." Looking around and finding that he had no support, and that I was not going to accept his challenge, he turned and vanished into the crowd. Although my attacker could have faced assault charges, I told my supporters that "I am leaving Toronto in about a week, and I never plan on coming back." Like my first experience with a dangerous incident, I sat back later in my office and realized how lucky I was. Instead of tapping me on the shoulder he could have stabbed me from behind or hit me with a tire iron or a baseball bat, leaving a four-year-old and a nine-year-old son without their dad. Even though I was wearing winter gloves and felt I had only tapped the back end of his pickup truck, it was me who triggered the chain of events that followed. Now I fight back urges of self-righteousness and moral outrage at bad behaviour, understanding I have no idea who will step out of a vehicle and threaten my life. On December 26, 1990, my wife and younger son boarded a plane to Vancouver, and my nine-year-old and I fled Toronto in our car, heading across the border between Windsor, Ontario and Detroit, Michigan, and started our journey across the northern United States to head home to my parents in Lake Cowichan.

Following My Path

<u>Album Cut</u>:
"Woodstock"
Matthews Southern Comfort
***Later That Same Year*, released 1970**

ONE OF MY BIGGEST ACHIEVEMENTS, that I take pride in still, resulted in a failed career. I set my sights on becoming a radio announcer at about eleven years old in grade five. I remember during a classroom conversation, in which Mr. Waters asked each member of the class, "What do you want to do or be when you grow up," that I knew for a certainty. When it was my turn, I said that I wanted to be a "disc jockey," to which the entire class laughed at me. As I was chubby then, my classmates misunderstood "disc jockey" for jockey and imagined me riding a racehorse. Of course, this did not deter me, and from that moment on it became my only career choice. In grade seven, I volunteered to be the deejay for the school sock hops at lunch. I remember at one sock hop Linda coming over and asking me to dance. I could not believe it and jumped off the stage excitedly. Later that night I was telling Mom about Linda, and Don came in and ruined my moment forever. He told me that he had asked Linda to come over and ask me to dance. It was one of the few times I was angry with my brother. I was shocked, embarrassed, and mad as hell that he had asked her.

Mom gave me my favourite birthday gift in 1972, a portable record player. In the same month, Gordon Lightfoot put out his eighth studio album, *Don Quixote*, and it became the first record album I bought. A couple of months later the Hollies put out "Long Cool Woman," and I bought the single. I played them both incessantly. By grade ten when we had to choose electives for grades eleven and twelve, positioning ourselves for graduation, I travelled to Burnaby with my parents to visit BCIT. I spoke with a counsellor and gathered information on the courses I would need to take in grades eleven and twelve to give me a chance to be selected to the Broadcast Communications–Radio program after my graduation. I then selected law, history, geography, and any course on the BCIT program list and graduated from Lake Cowichan Senior Secondary with academic honours. So far, my plan was on track.

I did almost change my future and miss my moment when I made a late admission to BCIT. Frankly, I cannot remember what caused me to delay applying. Despite my procrastination, as part of the admissions process I was invited for an interview with Terry Garner, a celebrity who at that time hosted the popular CBC TV show *Reach for the Top*. He had a deep, resonant voice and a welcoming manner. I liked Terry right away and explained to him my journey and my passion to be in radio. As I mentioned earlier, he did not sugarcoat it; he did caution that the industry was notorious for poor pay, bad hours, and limited success. However, I hoped that a combination of my academic achievement, my long-term plan and passion, and my leadership in the school as students committee chair would sway him.

I headed home with trepidation because of my late application and started to make plans for my twin brother Don and I to travel across Canada together in my Toyota pickup after graduation. Then just before graduation, I remember walking out of the post office in

Lake Cowichan with a letter from BCIT in my hand. With my heart racing, I opened the envelope and scanned the letter quickly, whooping with joy when I read that I had been accepted. With only twenty people a year out of about 450 candidates being selected to the radio program, I was ecstatic. The plan I had started back in grade five had finally paid off, and in that moment my life changed again. Don and I had to scrap our cross-Canada adventure, and instead we made a shorter trip across the bottom of BC, Alberta, and over the Saskatchewan border to Regina. We then headed northeast for three hours to Tisdale, almost at the Manitoba border, before turning around and backtracking to Alberta through Edmonton and Grande Prairie, finally arriving to surprise our grandma at her home in Spirit River. I had not been to Spirit River since I was six years old, and this was definitely the highlight of our trip.

Why Tisdale? What was the magic that drew us to this tiny farming community nineteen hundred kilometres from home? In the summer of 1975 only about eight hundred fifty people called Tisdale home. My goal was to visit my friend Ross. Ross and I had met at Western Mines during my second summer there; he worked underground as a mucker when I was a pot washer in the cookhouse. "Mucking" was the mining term for shovelling broken rock into tram cars underground after blasting had happened. Ross was tall, about six foot four and lanky, kind of geeky-looking with long, straight, blond hair, and he wore wire-rimmed glasses, which he really needed as he could not see much of anything without them. He was older than me, a university student working for the summer, while I had just finished grade eleven and was only seventeen. He got the job at the mine because his brother Fred had been working there for ten years. Apart from working at the mine outside of Campbell River, Ross had never been to Vancouver Island. So, one weekend when we had three days off in a row, which was a rarity, we decided to make a quick trip home to camp, to visit my parents.

That Saturday morning was a typical summer day in camp; dry and hot. The tar on the roadway that wound through camp would soften from the heat, and you could feel it shift beneath your feet as you walked toward the lake. We decided to go for a swim to cool off. Ross was not a great swimmer but managed to swim with me out to the dock, where we jumped off the diving boards, cannonballed into the lake, and generally relaxed and had fun. But in swimming the fifty feet from the dock back to shore, Ross's glasses fell from his nose and started to sink. Although I could hold my breath for a long time and was able to dive deep, the glasses sank to a depth beyond my lung capacity, and the lake swallowed them up without making a fuss.

Ross literally could not see a thing without his glasses, and on Monday we had to return to the mine. So, a hurried call home to Tisdale secured Ross a copy of his lens prescription, and off we travelled to Duncan, where he was able to get a pair of glasses made that day. We trekked back to the mine on Monday, and at the end of the summer Ross headed back to university in Saskatchewan while I entered my final year of high school.

A couple of months later, my brother Peter was out fishing in our rubber raft. We would start slowly from shore rowing past the dock, parallel to the shoreline, as trout would often strike there. The challenge was that if you dropped your fishing line too deep, it would snag on branches and debris at the bottom of the lake. This day Peter got only slightly snagged and was able to readily free his line. Bringing his line right to the edge of the boat, to inspect the line and the lure, he was surprised to find he had hooked a pair of wire-rimmed eyeglasses—in fact, the pair that Ross had lost swimming a couple of months before. Even to this day I am amazed at the odds of my brother hooking those glasses from the bottom of Kissinger Lake on his fishing line. One of those "what if" questions arose again: "What if one of the other kids had found the glasses?" Would they have thrown them back?

So, once we had to change our cross-Canada trip; Tisdale became the end point. I planned to drive to Ross's home in Tisdale and surprise him by showing up with his lost eyeglasses. I had never been to Saskatchewan before, let alone Tisdale, but we eventually came into town. I knew Ross's last name but had no understanding of where his family's farm was located. So, we went in to the local RCMP detachment and asked one of the constables where we could find the MacLean farm. We followed long, dusty, dirt farm roads for about thirty minutes and came to a stop in front of a farmhouse. A dog came out to greet us, barking and wagging its tail as the front door opened, and Ross's mom stepped on the porch to see who was there. Being a small community, everyone knew their neighbours, and our vehicle was definitely foreign with its BC licence plates. Don and I got out and walked toward the porch while Mrs. MacLean stepped down to greet us. I introduced us as friends of Ross's, and that I had worked at the mine with Ross and her son Fred. I explained about the eyeglasses and handed them over and told her that I had hoped to surprise Ross. She looked perplexed and said that Ross was not home; in fact, he was away in Manitoba. Thanking me for driving so far, she invited us to stay for lunch. We had been on the road for a week eating on a camp stove, and we gratefully accepted her offer.

A short while later her husband came in from the fields for lunch and caught up on our adventure. They were absolutely wonderful people. The lunch was massive and delicious. Fried chicken and potatoes, canned preserves, homemade bread, and pie; Don and I ate until we could eat no more, including second helpings of pie. To this day, the MacLeans's hospitality humbles me. After lunch they offered to take us into town and show us around. All four of us piled into their "corn binder," a brand-new International pickup truck. After the brief tour of town, we stopped at the Legion and had a cold beer with them, where they introduced us around to the locals and told the story of Ross's glasses and the bottom of the lake. Mr. MacLean needed to go back into the fields to continue his work, so he asked us to drop him off at a field where his tractor was waiting and asked us to take his new truck back to the farm for him. Dropping the truck off, and thanking Mrs. MacLean for her hospitality and generosity, we said goodbye and headed back toward my family in Alberta. I never saw Ross or the MacLean's again but have continuously carried our brief visit with them in my heart since.

Radio, Signing Off

<u>Album Cut</u>:
"W.O.L.D."
Harry Chapin
***Short Stories*, released 1973**

FOR ALL MY YEARS OF planning, effort, and dedication to purpose to become a radio announcer, I did not last long in broadcasting. While not unusual, because of the lousy wages and abuse from station managers, my leave-taking from this career was the most heartbreaking of all for me. The work was great, just as I had imagined, sitting in front of a microphone talking to a live audience and spinning records. From day one at BCIT we were told that we *were* broadcasters from that moment. Not students, not trainees, but broadcasters. It was all part of instilling confidence (and bravado) and have us identify instantly with being part of an industry. We were now entertainers, no longer simply applying for jobs, but auditioning for them instead.

One of the unique aspects of BCIT was how the school operated. Every instructor coached us to consider each day as if we were coming into work, not to simply attend classes. This was brought home to me clearly one morning by one of my instructors.

Doug was an old-school broadcaster, a class act. He was smart, he was fair, and he took an interest in people. I had been struggling to complete an important project for a class taught by the dean of the broadcast department. I found myself doing an all-nighter, drinking two pots of coffee and pounding out the final pages on my old Olympia typewriter at the kitchen table. By breakfast I knew it would not be complete in time for me to make my first class of the day, taught by Doug. So, I chose to stay at home, complete the project, and drop it off with the dean and then head to my next class. However, the moment I came into the studio at BCIT, Doug asked me to come into his office. After closing the door, he asked me where I had been. I replied with an apology for missing his class, but explained I had to complete my project and had decided I could make up his class later on. He sat there and listened carefully and politely, not reacting in any particular way. When I was finished with my explanation, he provided me with the most valuable insight I gained in my time during my two years there. He said, "Larry, if this was a job and you had not called in to let me know that you would be late, you probably would not have a job here anymore." He continued, "From this moment on, I want you to think of your time here as coming to work, and that you are responsible and accountable. Stop thinking about this as being at school where you can skip a class." He did not have to say anything else. I liked him, respected him, and took his advice to heart. He was a great guy, and I will never forget him.

My first job on air was by far the best. Our instructors tried to find summer jobs for us in radio stations around the province, and I was offered a job at CKLD in Princeton, BC. I did not even know where Princeton was but accepted without question. Hopping into my fastback, I made the five-hour drive from Vancouver, through Manning Park, into Princeton for my interview. The station manager had been in broadcasting for about ten years. Rob had graduated from BCIT in their first broadcasting program and always hired BCIT students for the summer. Princeton is a small town nestled in the mountains between the Tulameen and Similkameen Rivers, dependent upon primary industry: logging, a small sawmill, and Similkameen Mines. In those days, the radio station was situated in the basement of the Sandman Hotel, located at the top of the hill as you entered Princeton from Vancouver. It was a tiny operation, with one room for an office and one as a studio for our on-air broadcasting. We were live from 7:00 a.m. to noon with Rob and I sharing the airtime, taking a feed from the mother station, CJLD, in Kamloops for the balance of the day. One of my most memorable moments was a visit from a broadcasting icon. Terry David Mulligan was a class act. He stopped by on his way to a fishing trip in the local area to simply say hi. He told me that he had been listening to me on the way in and had enjoyed my music selection. Dressed in a plaid shirt and jeans with long hair and a beard, he came across as just another guy rather than a celebrity. He could have kept on driving, but instead he took the time to stop and talk to a random young kid on the radio, and I have never forgotten his generosity of spirit.

It was great to be alive. I was nineteen years old and was on the radio in a small town, and it did not take long for everyone to know me. I did my on-air shift, wrote advertising copy, recorded commercials, did the news, and after a month Rob went on vacation, and I ran the whole operation for three weeks. Princeton was an important transportation hub back then. Prior to the opening of the Coquihalla Highway in 1986, the only route into the BC Interior was on the Hope-Princeton Highway. Most travellers would refuel in Princeton, and the local Esso station at the entrance to town pumped the third-highest volume of gasoline in the entire province. They also hired teenage girls to pump gas in the summertime. I only filled the tank of my fastback at the Esso station that summer.

I also spent hours hanging with the RCMP constables, at first simply to look for news to report. After a time, a couple of the younger guys became friends. I went out on patrol one night with Herbie, riding with him from Princeton out to Hedley and back; another time one of the cops put me in the back seat of his cruiser and closed the door, and I became trapped. I rode around town for an hour like that, looking out the windows and listening to the police chatter on the radio. It certainly gave me a unique perspective. Every night I would go to the coffee shop at the bus depot and have coffee with four or five of them. I was this young guy with longer hair, large sideburns, and wearing denim, and they were all in uniform. One night when I came in to join them for coffee one of the new waitresses asked me if I was an undercover cop, which I thought was really funny.

I had not told anyone in Princeton that I had a twin brother. Don came up to visit me one weekend, arriving late in the afternoon with another high school friend, Sam. Don had my address, but in those days, no one had cell phones, and when he arrived and I was not home, he decided to go to the Esso and fill up his gas tank. A couple of the girls came out and started flirting with him, thinking it was me. He told them, "I am not who you think I am; I am Larry's brother Don," and asked them if they knew where I might be. Of course, they thought that I was playing a joke on them, so they simply laughed and let him drive away. He then noticed a couple of police cruisers at the bus depot and went into the coffee shop. I had told him I knew all the cops in town, so he thought that he would ask them. Not one of them believed him either, even when he showed them his ID. I had been at a dance in town, and when I finally got home and found him sitting in his car outside my place, I was excited, and he was frustrated.

It turned out that Sam had been working in a sawmill way up north in Mackenzie, BC, and he and Don were driving up there to retrieve Sam's gear. I decided to go on the road trip with them. Don had borrowed my dad's GMC Suburban, so three of us could sit on the bench seat up front, leaving the back of the vehicle empty for Sam's gear. It was a ten-hour drive if you did not stop, so that Saturday, after a late breakfast and getting organized, we headed out on the highway. There were few highlights. We kept driving north through 100 Mile House, Williams Lake, and Quesnel, and when we hit Prince George about seven hours later, our stomachs were grumbling, and we decided to pull over to buy food. We stopped at a Kentucky Fried Chicken and got their largest bucket of chicken, stopped at a liquor store, and got a dozen beer, and kept going. The first round of the chicken was delicious. But later that evening when it was no longer hot, and the beer had become warm, it was far less appetizing; by now the smell of cold, greasy, chicken permeated the vehicle. Three hours north of Prince George we finally arrived at Mackenzie. It was truly anticlimactic. It was after midnight when we arrived and started loading Sam's belongings into the back of the Suburban. We were like thieves in the night, stealing away in darkness about an hour later, retracing our journey. Although we took turns driving, we did pull over for a couple of hours of sleep, only to wake up to the last of the cold and even greasier remnants of the KFC Mega Bucket of chicken and the last of the beer. I swear it was about ten years later that I could eat fried chicken again.

After arriving back in Princeton at midday on Sunday, we all crashed hard. It had been a marathon trip. Late the next afternoon, we all went for a drive through town as I was going to show them the highlights of Princeton. We were cruising down Main Street when a police siren came on behind us, and looking in the rear-view mirror, we saw the flashing lights on the cruiser. Herbie stepped out of his car, putting his police hat on his head. Don got out of the driver's side of the Suburban, and I simultaneously stepped out of the passenger side, and we started walking toward Herbie. He stopped dead in his tracks, looked from side to side at both of us, shook his head, said, "I don't believe it," got back into his cruiser, and drove away. When I next saw Herbie a couple of days later, he told me he had went back to tell the other cops that I actually did have an identical twin brother, but they still did not believe him.

I dated a couple of the girls in town; nothing serious, though. The girl that I was really interested in was Deb. She had a smile that would light up the sky, brunette hair down to her shoulders, wonderful curves, and a boyfriend. A couple of single moms in their thirties also took an interest in me. I went to lunch a couple of times, had dinner at their places, and had brief, clumsy affairs.

Whenever I heard a siren in town, no matter how late in the evening, I would get into my fastback and race to the scene. In my reporter mode, I would be looking to report on the story. Because of my friendship with two of the constables, they allowed me access. I remember one night arriving at an accident scene on the outskirts of Princeton. Police cruisers and ambulances were already there when I arrived. Parking my car on the side of the road, I walked toward the flashing lights. Brandon, one of the highway patrol officers, walked toward me and asked if I would light and drop three flares on the road behind me to warn other drivers, placing them into my hands. After lighting the flares, I wandered back and asked what was happening.

Two local boys had decided to drag race their motorcycles on a long straightaway. One was a brother of one of the girls I had dated. He had made a fateful error in judgment. He had quickly beat his friend to the end of the road and then had turned his bike sideways to see how far behind his friend was when his friend's bike violently collided into his. He should never have turned his bike to look. The impact of the collision knocked his bike onto its side, pinning his leg underneath as it slid along the highway. His foot was severed, only hanging on to his leg by a thread (fortunately later successfully reattached). Brandon was using his flashlight scouring the highway for evidence and stooped down to pick up an object. He asked me what I thought it was, and I told him I had no idea. He told me it was a bone fragment from one of the boys. At one time I had thought about becoming a RCMP; that night I decided it was better to be a reporter than a cop working accident scenes.

I would occasionally go into the Princeton Hotel and talk to the owner and his son Gerry. Gerry was a university student and worked at the bar for his dad during the summer. It was a well-run establishment, and I liked Gerry. But being young and stupid I almost messed up badly.

Fred, one of the underage local guys, had approached me to buy him a couple of cases of beer for a party. I was really uncomfortable and did not want to do it, but he worked on me until I said yes. I went into the bar and bought two cases from Gerry from behind the counter. He looked at me quizzically, as I had only ever stopped for one beer at a time in the past, and I assured him they were for me. I should have stopped there, because my gut told me it was wrong to lie to Gerry and buy beer for underage guys. It was the longest night in my life. I found out that the party was twenty-one kilometres out of town at Bromley Rock, and I became terrified someone would get drunk and crash his car and be killed, and I would be responsible. I debated about whether to call Herbie or one of my police friends and admit what I had done and have them go to Bromley Rock and break up the party. I reached for the phone and put it back down a dozen times during the night, not sleeping a wink. In the morning as soon as I could I called Fred and asked how things had gone and if everyone had made it home safely, and when he said "Yes," I told him I would never buy him booze again.

Being a local celebrity of sorts, I was asked to spend a long weekend doing the announcing for a provincial women's softball tournament being held in Princeton that summer. Of course, I jumped at the chance. I spent the entire three days announcing the game—"Now up to the plate for Victoria, Jenny Smith the catcher"—except for five minutes. On Saturday about noon, Dan, one of the local aldermen, stopped by the broadcast booth to say hi. I covered local school board and town council meetings as a reporter, and so I had met him before. He asked me if I needed a bathroom break, and if so, he would cover for me. I said, "Thanks," and split for about five minutes; when I returned, he immediately disappeared. Dan was no dummy. Apart from being an alderman, he was also a local realtor. In the Monday morning *Similkameen Spotlight* was a three-page spread about the weekend tournament with a photo of Dan in the broadcast booth at the microphone. The caption read, "Local alderman supporting the community this past weekend at the provincial women's softball tournament." The bugger! He had set up a photo op with the local newspaper and had offered to cover my going to the washroom as a diversion. I was shocked, but more importantly the organizers of the tournament were angry with him. They printed a genuinely nice "letter to the editor" message thanking me for my efforts and support over the weekend as a correction to the paper, and they baked me a chocolate cake shaped and decorated as Fred Flintstone. It was heartwarming to see a community pull together in support of someone they knew had been wronged. I took my cake over to the RCMP station to share with my friends there. I could never look at Dan again the same way after that weekend.

When I left Princeton at the end of the summer to head back to my second year at BCIT, I was incredibly sad to leave town. It had been a tremendous learning experience working at the radio station and a glorious summer as a nineteen-year-old. Dozens of letters and notes were sent to the station wishing me well, and the *Similkameen Spotlight* put in a full-page advertisement to thank me. Small-town Canada cannot be beat.

My second year at BCIT was eventful in different ways. For about four months I dated Sally, who was in the TV elective in our Broadcast Communications program. She was fun and cute, and because I was not that confident with girls, it was most important that she took an interest in me. Her family was well off, having a sailboat and living in North Vancouver. She lived in a basement suite in Vancouver on her own and was two years older than me. She chose concerts for us to go to that I would not have considered, and we enjoyed them immensely. Chuck Mangione on November 12, 1976, introduced me to the magic of the flugelhorn; later in December 1977 he released my favourite song of his, "Feels So Good." We saw Janis Ian, who had a huge hit in 1975 with "At Seventeen." She had a lovely voice, a nice sense of humour, and a Jersey accent—and what a show she put on! She took a few questions from the audience, and some goofball in the back asked her what she thought about "Icky Bicky" (a derisive nickname for ICBC, the new public auto insurance body in BC). She replied, "What is an Icky Bicky?" and the audience laughed, relieved she took the question so well.

Since then, I have enjoyed dozens of concerts over my lifetime: country, rock, folk, blues, and comedy. George Carlin at the Queen Elizabeth Theatre gave me a taste of comic genius. My favourite rock concert was Elton John, shortly after releasing his album *Goodbye Yellow Brick Road*. He blew the Pacific Coliseum roof off closing with "Saturday Night's Alright for Fighting." Gordon Lightfoot introduced me to "The Wreck of the Edmund Fitzgerald" at his Vancouver concert, and Johnny Cash and June Carter Cash touched my soul in Nanaimo.

We also went out to dinner a couple of times, the first time at Mulvaney's on Granville Island, one of the better restaurants in town. They required men to wear a jacket, so I bought a caramel-coloured, corduroy sports jacket. It was my first time at a restaurant where a maître d' escorted you to your table and the waiter had a white cloth placed over their arm. Fortunately, I brought enough money, and unfortunately, I ordered prawns. The waiter brought a large plate full of unshelled prawns, their legs attached and eyes seemingly looking at me. I was at a loss as what to do. I did not know if I should pick them up in my hands or not, and I did not want to look unsophisticated to Sally. I turned to the waiter and quietly asked him the best way to approach the task. I made a mental note to order steak in the future.

We also went to Brother John's, one of the new and hip places in Gastown. Staff were dressed like monks, with hooded robes and string tied around the waist for belts. The food was good, and I did not have to worry about my dinner looking back at me this time. Everything went well, and when the bill came, I looked it over and left a generous tip. As we were leaving the restaurant, with Sally in front of me, I felt a tap on my right shoulder. I stopped and turned around and the waiter told me I had not paid enough for the bill. I was shocked and embarrassed. When I read the bill, I had not looked it over carefully enough, and had mistaken a subtotal as the full amount. So even with my tip, I had not paid enough. Fortunately, I had enough cash on me to take care of it quickly.

Sally invited me over to her place for dinner one night. It was really great. She introduced me to Harry Chapin, playing for me his *Greatest Stories Live* album, which to this day is still one of my favourite albums of all time. Later she asked me to stay over with her, which I happily accepted. Although we had lots of fun, and I enjoyed her company, she was a big city girl, and we gradually drifted apart; but she was an important person in my life, and I remember her fondly.

With experience and confidence gained from working at CKLD radio in Princeton, I applied for and was hired to be a "board operator" (now referred to as a "producer") at CHQM Radio in Vancouver during my second year. It was a busy job. Running the control board meant playing the music, running commercials, and opening the microphones for the news and sports announcers when their slots came up. You had to be quick. At CHQM, the intros, such as "And now the news with Terry Bell," were pre-recorded on a reel-to-reel tape recorder. You would watch the clock, time the music to end at ten seconds to the hour, play the news intro, and then open Terry's microphone. When he would say, "We will be back in a moment with the weather," you would close his mic and play a commercial, and then come back to him.

One night, I was about three minutes to the top of the hour and went to check the news intro only to find that the reel-to-reel machine was not working. My anxiety skyrocketed when I checked the obvious (it was plugged in), and it still did not work. I had to make a split decision as now I only had about two minutes left. I abandoned my control room and raced to the FM studio control room, unplugged their machine, switched recorders in my control booth, swapped the tape, and hit the switch for the intro. I was relieved and applauded myself for my quick thinking, but later was told it would have been better to simply tell Terry Bell that he needed to do his own intro. Live and learn.

My friend Rod did the same gig at CJOR radio, which was then a talk radio station hosting the biggest names in Canadian broadcasting, including Jack Webster and Pat Burns. Christmas Day 1976 found me sitting with Rod doing the all-night shift at CJOR. I arrived, and Rod showed me around the station and his control room. At that time of night on Christmas Day, no one else was working. We had not been there awfully long when we heard a loud banging on the outside door to the station. Looking out the glass door, we saw an irate man yelling and hollering. Rod made a mistake in opening the door to tell the man that the station was closed and to go away. He bolted inside and started screaming obscenities and was yelling that he hated Pat Burns and wanted to talk to him. Rod tried to explain that no one was there, and tried to escort him back out the door, when he grabbed onto a large fire extinguisher mounted to the wall and started yelling louder. Rod was a lean Scot, over six feet tall and imposing, and although the interloper was only about five feet six inches tall, he was wiry and determined, and we could not pry him off the extinguisher. While I kept a wary eye on him, Rod went and called the Vancouver Police Department, who promptly came and hauled him away. We just looked at each other and shook our heads.

It was a long night. Rod had brought turkey sandwiches his mom had made earlier in the day, so that became our Christmas dinner of 1976. We simply played tapes and records from 10:00 p.m. until 5:00 a.m. and talked. About 3:00 a.m. the log called for us to play a comedy selection for half an hour, and Rod told me to find a comedy record in their library. I flipped through a bunch of them and seized on David Frost. Rod threw it on his turntable, made sure everything was playing properly, and turned the volume down so that we could talk. About fifteen minutes into the record, I heard something that caught my ear and asked Rod to turn the volume back up. We were shocked to find that David Frost was doing a bit on masturbation. Back in 1976 this was outrageous to put on the air; so, we scrambled to find a different comedian. We kept waiting for the phone to light up with someone complaining but realized that no one was actually listening at 3:00 a.m. on Boxing Day.

During our second year we did a bus tour of radio and TV stations across the province. This entourage included the reduced group of eleven radio broadcasters and an equal number from both the journalism and TV programs, plus an instructor. We pulled out of the parking lot early one morning to the pungent smell of pot wafting from the back of the bus. What a trip! It culminated in an all-night party at the Yellowhead Inn in Prince George that included gallons of beer, pot, and magic mushrooms. Personally, I stuck to the beer. At one point in the wee hours someone asked, "Where's Dave?" No one had seen him for about an hour. Dave was in the journalism program, basically harmless, but a strange dude who seemed to always be on drugs. Short, with a pear-shaped body, long, tangled hair, and a matted beard to match, often wearing a beret. As we were occupying the entire third floor of the hotel, we had lots of area to cover to find him. Eventually I stumbled upon him passed out, buck naked, lying on his back in a sauna. God knows if he would have survived staying there, passed out for the rest of the night. But with another friend, we got him up on his feet and dressed, and off he went to rejoin the festivities. I do not believe any of our group were bad people, or had caused any damage, but the hotel management banned future trips from BCIT because of our rowdiness.

The one radio station that impressed everyone was CJLD in Kamloops. It was big, bright, very new, and professional-looking, with modern equipment and spotless on-air studios. The station manager greeted us in a sharp suit and neat haircut. We wore jeans and T-shirts, had long hair, sideburns, and droopy moustaches (check out *WKRP in Cincinnati*). I had worked at their station in Princeton the past summer and set my sights on CJLD for a position when I graduated. My friends were happy for me when I secured a spot. It was a pretty cool place to work. Most stations around the province were small and dark, with old equipment, run on skimpy budgets with profits going straight to the owners and little put back into the station.

I found a room to rent in a new home about twenty minutes outside of town. The owner was a single guy who managed an auto parts store in town, and he already had a friend who was a realtor renting one of the other three bedrooms. It was sparsely furnished but met my basic needs. Both guys were older than me and would bring girlfriends home. It was a little disconcerting to hear them having loud, exuberant sex in the bedroom, and then for the girlfriend to come out minutes later to sit and talk with me in the living room.

My on-air shift was from 8:00 p.m. to 2:00 a.m. A rather good shift: I could enjoy the sunshine and bomb around town in my fastback during the day and then live my dream job in the evenings. It was quite an experience. It was a mid-market station, so the talent was pretty decent; the calibre of announcer and individual was sketchier in the small-town markets. There were really good announcers around the station, but huge egos as well. I knew guys who would bring their girlfriends to the station to show off and then have sex in one of the studios. The announcer on the afternoon shift prior to me was Al; he was a couple of years older than me with a decent voice, but truly arrogant.

Generally, you came into the station at least an hour before your show to prepare, select the music you were going to play, and get loose. In those days you had autonomy in your music selection. It was a Top 40 station, categorized as MOR (middle of the road), so it played a balanced mix of pop, rock, and crossover country. Each announcer coming on shift had to play their section of the Top 40 hits, and then blend in their own music choices. Because the Top 40 songs played repeatedly over the day, I could sing them in my sleep.

One evening my shift had been changed to start earlier, but I was not informed. It just happened to be a day when my cousin Shelley and a girlfriend had come into town from Grande Prairie, Alberta to see me, and we enjoyed a nice dinner together. I left them at the restaurant to be back at the station at about 7:00 p.m., in time to prepare for my shift. Al had been on air as usual, and he believed I was going to be there to start at 7:00 instead of 8:00 p.m. When I arrived, he was angry at me and stood up and left with a record spinning on the turntable, which was unprofessional. He gave me no time to prepare or gather records for my show; he just bailed. I was frantic and grabbed a stack of records and sat down before his record finished; quickly collecting my thoughts, I turned on my microphone, and the show went on. From that moment on, I thought Al was a jerk. There. I finally got it off my chest after all these years.

My twin brother came up to Kamloops to listen to me on air as well. Of course, my station did not reach the Vancouver market, so it was cool he came up to see me and hear me live on the radio. I gave him a tour of the station and said he could sit in with me in the studio while I did my shift. He said no. He wanted to go sit in his car and listen to me on the car radio. It was a cool experience for him and for me. I loved him for it. My parents came up one weekend to visit. I am sure they also listened to me live on air; sadly, I do not remember talking to them about it. Hopefully, they liked listening and thought I was rather good. I remember when working the summer before in Princeton at CKLD that when I left town, one of my listeners, an older lady, gave me one of the best possible compliments. She wrote me a note wishing me well and saying that I did a decent job; that over the entire summer she "only had to turn me off once."

A cool experience was listening to myself on my car radio. In Kamloops at midnight the last news reporter and sports guy left the station. Between midnight and 2:00 a.m. I did news on the top of the hour as well as sports reports (baseball, boxing, and CFL football scores) on top of doing my announcing gig. When I left at 2:00 a.m., the station was totally automated. They had a rudimentary computer system that ran on a punched paper spool. The spool triggered a recorded syndicated radio program until 5:00 a.m. when live announcers came in. I pre-recorded news casts for 3:00 and 4:00 a.m. that also came up automatically from their computer system. So, when I left the station and drove home, I would listen to myself doing the 3:00 a.m. newscast: "Good morning, I am Larry, and this is LD news to 3:00." When I arrived home, I would sit in my car and listen to the news until the syndicated program kicked in, and then I would head to bed.

I was used to being alone in the station after midnight, so it scared me one morning when I had an arm reach around from behind me, squeeze my neck in a headlock, and lift me out of my chair. It was Steve, one of the veteran news guys. He was drunk and had come back to the station and thought he would get a laugh scaring me. He hung around until I had completed my shift, had the automation set, and was ready to go home. He insisted that instead I should go for a ride around town with him. Not knowing how to say no, we exited the station and got into his car. He drank from a bottle of cola, which I discovered later had been laced with rum. As we were driving through the outskirts of Kamloops, I looked past Steve through his driver's side window and saw an explosion and fireball light up the sky. I instantly alerted Steve, who, being a veteran news guy, instantly turned around and sped to the scene. We discovered that a sawmill had exploded and had set part of the building on fire. By the time we got there, police, fire, and ambulances were already on the scene. Steve wandered among the police and firemen gathering info. He was a retired RCMP himself, so he was given room to move about. After about an hour, we raced back to the radio station where Steve typed out a couple of news reports and recorded a couple of audio clips. Then we left the station again. I was beat and just wanted to go home, but Steve insisted I go over to his house with him first. Foolishly I went along. When we got to his house it was close to 4:00 a.m. and we went in the front door very quietly, as Steve said his wife was sleeping. This really made me uncomfortable, and I kicked myself for coming along. I should have at least brought my own car so that I could have left from there. Once at his place he took me into the kitchen, got a drink, and then left the room, coming back with an exceptionally large handgun. He said he was a collector, and then going back and forth from the room he brought two other guns to show me. I said I was exhausted and really wanted to go home. Finally, he agreed, but said he wanted to show me one more gun on the way out. I followed him down a hallway and he walked into their master bedroom. I stayed in the doorway afraid to move. His wife was sleeping there with her back to us, and I could hear her softly breathing, while Steve lifted the corner of her pillow and pulled out the largest handgun I had seen. After showing me the gun, he put it gently back and we left his house. I wonder if his wife ever found out what had happened, or even if he had pulled this stunt with other rookie announcers.

One weekend evening, I was on air with no one else around the station. It was routine to go into the newsroom to check the news feeds and to have a quick listen to a police scanner sitting in the corner. As I walked into the newsroom, I heard an urgent-sounding police call on the scanner. Quickly I figured out that there was a major accident a couple of kilometres out of town. A semi-tanker had flipped over onto its side, landing on top of a car, and was leaking its cargo of gasoline onto the highway. I knew this was going to be a big story, so I followed protocol and went to the list of news people to call. Starting with the news director and down the list of reporters, not being able to reach anyone—that is, until I hit Steve's name. This was all happening while I was running back and forth from my on-air studio doing my music and DJ gig. Steve quickly arrived at the station, dressed in a dark suit with a white shirt and wearing a bow tie that he had loosened. I discovered that he was on a wedding anniversary dinner with his wife when I had called (talk about dedication to craft). After listening to the scanner for a couple of minutes, he grabbed a microphone and the gear he needed and headed out to the accident scene. It was an exciting evening as I kept getting live feeds from Steve, while Vancouver radio stations started calling me as it became a big story around the province. Fortunately, people riding inside the car got out safely and the driver of the tanker truck escaped unscathed as well. However, the trucker's twelve-year-old son had been riding in the truck with him and was pinned inside. The drama continued for hours as firefighters worked at cutting the boy out of the cab of the truck, all the while with the load of fuel spilling onto the highway with gasoline fumes filling the air. On one of his cut-in reports Steve was beside himself. He was seeing hundreds of people lining up along the bank of the road to watch the rescue, as traffic continued to back up for kilometres down the highway in both directions, when someone near him lit up a cigarette. I cannot remember what he said in that report, but it had something to do with the stupidity of the smoker. Three hours later the boy was safely freed from the wreckage, scared but unhurt, and the urgency of the story dissipated. It was the most exciting day in my career, including an armed standoff I reported on in Port Alberni, where the RCMP shot the rifle out of the assailant's hands to arrest him. The rescue of the lad in Kamloops was far more emotional for everyone.

I was also on the air the night that Elvis died, at only forty-two years of age, on August 16, 1977. The world wept for the King, and every radio station in the world, I imagine, played at least one Elvis tune. His death overshadowed the passing of another legend: Groucho Marx. I loved the comedy of the Marx Brothers and especially Groucho; so, with management permission, I played not only "Jailhouse Rock," but also the Marx Brothers' "Hunga Dunga" skit. I might have been the only radio announcer in the entire world who played both.

One of the more fun experiences I had at CJLD came when the sales manager asked me if I wanted to make extra money and do reporting for him. Gary was a horse racing enthusiast and the station needed someone to go out to the racetrack and do live reporting on the races at Spoolmak Days (Kamloops spelled backwards), which was the area's big annual summer festival. My parents had taken me to the racetrack with them near Victoria when I was young; apart from that, I did not know a thing about the sport. Of course, I told Gary yes. I needed the extra cash, I knew it would be wonderful experience broadcasting live from the field, and I thought it would be fun. Gary filled me on the basics: "win, show, and place" and how each race would unfold. Arriving at the horse track, I introduced myself as a reporter and was led to a low building close to the track. It was from here I would telephone the results of each race in live to the station. I had a blast! I would watch each race, and once I heard the official results, I would run back to the building, call in my report, and then run back out to the track to watch the next race. I sprinted back and forth doing reports all afternoon for the eight races held that day.

An interesting part of being a radio announcer was the women you attracted. Every night the phone would ring in the control room while I was alone on air, and I would find myself talking to someone who was lonely. One night I remember talking to a woman who said she wanted me to come over to her place after my shift at 2:00 a.m., and she described what she would do with me and offered to make me breakfast in the morning. It was exciting in its own way for a twenty-year-old kid to get this kind of attention, but I never bit. I was too cautious. One night I told a lady who called in wanting sex that she did not even know what I looked like. I told her that I could be "forty years old, balding, with a paunch." She said she could tell otherwise by my voice. Of all the offers that came my way, only once did I arrange to meet someone. She was one of two or three regulars who called to talk with me almost every night while I was on air. Her voice seemed deep and husky to me—incredibly attractive. So, one day we agreed to meet at noon at a water fountain in the centre of town. When I got there, I found an attractive redhead who was only sixteen. She was a lovely person, and we talked for about an hour and then said goodbye. If she were older, I definitely would have been interested in her, but instead we simply continued to talk at night on the phone when she called the station.

As the junior announcer at the radio station, I was given the task of delivering stacks of the Top 40 Hit List to stores all around Kamloops. The list came out weekly and was much sought after, highlighting the most popular artists and songs in Canada. One of the stores I delivered to was a Sam the Record Man outlet in the Sahali Shopping Mall. About my second week delivering to Sam's,

I met Kelley, who was working that day. I thought she was cute, so I took time to talk with her for a while and then left on my rounds. The following week delivering the Hit List to Sam's, I walked in hoping she was working and was happy to find her on shift. We talked longer this time, and I was bold enough to ask her out. She indicated that I should buy a record first and then ask again the following week, which of course I did. When I came by to pick her up for our date a couple of weeks later, she was a little startled to see that I was driving a slightly battered Volkswagen. We ended up going to a McDonald's, and she had the first glimpse of how little radio stations paid junior announcers. It was April 1977, and I had turned twenty in February, while she would not turn nineteen until September.

She was from Penticton but was living in an uncle's trailer on her own, as her uncle worked away in the Arctic for three months at a time. Another uncle, aunt, and three cousins also lived in Kamloops, so she had family close by. After graduating from high school, she had left Penticton as her terminally ill grandmother had moved into her family's home, and it was overwhelming for her.

We had fun over that summer, spending time exploring together. My parents came up from Vancouver Island to hear me on the radio and I introduced her to them, and one weekend we drove down to Penticton where I met her parents for the first time. As I got to know them better her mom treated me like a son, and her dad and I were almost Archie Bunker and "meathead" from the TV sitcom *All in the Family*--the difference being that I did not argue with him. They were good and generous people, and I grieved when they both passed on.

Her dad was rightly protective of his daughter. Almost six months after I had met Kelley, her dad asked me to come help him check a tire on his car in the driveway of her place in Kamloops. He made a point of tapping a tire iron in his hand and threatened me that I had better treat Kelley right. I had just accepted an offer to work at CJRV Radio in Port Alberni, and his threat was a result of our announcement that Kelley was going to leave Kamloops to live with me in Port Alberni. That chance meeting in Sam the Record Man changed my life forever. Two children, and thirty-two years of marriage filled with fun, joy, love, and devastating heartbreak followed. Perhaps starting so young, or moving in together too quickly, or a combination of bad decisions along the way doomed us. In any case, our marriage sadly collapsed, nearly thirty-four years to the day from me walking in with my Top 40 list.

Although twenty years old, and having worked since I was fifteen, I still had things to learn about how to deal with stress. One night I found myself overwhelmed. It was May 17, 1977, and I had been working at CJLD for a little over a month and had settled into a rhythm, but that night it was hectic. News stories were coming at me fast and furious: Muhammad Ali was fighting Alfredo Evangalista at the Capital Centre in Landover, Maryland, the BC Lions were beating the Winnipeg Blue Bombers 25–17 on the road in CFL action, I had my show underway, and a sports report was due. Normally the sports scores and rundowns were ready for me, but that night they were not where they were supposed to be. So, I scrambled to put something together while running back and forth to the studio to introduce the next song and then rush back to the newsroom while keeping an eye and ear on the football and boxing matches on the TV in the newsroom. Somehow, I got through my shift, ready to go home. It was two o'clock in the morning and I was tired and worn out; so unfortunately, I acted without thinking. I left a snarky note for the newsroom about not having the sports scores ready for me.

I came in early the next day to prepare for my on-air shift and was greeted by the sports director, whom I knew but had never really had anything to do with previously. Ken was not particularly well-liked, and I quickly found out why. He asked me to come into his office and closed the door behind us and waved a piece of paper under my nose. It was the note I had left for the sports guys, from my shift the night before. With the paper inches from my face, he told me that if he ever saw a note like this again, he was going to "shove it up my fucking ass." It took me off guard. What I did know from my experience with bullies was to stand my ground. I told Ken that I should not have left the note and that I was sorry, but that unless he was prepared to talk to me in a civilized manner I was leaving. I turned on my heels and left the room and the station and walked down the street for a couple of blocks to calm down. This single moment ended my gig in Kamloops. Afterwards I never felt welcome by the management at the station. Looking back on that time I now understand three things:

1. I was pretty stupid to leave a sarcastic note.
2. Ken acted inappropriately. Instead of using this mistake as a teaching moment and mentoring a rookie at the station, he was a bully and abusive.
3. Regretfully, I do not remember making peace with the guys in the sports department. I was too embarrassed.

Perhaps it was mostly in my head that I was no longer welcome, but after working there for six months I left Kamloops and CJLD and moved back to Vancouver Island, landing in Port Alberni at CJRV Radio. It was one of the emptiest, most heart-wrenching departures I'd had. After my last shift at CJLD at 2:00 a.m. in September 1977, I left the station keys on the front desk counter and walked away with no fanfare or goodbye, the door and my time in Kamloops both closing behind me.

My former boss at CKLD in Princeton thought he was doing me a favour in suggesting CJRV in Port Alberni. He had worked there briefly in the past, so he reached out to management with a strong endorsement for me. By accepting a job there, I found a couple of big pluses: I was reunited with two friends who had graduated with me from BCIT, Rod and George, and I was given the afternoon drive time slot from 4:00 to 6:00 p.m. The two most prestigious slots in radio were the morning drive and the afternoon drive slots, so this was a bonus. However, the pay was disappointing. I had been working the 8:00 p.m. to 2:00 a.m. slot five days a week in Kamloops for eight hundred dollars per month, and the CJRV management offered me four hundred dollars per month and three percent commission on advertising sales, as my new gig included selling radio "spots" or commercials. When I accepted the position, I believed that the commission aspect would supply enough extra money to put me ahead of what I had been earning at CJLD. That quickly changed.

I adapted to the drive show easily and enjoyed my new slot. It was fun to be working with George and Rod and having a daytime audience in a smaller market was great. Going back to BCIT days we were always trying to break each other up while on air. At BCIT one day I had started shaving Rod's moustache while he was reading the news, and he could not do a thing; our instructors had hammered into us that "the show must go on." Our job was to entertain people and take them away from their daily troubles. We were told that no one cared about whether we were sick, or if our relationships were going to hell, or if our dog had bitten the mail carrier; we were to suck it up and go on air with smiles on our faces and help our listeners forget about their own daily challenges.

One day Rod had about six of the other staff stand outside of my control room while I was on air, and every time I turned on my microphone to speak, they would hold up score cards (like the Olympics). It was pretty funny at the time, and I broke up. I did not always need my co-workers in order to lose my composure. It is embarrassing now, but you had to be there, I guess. I was reading a newscast and had made the cardinal sin of not pre-reading all the stories before I read them live over the airwaves.

For reasons I cannot explain, when I read the story, I had a visual in my brain that struck me as hilarious. The story was about a man who had been riding his motorcycle down a road in the Interior of the province and had rounded a corner and struck a moose broadside. Funny, right? I started laughing so hard while reading the story that I had to shut my microphone off and try to compose myself, but each time I tried to finish the story I would break up and shut off my microphone once again; it took about three tries. Not having pre-read the story, I was disturbed learning that the conclusion of the story was that the motorcyclist had died. Not my most glorious broadcasting moment.

Advertising sales was one of the toughest ways to make a living that I have done. To start, the sales and program manager, Mike, had given me a phone book of the area and a "rate card," a sheet with the prices of our radio advertising listed (ten dollars each time a thirty-second commercial ran, or twenty dollars for a sixty-second commercial). I also found out that Mike had locked up all the most lucrative accounts in town for himself. Essentially, I had to bring in all new contracts, by literally knocking on doors of businesses all around Port Alberni. I worked my butt off. Seriously. Using my own car and gas, I had to hustle to eat, eventually bringing in an added three thousand dollars per month in revenue for the station while only pocketing three hundred dollars. With my four-hundred-dollar salary, I was working ten hours a day for less than what I had earned in Kamloops.

I remember having success one day signing on a new client and had rushed back to the station excited at having made a sale. I was paid a meagre four hundred dollars per month plus ten percent commission, so it meant gas in my car and food on the table. When I arrived back at the station, however, I found that the merchant had changed his mind before I got back to the radio station, deciding instead to pay for newspaper advertising. I was upset and disappointed but would normally have let it go. However, co-workers badgered me to go over to the merchant and chew him out, which to my later regret I did. I knew it was wrong; I felt it in my gut. The sad reality was that it did not change his mind, and although I went back and apologized, it damaged my reputation. To this day when I think about it, I am embarrassed and mortified at my bad behaviour and lack of grace (Dad would have taken me out to the car if he knew).

The station management mandated that on top of our regular work we had to broadcast the local men's hockey home games. I do love hockey, and it was a good learning experience, and it was fun. I did the colour commentary and one of the news guys did the play-by-play. We would go to the station, gather up all of the equipment we needed and head over to the arena. After getting set up, I would go and interview the home and opposing coaches and then hustle back to the broadcast booth at the start of the game. The booth was completely exposed and there were no heaters, so we sat and froze our butts off for almost three hours. After the game I would go back down and talk to both coaches, and record clips for the sports guys to use later. One night I found that a high school friend, John, was playing for the visiting team. During the game I praised John every time he touched the puck, or made a good play, and after the game I named him the Second Star of the Game. After wrapping up at the arena, we would then go back to the station and put all the gear away before heading home, having now worked for about a thirteen-hour day. The play-by-play announcer was paid an additional twenty-five dollars for his efforts and for doing the colour commentary, I was paid a meagre ten dollars extra. Life in the fast lane.

After working there for six months I was exhausted and felt I had proven my worth. I asked to meet with one of the station owners to ask for a raise; his partner Joe was away at the time. I outlined my success with the advertising sales and highlighted the extra revenue I was bringing into the station. I reminded him that on top of the effort I was putting out, that I was also using my own vehicle and burning my own gas to do my job. My request was modest. I asked for another hundred dollars per month on my salary, and money for gas, or the use of a company vehicle when I was out doing the advertising sales. To this day I can still see Will. He leaned back in his swivel office chair behind his desk, tanned and relaxed. I knew that he had recently returned from a Hawaiian vacation. He looked me in the eye and said, "I am sorry; we cannot afford to pay you more right now. You are just going to have to work harder." He went on to add that if I did not like it, he could hire any sixteen-year-old kid to take my spot. Arrogant, smug, and dismissive of my Broadcast Communications diploma and my experience. I despised him for his answer, but unhappily I went back to work. Two days later, Mike offered me a carrot, which in the moment I thought was decent. I would be given Fletcher's Furniture as an account. They spent a good deal on radio advertising, and it would boost my commission income, so I initially thought it was good news, until in the next breath he told me that he had already secured a contract for the next six months and that I was now expected to service their account with no financial benefit for those six months before I would see any financial gain.

I had to start thinking of alternatives, including looking for a new gig at another radio station. So, in the evenings when the station was empty, I started preparing audition tapes in the recording studio. At about the same time one of the news reporters quit his job. Although it would mean no longer spinning records and being a DJ, taking his spot in the newsroom gave me an opportunity. The pluses were that I would no longer work directly under Mike, would no longer have to spend my own gas money, and would earn a steady eight-hundred-dollar salary. A guaranteed payday at an amount higher than what I had been busting my back to earn. However, taking the job in the newsroom sadly meant the end of my career as a DJ.

The station had hired a new news director from the Victoria market. The guy had a good voice and seemed to know what he was doing and because he came from a much larger market, I must say I was impressed at the time. We became friendly, and I did not concern myself that he was my new boss. I had him and his wife over for dinner and they reciprocated. Meanwhile I plugged along in the newsroom covering news stories, including city hall meetings and events around town. One day Otto Lang, the Liberal minister of transport for Canada, arrived in town to make a presentation. He had done a tour of the famous Alberni Canal on a fishing boat and was about to disembark at the dock. I was there with my microphone to try to get an interview with him, along with the local newspaper reporter and his photographer. It took a while for the docking process and for the crew to put down a gangplank, so while he was waiting the photographer turned and started taking pictures of a family of ducks floating by. His timing could not have been worse. Otto Lang decided to make an impromptu vault over the side of the ship onto the dock, and ignominiously landed square on his pants, very undignified in his suit, on his back with his hands and feet in the air. The only photographer present was taking pictures of waterfowl. The missed photo would have been in every newspaper in Canada… ducks in the canal; not so much.

I plugged along for about another five months and then took a two-week vacation, heading back up to Kamloops. Now that I was applying for jobs in news, I decided to stop by CJLD and speak with the news director and discuss job prospects. He told me he had just hired a guy and had no openings, but he gave me a tip that he had heard that CJRV in Port Alberni was looking for a news reporter. In a heartbeat I understood that while I was on vacation, I was being replaced. Damn. It certainly put a damper on my vacation. I was apprehensive to go back; but at the end of two weeks, I arrived at work for my 5:30 a.m. newscast. I also read the 6:30 news, and then just before doing the 7:30 news the news director came in and asked me to go and see Mike. Once inside his office, Mike closed the door and took out a three-page letter written by the news director. It said that I could not read or write well, that I was negligent in my reporting, that I was a liability to the station, that I had missed a critical news story, and he finished by saying that he did not want me in his department. After reading the letter, folding it, and placing it on his desk, Mike asked me to resign. Alternatively, he said he would fire me. He said it would be better if I quit, because then I could collect Employment Insurance benefits.

I hit him hard with a barrage of expletives; I am pretty certain I referred to the letter as a pile of BS. I told Mike there was no truth in anything written in the letter and I was not going to quit. If he wanted to, he should go ahead and fire me. Then I went home and phoned the BC government Employment Standards Branch, to see what rights I had against wrongful dismissal. They advised that the worst thing that I could do was to quit, because then they could not support me. So, after lunch I went back to work. When I walked in the door, Mike was ready to pounce and brought me back into his office. He again said it would be in my best interest to quit and I told him adamantly that I would not. The news director made himself scarce while I did the rest of my shift for the day. The next day, when Mike realized I was not going to buckle and quit, he said that he was going to move me out of the newsroom, back to being a DJ, but that I would have to do the midnight shift. Management had brought me to CJRV to do the prime-time afternoon drive show, and so I refused to do the night shift reserved for rookies. For two days I continued working in the newsroom, and every thirty minutes Mike would drag me into his office and harass me, each time telling me he would fire me if I did not quit. On the third day I walked into his office and handed him my keys to the station and walked away from broadcasting. I had signed off for the very last time; the show had ended.

Back to the Woods

<u>Album Cut</u>:
"Honky Cat"
Elton John / Bernie Taupin
***Honky Chateau*, released 1972**

I REMEMBER STANDING ON THE deck of a ferry boat heading over to the Mainland from Vancouver Island, shortly after leaving CJRV in Port Alberni. Staring down at the water rushing by the side of the ship seemed to be a reminder of how swiftly my broadcasting career had come and gone. It was the first time I had a moment to pause and reflect, the first time I had a moment to grieve. I consoled myself with the understanding that, if for even a brief time, I had lived my dream.

But I was now in a dilemma. My departure from broadcasting happened at the end of the month, and I had actually given a month's notice at my apartment in Port Alberni to move out, expecting to move into a little bit nicer place in town. With no job, my belongings already packed in boxes, and a bad taste in my mouth, it was not hard to make the decision to leave Port Alberni. But to where, and to what?

As radio had paid so poorly, I had no financial backup, so the first priority was to find work of some kind and in turn a new place to live. Long-term planning was of no consequence at that moment. So, being on Vancouver Island, I retreated back to Lake Cowichan and my parents. I was now twenty-one and living at home out of a suitcase, with Kelley. The best-paying jobs in the area were in logging and working in the sawmills. So, I drove one morning to Honeymoon Bay and asked to see the mill manager, Keith. Although I had never met Keith, I knew his son and daughter from school days. I put a smile on my face and gave Keith my story, straight up. I told him that I was home because my first career had ended and I was at a loss as to what my future career might be, but in the meantime, I really needed work and would appreciate whatever job he could provide. Good people made a difference in my life; Keith was one of those. He knew I would never stay for the long term, but he could easily see that I was in a tough way. He hired me on the spot and told me to show up the next day. Years later, at our ten-year high school reunion, I bumped into his daughter. I asked about her dad and found that he had moved to the Maritimes and was well. I told her what a difference her dad had made in my life at that time, what a decent guy he had been, and asked her to give him my best.

Working at the sawmill was the best paying job I had had to that point. I worked at the mill for about six months and was able to bank money for the first time in years. My primary job was to "pull lumber" on the gang chain. Logs would be cut inside the mill into different lengths and thicknesses: two by fours, six by sixes, and so forth. They were then sent down the chain (a conveyor belt) where men stood on each side. Each man would have about four different piles to stack, and as the boards came down the chain, I would grab my piece and quickly slide it onto the pile behind me on the ground. It was all upper body work; grab the board, turn, and slide it off the chain onto the pile. The higher the stack the more work, as the boards now had to be lifted to a height of over six feet. Once the pile reached the proper height you banged a metal bar on a pole to signal a carrier to take it away and then you started a new pile; and on it went. You had to be very quick, as the chain did not stop, and the boards kept coming. After years of sitting in front of a microphone I was doing something physical, and the best part was that I got into really decent shape quickly.

One day while working, the guy standing next to me pointed to the fellow directly across the chain from where I was working. He was in his fifties, and his nickname was "Shorty." He said, "See Shorty over there? He's been standing in that same spot for seventeen years, and you are going to end up like him." It was the best motivator for me to start thinking about what I was going to do next; there was no way I was going to spend my life pulling lumber off a chain for the next forty years. As it turned out, before I had time to determine a plan for my future, the sawmill closed. The economy had changed, the mill was old, and the owners decided it was time to shut it down.

Luckily, I had banked money, but not a large enough stake to make new plans. I had also moved from my parents' and was now renting a duplex about five minutes away. I seemed stuck again. Asking around, I was given advice to get work jeans, a hard hat, and caulk boots (pronounced "cork") and go back to camp and seek work there as a logger. With no other choices on the horizon, I drove back to Nitinat early one morning and met with Harry, the Crown Zellerbach camp manager. Of course, I knew Harry from growing up in camp, and he knew me. By this time, my dad was no longer cooking there, as my parents had moved a couple of years earlier to Lake Cowichan and Dad had become the bar manager at the local Elks Club. I had a conversation with Harry that was remarkably similar to one I had had with Keith about six months earlier, and, like Keith, he gave me a break when I needed it most. Crown Zellerbach hired me to work on the "boom crew," and they recommended bringing along a dry set of clothes the next day when I reported for work.

At that time, all the logs that were hauled from the forests around the area were dropped into Cowichan Lake and dragged in booms by tugboats, forty-two kilometres to the southern end, where they were loaded onto railcars and shipped away to be cut into lumber or made into pulp. Huge logs—hemlock, Douglas fir, spruce, and cedar—were lifted from the trucks using A-frame hoists. One-hundred-ton loads lifted high in the air and then dropped into the lake with a huge splash. As kids we would go down to the lake and watch the unloading; it was almost as entertaining as waiting for bears to come out at the garbage dump.

Like herding cattle, small "boom boats" hustled in and started herding and separating the logs into different booms, cedar with cedar, hemlock with hemlock, and fir with fir. The booms could be immense and standing on a hill looking down over the lake when you saw one of the large lake tugboats hauling a half-dozen log booms southward, it was breathtaking in its own way. My job was like branding; I was to stamp the ends of each log floating secured inside these large booms, so they could be identified as to which logging company they came from when they arrived at a sawmill. To do this, I walked out from shore with a small hammer in my hand brandishing the Crown Zellerbach stamp, and then after selecting a log I smacked the end of the log forcefully to make an imprint. Then I moved to the next log, and to the next. Thousands of logs, bobbing in the lake waiting, unaware of my intent.

It became clear that to be successful you had to have excellent balance and dexterity and be very quick on your feet. I put on my life jacket, my caulk boots, and panicked. I had serious concerns about my balance, dexterity, and swiftness of foot; fortunately, I had great confidence in my ability to swim and tread water. Which was important because I ended up falling off logs twice before the first morning coffee break and once later in the afternoon.

Cowichan Lake was frigid in April, and I worked the majority of the day soaking wet. Someone watching might have found it comical, as I found new ways to fall in each time. I found that the smaller logs would sink as you walked from one end to the other, so you had to walk to the end and turn on the log and head back quickly; my first plunge in the lake made it clear the small logs were my nemesis. After falling in, and then changing into my only set of dry clothes, I hung my wet gear around a heater in a small shack that was used by the workers for coffee and lunch breaks, and reluctantly headed out to try again. This time I knew the best plan would be to walk on the huge logs, as they would not sink on me. However, I did not realize that they would roll, spinning so fast they could spin you off into the lake. If you have ever seen a loggers' sports event, two men stand on the same log together and work at spinning the other off and into the water. Feet fly, and then they "put on the brakes," stopping the log from spinning, and then make it spin backwards as fast as they can, and "put on the brakes" again, until one of them ended up in the water. I needed no one else to be spun into the water; my second plunge was while I was on one of the largest logs I could find. So much for Plan B.

Heading back to the coffee shack I found that my clothes had not had time to dry, but as they were semi-warm, I swapped and found my way back out. Like Goldilocks, this time I targeted the medium-sized logs to see if they were just right for my level of ability. They also challenged me. When I realized I could not keep my balance on one log, and was on the verge of falling in, I decided to jump to another, more stable log. This actually worked a couple of times until the second log started to move when I stepped on it, and then the worst thing happened—doing the splits while both logs separated until I fell in the water between the two logs. This was the most dangerous event of all. Even with a lifejacket on, you could fall in the water between two logs, have them close back together while you were submerged, and you would drown while futilely trying to get above the surface again. Going home that night, wet, cold, and dispirited, I had no desire to go back the next day. But not only did I need the money, I had been given an opportunity as a favour, and I needed to honour that generosity. So back I went the next morning. I must have had a little more luck, as I made it to lunch and was able to stay dry. But there was a constant level of anxiety knowing I could fall in at any moment. I also found it disconcerting that while standing on a log in the centre of a large boom, I had no idea which logs I had stamped already and which I had not.

After lunch I found myself standing on the deck of one of the boom boats and was shown another task that was expected of "boom men." Each boom was tied together by heavy metal chain links; so, to open a boom up so that the boom boat operators could sort the logs, the chain link had to be pulled up out of the water using a long pike pole that was kept standing vertical like a flagpole on each boom boat. So, grabbing the pole while the operator eased the boat gently against the boom, I leaned forward with the pole, submerging the entire length, then pulled the chain up. I felt good about my first success. So, we went to another boom to do another uncoupling. I was really happy to be standing on a solid boat deck. The second time while I was bending over with the pike pole to pull up the chain, the operator gunned the motor in reverse, purposefully throwing me off balance and into the lake. I was an unhappy man.

After lunch, the boom foreman came over to me, and after one and half days he looked at me and said, "I don't think you were cut out for this job." I told him I could not agree with him more. The next day the boom manager transferred me to the grade crew, and I started building new logging and access roads high in the mountains—happily on dry land.

The grade crew was made up of two-man teams. Blasters ran the heavy rock drilling machines and held blasting "tickets" or certificates qualifying them to work with explosives. Their helpers were "drill swampers." I worked as a "Cat swamper," meaning I helped the bulldozer operator actually push the roads through the forest. "Cat" was short for Caterpillar, named for the bulldozers that company built. Clyde ran a D9 Cat, which was the largest that Crown Zellerbach ran at the time. The operator or "Cat skinner" sat about four feet off the ground on top of a tremendous amount of power.

The road building process was fairly simple. Surveyors would lay out the path of the road by tying pink, fluorescent ribbons on the trees that needed to be cut. Fallers would then come into the wilderness with their chainsaws, axes, and wedges and cut a swath of trees wide enough for the road to be built. The big bulldozers would come in and winch and haul the fallen trees out of the way and push them into piles to be later collected and taken out with logging trucks once the road was finished. Once the logs were cleared out of the way, the bulldozer would be used to create the roadway. When the bulldozer hit boulders or a rock outcropping, he would pull back out of the way and sit, allowing the drill crew to move in and drill, load their holes with dynamite, and then blast a path through. Sometimes there would be so much rock to get through they had to repeat their process more than once before the bulldozer could get back in. I remember watching the dust settling down over a blast site, the air rank and toxic. We had to climb over the rubble and check to see if any of the explosives had not blown. Occasionally you would find an unexploded stick of dynamite. Although I was a Cat swamper, occasionally I also did shifts as a drill swamper.

An important incentive to hustle the roads through was given to the machine operators. They were paid bonuses on the amount of road they pushed through each day; understandably, Clyde hated sitting still. The unfair part of the monetary incentive was that the swampers never got a penny of bonus but were continually driven to hurry up, to my mind a fault in the union's collective bargaining agreement. Cat swamping was often demanding work. We built roads through mountainous terrain, and there was inevitably a side of the road with a steep upward bank, and on the other side, a cliff to look (or fall) over.

Running off the back of the Cat were two winches: the larger spool lower to the ground with a very heavy braided metal cable, and the upper spool holding a lighter cable. If the swamper wanted to move logs off the high bank side, he would unspool a large length of cable on the ground at the base of the Cat and, taking the end over his shoulder, drag the cable up the bank over uneven ground, broken tree limbs, boulders, and around stumps to reach the log that needed to be hauled out of the way. The cable would be wrapped around the log, and then the swamper would move off to a safe distance and signal the Cat skinner to start winching it in. It was a dangerous process, as a cable could snap and whip through the air with enough velocity to cut a man in half. Or a log could break free and start rolling or catapult down the hill, risking the swamper if he were not standing clear, or even the Cat skinner if the log came crashing down and struck the bulldozer.

You might think that it would be easier to get logs on the lower side because you did not have to drag the cable up the hillside; not so. You unspooled metres of cable, looping it on the ground (like a garden hose), and then you would take the heavy cable by the end and swing it vigorously through the air, aiming at the log you had selected. The lower slopes could be steeper than the high side, which made them treacherous to climb down. Wearing heavy work gloves, you would grasp the large cable and rappel down the bank, being careful not to dislodge rocks or tree limbs that could come crashing down on your head. If you valued your life, the veterans told us from day one, never go underneath a log to wrap the cable around it. The trick was to throw it over the top of the log so that the cable was left dangling; you could then reach underneath the log with your arm and grab the cable to pull it around and tie it off on top. You did not want to have a log weighing tons dislodge and roll on you while you were underneath it. I met a couple of crusty old loggers; brothers they were, both over sixty years of age. They had done nothing else all their lives. They knew all the tricks and were aware of all the risks. One day Freddy climbed under a log to wrap a cable; the log shifted, and Freddy was crushed and died instantly, after doing the job for decades. In my experience, workplace injuries happened when someone let their guard down, or tried to take a shortcut—certainly much more often than because of a mechanical failure. Poor Freddy lost his life over a mistake he might not have made on a different day. Sometimes, though, there are accidents that we can never see coming or protect ourselves from.

Years earlier, while at Western Mines my first summer when I was sixteen, tragedy struck. I never knew John, but I saw him around the mine site. He worked underground, and one day he sat down in a tunnel with two other co-workers to eat their lunches, with John sitting between the other two. A large piece of rock gave way from the ceiling above their heads, striking John and killing him instantly while not touching either of the other two workers. I found out later that one of the survivors quit on the spot and the other went on disability due to the trauma. When the accident happened, a loud siren blew through the whole camp, shutting the mine down completely, while an investigation was done and John's body retrieved. What always struck me about John's death was seeing his car, a Lincoln Continental, sitting forlorn in the parking lot for days afterwards until family came and retrieved it. John never saw it coming and never had a chance.

When building logging roads, the Cat skinner was in charge; the swamper took his lead. However, a good swamper knew what to do and could survey a hillside and quickly figure out which log would need to be pulled first to make it easier to get the rest out, or in fact which two or three logs could be winched out at the same time. It was a skill that was developed by practice and experience. When I was put on a crew to work with Clyde, I did not know the first thing about road building or how to be a swamper. Clyde was upset when he was given a green rookie; remember, he was working for bonuses, and a rookie would slow him down. So, on our first turn (where you stopped pushing road to pull logs out of the way), he manoeuvred his bulldozer around with the back end pointing over the edge of a steep bank. He showed me the cables and winches and explained how to unspool and then throw the cables over the bank. He pointed to a specific log among a jumbled pile and told me to go and hook that one up. It was hard to see which one he was pointing at, and even more difficult when at the bottom of the hole. He kept yelling and waving his arms around until I got the right one and then yelled at me to grab the cable and climb out of the hole and then he winched it out. He dragged it down the road about one hundred feet and had me unhook it, and then while he reeled his cable in and turned the Cat around and came back, I ran back up the road to decide which log would be pulled out next. This process would continue until we pulled all the logs out—which could take hours. I was always exhausted on days when we had to pull logs from start to finish. Over the first four days Clyde would get off the Cat, throw his hard hat on the ground, and swear at me out of frustration that I was not doing it right. I put up with the abuse because I needed his guidance. On the fifth day he jumped off his Cat to go through his usual routine, and I stopped him cold before he could cast his hard hat on the ground. I told him that I had the basics figured out and I needed him to shut the hell up and let me do the job so I could get a better feel for it. I told him the only time I needed to hear from him was if he saw me inadvertently putting myself in danger where I could be injured or killed. After that, we got along fine. We worked together for almost a year and built hundreds of kilometres of gravel logging roads through the mountains. We also shared one of the most wondrous experiences of my life together.

One morning shortly after 6:00 a.m., we were in our Ford pickup truck heading up a steep logging road to where the Cat was parked, ready to go for the day. It was not quite light yet, and it was grey and cool with a mist sifting through the air. As we rounded a corner in the road, Clyde brought the pickup to an abrupt halt. In the very middle of the road was a deer, a fawn born only a short while before. It lay there wet from the afterbirth and shaking slightly. The mother was nowhere to be seen. We sat for at least half an hour before the fawn started to move, gradually standing on wobbly legs. Clyde finally spotted the mother, standing alertly near the edge of the road, her ears and eyes just above the brush. She never moved a muscle but watched her baby intently. Through a signal from its mother, or by instinct, the fawn started taking steps, moving slowly and haltingly toward Mom. Once started, it did not seem to take long for it to get to the edge of the road and to disappear into the brush; mother and baby were gone from our view forever. The miracle of birth in the silence of that mountainside, in the cab of our pickup truck, was one of the joys of my life.

In the summer it would get extremely hot and dry, to the point where the BC forestry service would come in and shut the operation down to avoid a forest fire. It could be weeks before enough rain came to make it safe to open it up again, and men would collect unemployment insurance. Other times the company would shut down operations due to a labour dispute. Every morning a bus would swing by our homes in Lake Cowichan and take men into camp early in the morning; from there we would unload and disperse into our respective crews to head out to our job sites. One morning, as the bus pulled to a stop in the yard, the union rep Ken stood up and told everyone to stay sitting where they were and not get out, explaining that today we were going to go on a "work slowdown." I did not like it at all. To me, we were playing childish games. Foremen came over, looking for their crews, and were told to bugger off, sending them scrambling back to the camp manager. We sat on that bus for about half an hour until Ken gave us permission to get off and load into our respective pickups and crummies (trucks with passenger boxes in the back that could seat six- to eight-man crews). Days later, Ken orchestrated a different kind of slowdown. He was a machine operator, and, using a knife, he cut one of the hydraulic hoses on his loader. Hydraulic fluid spilled on the ground, the machine became inoperable, and his whole job site was instantly shut down. A mechanic had to be called out from camp with a new hose and more hydraulic fluid to repair his loader, taking about two hours. He was also notorious (along with others) for stealing motor oil, rope, flashlights, and other supplies, stuffing them into his backpack, and sneaking them home. I had no time for him. Employee theft was, according to these types, always justified; the thieves would always say things like, "The company is so big they will never notice it," or, "they do not pay me enough, so this gets me even." My parents taught me to be honest, and I hated to see this happening. Years later, working in retail management, I got to see more clearly the actual cost of employee theft in a different context.

In the winter months logging would be miserable. Although we wore superior-quality rain jackets and pants, we would be soaked within minutes. Water would run off our hard hats and down our necks. The work gloves we wore would be muddy and sodden. You would take them off, rinse the mud off in a puddle if you could, then wring them out and put them back on, repeating the process continually throughout the day. Your hands and fingers would be white and wrinkled by quitting time. The ground would become even more treacherous as rocks, logs, and underbrush became slick. Then it would snow, and things would get more miserable and even more dangerous. Overburdened tree limbs above your head could snap and plummet with enough force to maim or kill.

Loggers would call these limbs “widow-makers.” Eventually, when the snow became too deep for safety (or productivity), the whole operation came to a halt. This was the other unemployment insurance season.

Winter of 1979 came ‘round in typical Lake Cowichan fashion. Rain, clouds, rain, more clouds. Temperatures dropped below freezing in the mountains where the bulk of the logging was happening. Decades of logging meant the logging companies had to go higher and higher to get at timber because the lower levels had long ago been clearcut, and the new growth would take decades more to become viable for more accessible operations. Snow had been falling, and logging became more difficult and much more dangerous. As in the summer, Crown Zellerbach held out until it became impossible to continue and logging operations were finally shut down. Most loggers would go on unemployment insurance and sit in the warmth of their own living rooms rather than finding other places to work. This was not reasonable for my brother Peter, who packed his gear and headed out to the Queen Charlottes (now Haida Gwaii). The foreman asked me to go work at a remote logging camp at Kyoquot on the northwestern coastline of Vancouver Island. Frankly, I was surprised to be called out for work. The IWA (International Woodworkers Association) was the dominant union, and seniority was followed. I had been working for less than a year, and men who had seniority above me chose to stay warm and dry at home and collect unemployment insurance. I needed the money, so I accepted the job, although it meant living away from home for fifteen days and being home for only four days on these shifts.

I was picked up in Lake Cowichan and rode the two and a half hours north on the Island Highway to Campbell River in a six-man crummy. A couple of years earlier I had made the same trip on my way to Western Mines, but now continued north for another hour and a half turning westward at Woss, a community of two hundred people in the Nimpkish Valley—a "speck on the map," as we referred to it. We passed through the logging community at Zeballos about an hour south of Woss before making our final turn toward the West Coast to Fair Harbour. Overall, an arduous twelve-hour ride in a crowded crummy to finally arrive at Fair Harbour. This was literally the end of the road; ocean and a small marina marked the end of our land journey. Grabbing all of our gear we boarded a tough little water taxi to battle the waves for an hour to mercifully land at Kyuquot.

One of the logging adventures my brother Peter had, was arriving at the shoreline at Kyoquot with a crew to establish the camp about a year and a half earlier. Bulldozers were brought in by barge and landed on the shore, smashing their way uphill, carving a road about one hundred yards from the shoreline to level ground where the camp was set up: cookhouse, bunkhouses, mechanical shop, and office. I landed at the dock about eighteen months later. Rugged and remote, with only a radio telephone to connect us with the outside world; we raced on foot to the bunkhouses to stake out our rooms. Each room housed two men, and the veterans knew which were considered the prime room locations, and they also knew whom to avoid as roommates. My first tour up there I was stuck with Clarence, a nice guy but a prodigious snorer. Even with my ear plugs in, he would wake me from an exhausted sleep. I would have to get up in the middle of the night and walk over and vigorously shake him so he would roll over and stop snoring, only to have to repeat the process a short while later. One night I was so fed up I pushed his bed so hard with my foot that he bounced in the air and landed back in his bed. He kept on snoring. My next fifteen-day shift I ran a little faster to the bunkhouses to avoid sharing with him again. Clarence was wiry and short and could eat more than two men combined. I watched in awe as he would eat a dozen fried eggs with toast and bacon for breakfast and take a lunch box with four sandwiches, apples, bananas, cookies, and cake with him, and come back later for a full dinner. He was a drill operator on the grade crew, so it was not like he spent a ton of energy to work up an appetite. His lunch box did save me on my first day there, though. I had made the mistake of not bringing a lunch box to Kyuquot with me. I thought I would use paper lunch bags offered at the cookhouse instead. After breakfast, the morning after arriving at camp, I grabbed my hard hat, rain gear, and lunch bag and walked to the marshalling yard to be assigned to a crew. While waiting, I set my lunch and gear on the ground and started talking to one of the other men next to me. A minute later another logger tapped me on the shoulder, and, turning around, I saw a flock of seagulls devouring my lunch; nothing could be salvaged. Foremen arrived, and I was luckily assigned to work as a swamper with Clarence; there was no time to make another lunch, and fortunately he shared his bounty with me.

I have never seen such enormous timber in my life. Old-growth forest as far as you could see. Cedar trees that were so big around that one log could not fit onto a logging truck without being split down the centre first. A high school friend, Eddy, was one of the other drill operators in camp. I loved Eddy, as he was one of the most easygoing guys you would ever meet. In elementary and secondary school, he was as swift as the wind, winning Island track and field championships. I had not seen Eddy for years, and he had changed dramatically. He was definitely out of shape, a heavy smoker, and had become very scruffy-looking, with long, frizzy hair and a continual four-day growth of beard on his face; but his heart was still golden and his laugh still contagious. One day Eddy was asked to load dynamite charges along the length of a gigantic red cedar log that was too heavy to lift by the loader and too large to fit on a truck. If the work was done correctly, the tree would be split down the centre along its entire length, effectively cutting it in two. With the loader operator, truck driver, and a couple of foremen watching from a safe distance, Eddy blew his charges, and the forest behemoth nestled in the underbrush was instantaneously transformed into millions of toothpick-sized pieces of cedar. Two hundred years of growth and thousands of dollars in lumber were obliterated in the blink of an eye. It would have made any environmentalist weep.

Eddy and I shared daily adventures building road. Although I did work swamping behind a D9 Cat as well while in Kyuquot, I spent two-thirds of my fifteen-day shift working with Eddy. Eddy and I got along well, dynamite not so much. The nitroglycerine that seeped from dynamite sticks found its way through the pores of my hands, the fumes found their way into my lungs, and I would get monumental headaches. I held my breath each time we transferred dynamite and blasting caps from the storage shed to our pickup truck. Heavy rubber gloves were necessary to avoid the nitroglycerine entering through the pores of my hands. Eddy worked mostly night shifts, and I remember one night out in the forest, standing hunched behind our pickup truck in pitch-black stillness, wishing I would die because my head was exploding from a nitro headache. My introduction to explosives had been earlier at camp. One day my boss asked me to help load a pickup truck with dynamite. Once loaded, we drove out into the woods to where it was needed, the driver and me both getting out to unload. He climbed in the back, we dropped the tailgate, he passed a box to me, and I carried it to the blast site and set it down on the ground very gingerly. I had seen Wile E. Coyote blow himself up hundreds of times on cartoons. I made three trips, and on the fourth trip, instead of passing the box of dynamite to me, the driver tossed it to me purposefully short of my reach, and it crashed heavily on the ground. I almost had a heart attack, and my face drained of all colour; he killed himself laughing at the expression on my face. It was a mean-spirited prank on a rookie; dynamite needed a blasting cap to ignite and dropping it on the ground was safe (although not recommended). Old-timers in the logging industry had the mentality that "I learned the hard way, so you should too." I found this harsh and stupid. I always looked to my dad's example of patience and guidance and took the path of sharing my experiences and mistakes to help others, rather than insisting on them learning the hard way.

The driller had to use his knowledge and experience to be effective. His practised eye had to evaluate the type of rock he was having to blast, the grain and hardness, and the size of the area to be cleared. The number of holes, the depth and angle of each hole, and the amount of dynamite used were critical factors in the effectiveness of the blast. Once all of the holes were drilled, we would take a spool of blasting wire and boxes of dynamite to the site and start loading each hole. A special tool was used to puncture two holes in the first stick going into the hole with the cable being threaded through the stick. Placing it in the hole, the swamper would then tamp the dynamite stick to the bottom with a long, plastic pole. More sticks were tamped down until the driller was satisfied, then trailing the cord to the next hole, the process would continue until all of the holes were filled. When finished, there was a red spiderweb of blasting wire across the rock face. The last step was attaching a blasting cap to the end of the wire with enough of a fuse to get away to safety in our pickup truck before the explosion. One night in complete darkness, Eddy drove the truck backward as fast as it would go, bouncing over holes and rocks with our heads hitting the roof of the truck to get to safety in time.

We were just starting a shift one day, and it was still light outside. The weather had been awful for a couple of days, but today the wind was hammering camp ferociously. Camp management decided to continue operations and had sent crews out into the woods. Eddy and I were driving in our pickup to our job site, being buffeted by the wind, when we pulled over on the side of the road. A logging crew was working on a higher road near the top of a hill above where we sat. From our position we could see machinery and pickup trucks far in the distance. All of a sudden, I saw giant Douglas-fir trees start toppling, one after another like bowling tenpins, around the loggers. I grabbed the radio microphone in the truck and yelled at them to clear out. It was both awesome and fearsome to watch the force of the wind uproot dozens of old-growth giants in seconds.

I had done a couple of fifteen-day stints at Kyuquot and desperately wanted out of logging. On the referral of a friend, I had interviewed with Sears in Nanaimo on one of my four days off, and they had offered me a job. I decided I would make one more trek to Kyoquot before starting my new career. While working at Nitinat for Crown Zellerbach, I had earned my Industrial First Aid (now Occupational First Aid) level C ticket. This was the lowest level of ticket, and to be a first aid attendant in a remote camp required an A ticket. On my last trip I made a fateful error in judgment.

Shift changes were done by sending a crew out on a water taxi back to Fair Harbour, where another crew was picked up and brought to camp in Kyoquot. That day, the first aid attendant on duty wanted to leave early and not wait for the new attendant to arrive. He persuaded me, with my C ticket, to take over for him until the new guy arrived, as it would only be about three hours, and he assured me that "nothing would happen" in the interim. Reluctantly I agreed, as I was not secure enough to say no to him. I watched the water taxi leave the dock with the attendant vanishing forever from my view. I sat down in the first aid room and prayed that I would get through until his replacement arrived. Fortune was not on my side.

A radio call came through a fleeting time later; a faller had badly cut his hand with his chainsaw. Fallers worked in pairs and had small first aid kits with them for emergencies. I raced in the ambulance out to the job site, and by the time I arrived the wound had been wrapped and bound by his partner. I examined his hand

and decided I would leave it the way it was. His partner had done a respectable job and had staunched the wound, so I took the faller back with me in the ambulance to wait so he could be taken out on the next water taxi for medical attention at the hospital in Campbell River. My heart was racing, and I was shaking; I was in way over my head. I had hardly settled back into the first aid room when a second call came in over the radio. This time I was informed that a surveyor had fallen off a small bluff and broken his leg. Another worker had splinted his leg, and they had walked out to the road and called in for help. Within an hour and a half, I now had two seriously injured workers, both in considerable pain, under my care. In a medical situation, the first aid attendant overrode all camp management in regard to decisions about care. I understood the torturous hours long water taxi and ambulance ride over bumpy logging roads that the surveyor would have to endure to get to the hospital in Campbell River. I told the camp manager to order a helicopter to come in to fly both injured men out for care. He refused, and although I technically held authority, I could not make him budge. I was extremely relieved when the replacement first aid attendant arrived to take over about half an hour later. Bouncing over the waves in the water taxi to Fair Harbour and then on the logging roads on my way home, I prayed he had had better success in securing that helicopter. The manager had put cost ahead of the well-being of his men, and his negligence was deplorable. I was happy and relieved to be leaving logging forever.

Satisfaction Guaranteed

Album Cut:
"Money for Nothing"
Dire Straits
***Brothers In Arms*, released 1985**

AFTER MY SHORT STINT IN broadcasting and my exposure to sawmill labour and logging, I made a long-term career decision. My time logging was important to me in a couple of ways. From a practical view I had a year of good wages that enabled me a more normal life and allowed me to save money. From a life view I finally grasped the full scope of the work, the environment, and the danger that all those dads in camp had faced every day they went into the woods when I was growing up. After logging I spent the next thirty years wearing a suit and tie, but never undervalued or forgot about my time wearing a hard hat and caulk boots.

As I mentioned, a friend had tipped me off to interview at Sears Canada's retail store in Nanaimo. The HR manager (personnel manager in those days) was a nice man. Vic listened carefully to my story and my history, had me do a couple of tests, and then offered a choice of two job options. Behind "door number one" was a job in commission sales in their menswear department, and behind "door number two" was an opportunity toward a leadership path as a manager trainee. He explained to me that commission sales would probably pay more over the short term, but manager trainee would perhaps pay off better overall. He also asked me how long I planned to work for Sears and what job I might aspire to down the road with the company. I was frank and told him that I had never considered working in retail or business before, but if it worked out that I could stay for years. As far as possible career options were concerned, I told him, "I would like your job." Even then I understood my strengths in respect to working with and interacting with people, so becoming a personnel manager seemed reasonable. So, when it came down to it there was not even a real choice; I jumped at the leadership opportunity and started on an eleven-year journey with Sears.

It was now the spring of 1980, and I was twenty-three years old and had been married for almost two years—a little tattered and battered, but still ready to tackle the world. It was near the cusp of the old-school retail model. Customer retention was important, so Sears hired enough staff to be available in all departments at all times and trained them to go the extra mile. "Satisfaction guaranteed or your money refunded" was the slogan on the sign over the door, and we embraced it. Everywhere today the model is closer to self-serve, and you can wander enormous stores and never find a staff member to help you.

Sears was a wonderful place for me to land. The majority of my bosses were good to me and gave me significant latitude to make decisions on my own; to fail and to learn as I went. My fellow managers were also young and starting families themselves, and we became great friends and socialized, partied, and supported each other. "Farley," "Snowman," and "Grounder" were more experienced and successful managers, and they took me under their wings and mentored me and always went to bat for me.

I was placed in the furniture and carpeting department with Farley as my boss. In the store hierarchy, departments were categorized as either big ticket or small ticket, "ticket" referring to price points. Furniture and carpeting, hardware, sporting goods, and major appliances were all big ticket, selling all of the high-priced merchandise and services. Prestige and higher salaries came along with running big-ticket departments, so managers strived for one of those positions. It was great fortune that I was placed in furniture and carpets as a manager trainee. We had five full-time, commission salespeople, and Liz for clerical support. My first six months were invaluable. Few other departments had the scale and scope, and I was learning about staffing, display and merchandising, inventory control, and customer relations. In Nanaimo, our department was separated from the main store, in its own space down the mall. This made us feel that we had autonomy, and we looked at it as if we were running our own business.

Seven years in Nanaimo elapsed quickly, largely routine. However, there were events that still stand out after all of these years. With Farley away over a weekend I was effectively the manager for those three days he was absent. It was summer and our front doors were open for air to circulate. I was at the back of the store doing paperwork and heard a commotion at the front doors. Profanities were carried to my ears with voices becoming louder. I hurried to the door to figure out what was going on and to manage the situation. Walking out the front doors, I saw a tow truck connected to a pickup truck with a sofa loaded in the back, the customer standing patiently to the side, and the tow truck driver swearing at my salesman, Patrick, who was red in the face and bouncing on his heels.

The truck driver was about six feet tall, towering over Pat's five foot six inches. Pat's advantage (which the tow trucker driver was unaware of) was that he had been a Golden Gloves boxer as a youth. I stepped directly between the two of them and putting a hand on each chest I physically pushed them apart. I quickly grasped the situation. Pat had been helping his customer load a sofa that he had just bought into his truck, and the tow truck driver had started hooking up the pickup to tow it away while Pat and his customer had gone back into the store to gather the armchair that was part of the set.

Along the entire perimeter of the shopping mall was a "no parking" zone, painted bright yellow. The tow truck driver had been waiting in a corner of the shopping mall parking lot, ready to pounce. The situation had been turned into a "might vs. right" moment, with the truck driver adamant he had the right to tow the pickup as it was parked along the yellow line, and Pat trying to make him understand that the customer had store permission to stop there as he was taking merchandise away. The truck driver was not budging, forcing me to intercede. I tried logic, explaining again that the customer had the permission to park in that spot and asking him to please release the pickup and move on. He refused. I told Pat to go back into the store and call our security manager to attend, while the stalemate continued. Although also small in stature, our security manager John did not take flak from anyone. He took control swiftly, and the driver reluctantly released the pickup and slunk over to a corner of the parking lot. By successfully defusing a volatile situation while standing up for the rights of the customer and in support of Patrick, I gained confidence in myself and respect from Pat. It was also enlightening. I had never come across someone with whom common sense and logic had no effect; the driver had been intractable. It was also a lesson in teamwork and the value of asking for specialist support.

Crazy stuff happened. We had a store sale on folding lawn chairs that summer that just exploded. We quickly sold out and took orders for chairs we were expecting to come from our Burnaby warehouse in by the weekend. I had presold four chairs to one lady and assured her that I would call her as soon as stock came in.

Stock came in on Friday evening, and I called her home phone number on Saturday morning. The phone rang and was picked up at the other end. I said, "Good morning. I am looking for Mrs. Smith, please; her lawn chairs have arrived." The male voice on the other end snarled back at me, "She just died, you asshole," and slammed the phone in my ear. I was dumbfounded and sat there shaking with an expression of shock on my face. After composing myself, I looked at her sales receipt and noticed she had also added a work phone number. I called her work and was told that she was away and would be back on Monday morning! Of course, the first thing I did on Monday morning after opening the store was to call her work number. "Good morning, Mrs. Smith," was the response on the other end of the line. I introduced myself and told her that her lawn chairs had arrived and were ready for pickup at the furniture department. I was sorely tempted to mention the conversation I'd had on Saturday; instead I decided to wait until she came in for the chairs and see who came in with her. A couple of days later the Smiths came for the chairs. Had I dialled the wrong number the past Saturday, or was he simply sadistic? Even dialling the wrong number should not have elicited the extreme response I'd received.

One duty not explained to me when I was hired was the responsibility of aiding our security team in running down and arresting shoplifters. There was a system based on codes, which were announced over the PA system in the store; for example, "309" meant to rush to department 9 (hardware) or "306" to department 6 (sporting goods). One of the security team—John, Sandra, or Ted—would be discreetly watching their suspect, and we would nonchalantly stroll by or busy ourselves nearby. An arrest could not be made unless the suspect stepped outside of the store with the goods on their person. Once outside, security, followed by us, would exit quickly and arrest the shoplifter, who was then brought into the store, and the police were contacted. However, when confronted, shoplifters instinctively sped away on foot, forcing us to chase them down. I remember racing after shoplifters down the streets in Nanaimo until I was out of breath. Other times John would ask me to come with him to one of the nearby local strip joints to look for a suspect, as they were popular places at which to sell stolen leather jackets. Ted was young, tall in stature, and extremely cocky. To my horror one day, I watched him drag a shoplifter down the aisle to the security room, choking him by the neck, with the man's feet almost off the ground. I filed a complaint with personnel.

Once apprehended, the shoplifter would be taken to the security room, the police would be called, and the arresting security team member and at least one manager would wait in a tiny room with one chair and a desk until the police arrived. One time, Ted had arrested a man with his twelve-year-old son in tow. The boy was crying and in distress; I do not know if he was aware of what his dad had done. Ted sat behind his large, wooden desk, with the man sitting in the chair in front of him with his son by his side, and me standing opposite to them, leaning against the wall. The father kept telling his boy to stop crying to no avail, so I suggested to the dad that it would be best if the boy waited outside, to which he agreed. I stepped outside the office and signalled a staff member to come and stay with the boy, and then went back into the security office. Ted was a jerk. Period. He sat behind his desk with a smug grin on his face and taunted and belittled the man. It was obvious he was trying to provoke him, and the shoplifter was getting increasingly agitated. Finally, I told Ted to get the hell out and go and check on where the police were. Once Ted was out of the office, the man swore and said he wanted to punch his lights out. I told him I could understand why, and that Ted had not been acting professionally or respectfully. I also explained that punching Ted would be a bad idea as that would mean an assault charge on top of shoplifting, and that frankly he was not worth it—and that he should think of his son. Minutes later the RCMP took them away, and I chewed Ted out for being an ass. Years later, long after I had left Sears, I heard that Ted had changed careers and ended up a prison guard. Perhaps he had matured by that point. Arrogance, a uniform, and a nightstick would have been a terrible combination otherwise.

One day I spotted a man walking around the store with what looked like a handgun sticking out of his right pants pocket. I alerted security, and they had the RCMP waiting for him as he walked out the exit door of the paint department. After speaking with him, and then searching him, they found a replica BB pistol in his pocket. If that did not scare me enough to refuse being involved in shop lifters arrests, another episode did. This time a security member caught a two-man shoplifting team and tried an arrest of both; however, one made his escape. Our customer service manager, Ken, helped security out on this particular arrest and took his turn standing in the security room with the offender. Minutes later, prior to the arrival of the RCMP, the door was banged open, and the second shoplifter was back to help his friend escape by holding a gun to Ken's head. After I heard this story, I refused any further requests to help security. I had a baby boy and a young wife at home, with a life ahead of me, and my near-miss on Abbott Street years earlier haunted me still.

We had a small grocery store a couple of blocks away from where we lived in Nanaimo, called Terry's Market. I used to pop in occasionally on my way home if we needed something and I did not want to go into the supermarket. Terry closed shop at 10:00 each night, and one evening I drove over to get something at about five minutes prior to his locking up. As I pulled into my parking space, I noticed two things: I was the only car in the lot, and I saw a man run across my field of vision in the dark and dart behind the market. It appeared to me that he was chasing a large dog, and he was holding a handgun. My first thought was that he had a pellet gun and was chasing the dog. I did not think too much more about it, as I wanted to get in and out before Terry closed. I went in, quickly found my item, and went to the counter to pay Terry. It struck me that he was acting a little off; he did not engage in any conversation, and he seemed to want me out of the store quickly. I did not worry about it too much, thinking that he was just in a hurry to close up. When I exited the store a minute later, I noticed two sedans parked at opposing angles to my car. The man with the dog was standing close by watching two other men putting a third man in handcuffs into the back of an unmarked police car.

The next day I went back into the store to get the story from Terry. Apparently, I had almost stepped into an armed robbery. The police were aware of an armed robber who was knocking off grocery stores at their closing times around Nanaimo and had been tipped off that he was going to hit Terry's next. My timing could not have been worse. What I did not know driving up to the store, was that the robber, armed with a rifle, had already made his approach to the back of the store, and was going to rob it within minutes. When the police saw me pull up, they decided to make their move to avoid chaos inside the store. The man I saw with the handgun "chasing the dog" was actually an RCMP constable with his police dog going in to make an arrest. My infant son, David, would be robbed at gunpoint on Mother's Day in Langley eighteen years later, while working at an Esso gas station. Two punks on drugs and driving a stolen car had come in looking for cash for their next fix. They were eventually caught and arrested and given a slap on the wrist. The one who did the actual robbery spent about a year in jail waiting for trial; the one in the getaway car stayed out on parole. In court I was infuriated to hear their defence lawyer say it was "no big deal" because the gun was a fake. I wanted to shout at him and ask him if he would have thought differently if it was his son instead who had a gun waved in his face.

The Sears store had a mixed softball team that I joined soon after starting in Nanaimo. After the first year, I settled into the catcher position. I had a good arm and loved to pick off runners trying to steal second base. We would play other businesses around town and had games weekly; we did not have a league, there were no standings, and it was all played simply for fun. There was little I enjoyed more on a summer evening than playing ball; it was a very social event among my friends at the store. Spouses and kids brought blankets and lawn chairs to sit on to watch the games and cheer us on. We would win one game and lose another, and none of it mattered for me. The camaraderie, the summer sun on my face, and the joy of playing a sport I loved so much were worth every minute. I played for about six years until I was twenty-nine years old and suffered a serious shoulder injury.

It was in the eighth inning, and we were ahead by a fair amount. I had been having one of my better games and had hit two home runs, which was an exception for me. We had already retired two batters, and I was crouched behind the plate in my catcher's position. The batter drove a sharp line drive past our shortstop into shallow field, and the runner on third base made a run for home. I stepped just in front of the plate, ignoring the runner, instead focusing on the throw from the field, hoping to make the out. Rather than slide under me or touch the bag and step around me, the runner had run full tilt from third base, intent on hitting me with full force to knock me off my feet. He turned his shoulder into mine and collided with me at full speed and lifted my body off the ground into the air, throwing me backwards where I crashed heavily to the ground. I was mad as hell. Lying on my back, I tried to kick at him with my feet and then quickly jumped up to fight him. By that time, both teams had rushed in to separate us. With two batters already gone, we needed one more out to end the inning, and so after dusting myself off I went back into my crouch behind the plate. I quickly realized I could not hold my catching arm up, and instead had to rest my left elbow on my knee to position my ball glove. The batter took the first pitch and hit a weak ball toward our first baseman, and the inning was finished. As I went to the bench, I realized I could no longer move my left arm, and I was in considerable pain.

After the initial impact, my body had gone into shock, and I was able to function for a brief time. Luckily our third baseman, Penny, was a nurse, and she drove me to the hospital. After I was examined, a sling was put on my arm, and I was happily given meds for pain. Although I did not realize it at the time, that injury ended my ball playing for ever and would cause me years of pain and suffering. I was so angry the next day I did stupid things, like go to work and mow my lawn. Years later while working in Toronto, I read in a newspaper article about an almost identical incident in a softball game in Winnipeg. In that case, the backcatcher had successfully sued the runner for damages and suffering; I wished that I had done the same in Nanaimo.

Prior to my injury I also played floor hockey once a week for about four years in Nanaimo. Great exercise and great fun. We would run around, literally for an hour and a half without a break, at one of the school gymnasiums in town. As an adult I played softball, floor hockey, and ice hockey on "no hitting" teams. We all agreed that considering we had young kids and jobs, no one wanted to get injured and be off work.

However, one night I was intent on hitting anyone I could. I was warned a couple of times, but did not care, and kept banging and bumping along the walls and in the corners. Finally, Snowman pulled me aside and asked me what the hell was going on. I tried to push him aside and swore at him; but he was about six foot two inches and broader than me, and he was not going to let go. I loved Snowman, but I was so angry I was beside myself. I had been told earlier that day that my younger brother Peter had lymphoma. He was about twenty-four years old, and I was twenty-six. I wanted to know, "Why him? Why not some scumbag instead?" Why did my little brother have cancer? He was the logger, the fit, healthy guy. While Don and I had struggled with our weight growing up, Peter had always stayed slim, and then had gotten strong and muscular doing arduous work, climbing hillsides logging. It took me years to come to grips with the fact that there was no answer to my questions. Peter's physical and mental strength helped him survive.

I took a call one day from the medium-security penitentiary outside of Nanaimo, about coming to the prison to play floor hockey against the inmates there. I agreed without consulting the guys. The majority thought I was crazy and declined to play. In fact, only five of us walked through the prison gates to play the inmates a couple of nights later.

While at BCIT, I had gone to interview prisoners leaving Oakalla Penitentiary in Burnaby. Oakalla was a notorious lock-up for serious offenders. It was built in 1912 and closed in 1991 following a bloody riot and the escape of thirteen prisoners. The prison had housed male and female prisoners and saw the execution by hanging of forty-four inmates until the abolition of the death penalty in Canada in 1976. Armed with a tape recorder and microphone, I sat and interviewed about half a dozen prisoners in their halfway house. These were prisoners completing their prison terms and on the verge of departure. I was nervous but tried to show confidence and no fear. My recollection was that it went well, and I came back with what I had hoped would be a great report; however, the fluorescent lighting in the building had caused a background hiss on the recording tape, and it was not broadcast-worthy. Although it was embarrassing, I contacted the prison and planned to go back a second time and do the interviews over again.

Years later, walking through the gates at the Nanaimo Correctional Centre and having them close behind me was more disconcerting, even though it was only a medium-security facility.

We were escorted into a recreational building to play our floor hockey game and shown into a small room to change into our gym gear: running shoes, shorts, and T-shirts. A guard explained how they would ref the game and cautioned us to not go into the corners chasing the ball, as the week previously, when a different team had come in, a brawl had erupted. After the guard left, we looked at each other and wondered what we had gotten ourselves into.

Leaving the change room, we moved into the auditorium and were instantly intimidated. Dozens of inmates, mostly shirtless and well-muscled, were running around firing balls off the walls, hooting and hollering boisterously. Long hair and headbands were common. Two goaltenders were dressed in full goalie gear, including padding and face masks; we felt practically naked in T-shirts and shorts. At the far end of the auditorium floor was a stage with free weights and exercise equipment set up. Looking up, we saw an open walkway on the next floor of the building, with guards watching the inmates from above. It could easily have been a scene from a B movie.

We had been playing together for years and were fairly fit and adept. The score went up in our favour quickly, and to stay alive we avoided bumps and going into the corners. They had given us one of their extra goaltenders and one inmate for a spare; and although we were more skilled, they started to wear us down. We could only substitute one player at a time, while they were rolling full lines, and we started losing momentum from sheer exhaustion. I remember sitting on the edge of the stage gasping for air and sweating profusely on a quick break, with one of the inmates sitting beside me. Foolishly I asked him what he was in prison for, and he said, "assaulting a police officer." I decided not to ask any further questions. We were the only ones to escape the facility that night. We all agreed it was an experience none of us would ever forget, but declined invitations to go back again.

While at the Sears store in Nanaimo I became interested in salmon fishing. Although I had spent mornings in my youth trolling for trout in our family's rubber boat in camp, I had never fished on an ocean before. There were avid fishermen working at the store, and most had their own boats. Jerry worked in sporting goods as a commission salesman. He was a really nice guy and sold me a short, sturdy "trolling rod and reel" meant for fishing from a boat. We then went out one beautiful and calm morning from Nanaimo Harbour and found ourselves slowly drifting past Five Fingers Islands when Jerry stopped his boat and said we were going to "jig for cod." This was another new experience, and quite fun. Jerry put a heavy lure with a large hook on a line, handed me the rod, and asked me to let the line out until it hit the bottom. Once on the bottom, the technique was to lift the tip of the rod slowly a couple of feet and then let the line settle again to the bottom, attracting bottom-feeding fish like cod. It was not long when I found the line had become very heavy, but there seemed to be no fighting at the other end. Jerry explained that cod did not fight; you just had to pull them up. So, I continued winding and winding and eventually saw a large orange shape coming up from the ocean depths. It seemed I had great fortune and had caught a twelve-pound red snapper. The fish seemed to be mostly head, and it was bright orange. Minutes later I noticed its colour had changed to being almost white. Jerry explained that as they came up from the ocean floor they depressurized, and the shock to their system would turn them pale, but gradually they would return to their bright-orange colour. He also told me they were extremely "good eating fish." After fishing for about another hour and catching more cod, we pulled into a sheltered cove on one of the tiny islands, beached the boat, and got out to enjoy the sunshine and stretch our legs. We climbed a small hillock and enjoyed the panorama of blue sky, ocean, sea birds, sailboats, and other fishermen. I loved the salt air and was at peace. We made our way back to the cove and Jerry took out a fillet knife and showed me how to fillet cod to get the most usable meat. His knife was razor sharp and his movements quick and efficient, and he completed his work in a flash.

But although I enjoyed my day immensely, I did not have a boat. I also wanted to catch salmon, which were plentiful in the area. I asked around and found that there was a spot within five minutes of my home, called Rocky Point, where you could fish from shore. The first time, I went down to check it out was on a cool April Sunday morning, and there was thankfully only one other person down on the rocks fishing. I had my stubby trolling rod, Buzz Bomb lures in assorted colours and sizes, and a large, green garbage bag in my back pocket in case I was lucky enough to catch something. I found that when the tide was high you were standing only a couple of feet from the water, and it was easier to bring a fish in. When the tide was low it was trickier as you had to climb down rocks, slippery with seaweed, and find a ledge large enough to stand on and to cast from. This particular day, my first time out at Rocky Point, happened to be at low tide.

I settled into my spot about fifty feet from the other fisherman, tied on a pink Buzz Bomb and started casting and retrieving. The ocean bottom was all sand with nothing to snag on, so I would cast out as far as possible and let the lure sink until the line went slack, and then slowly retrieve it and cast again. I was fumbling and unsure of myself but was glad to be out there. Only minutes had elapsed since I started my casting and receiving when I heard a shout from the other fisherman, and I saw his fishing line taut and his rod tip bouncing as he had latched onto a salmon. Before I knew it, I felt a strong tug on my line, and I was also bringing in my salmon. While bringing my line in, I kept stealing glances at the other fisherman. He would bring his line in steadily for a minute and then he would stop, and his line would be hissing as the salmon fought back and tried to get away. When he finally got his fish to the rocks it was played out and he reached with his hand into the water, grabbed the salmon and threw it up on the rocks behind him. Then he turned and watched me, and started shouting advice, telling me to keep it away from the kelp beds where it could escape. He climbed over the rocks to assist me, and once my fish was close enough, he reached into the ocean again and threw my salmon on the rocks beside me. On my very first attempt I had caught a fifteen-pound spring salmon. I was exuberant and thanked him profusely. I gathered my gear, putting the salmon in the large, green garbage bag, and I went home. It was the largest fish I had ever caught.

I found that as much as I loved being close to, and being on the ocean, it did not love me back. Unless the water was pretty calm, I found I would get violently seasick. At the worst of times, I would want to die to be put out of my misery. I became a "sucker for punishment." Even if I knew better, I would still accept an offer to go out fishing even though I knew how horrible it might be. It was always the promise of a glorious day that drew me back.

Peter and I hardly saw each other after I moved away from camp. So later, after moving to Nanaimo I would jump at the chance when he asked me to go fishing with him in his boat. One time Peter, Dad, and me went out for a camping/fishing trip out to Port Renfrew, and it became one of my favourite days ever. Peter had already set up a trailer at a campsite there days before, and so we simply had to tow his eighteen-foot aluminum boat to Port Renfrew. The first thing we saw as we came into the camping area was a man carrying two salmon, about thirty pounds each, in his hands. It was too late in the day for us to go fishing. So instead, we took a quick boat ride, dropped his crab traps in the water, and then returned, tied up the boat, unpacked, and set up camp. There was still enough light left after setting up camp to go out and check the traps, so we went to see whether we had caught any crabs for dinner. I had not "crabbed" before, and it was fun pulling in the long rope to see if there was anything in the cage. All of the traps had three or four crabs in them, and we kept a couple that were large enough from each trap for our dinner. By the time we were back it was almost dark, and Dad put a large pot of water on the campfire, and Peter passed cold beers around to everyone while we waited for the water to boil.

We noticed that while we were out collecting our crabs, a small tent had been set up in the adjacent campsite. Two guys about Peter's age and a girl were trying to get a campfire going without success. We offered our help, and when we got them set up, we invited them over for a beer. One of the guys told us that they had been out for a drive from Victoria and had picked up the girl hitchhiking, and they all decided to head to Port Renfrew. By this time, the water was boiling and after dropping the crabs in the pot, we asked them to stay for dinner. Like me, those guys must have had a story to tell for years. Picking up a pretty girl for company on the road, and then getting cold beer and fresh crab for dinner, should have been pretty memorable. The funny thing was that the girl refused the crab because she had seen warning signs about "red tide" and thought they were contaminated. Peter told her that red tide only affected shellfish and not crabs, and in fact that we would not be eating them ourselves if they were not safe, but she still declined.

The next morning, we were up before the sun, had coffee and a quick breakfast around the campfire, and then were out in the boat ready to catch salmon. Peter knew what to do and where to fish; he had been fishing at Port Renfrew for years. However, after fishing for a couple of hours at his favourite spots we had not even had a bite. He decided to go out further into the open ocean, and fortunately for me the water was quite calm that entire day. After travelling a long way out to sea, Peter cut his motor, and we sat there and drifted. Ahead of us from as far as we could see to the left and right was a sweeping panorama of commercial fishing boats, taking turns circling with their nets. No wonder there were no salmon for us that day. We gave up the idea of salmon and decided to take our time and follow the shoreline back into the campground and jig for cod. It was simply astounding to me. We would stop and the three of us would drop our lines over the side of the boat, and before the lure even hit the bottom, we would all have fish striking our lines. We hauled in dozens of fishes, putting most back, keeping only the sea bass and sole. There were so many fish at the first stop that Peter decided to motor further down the coastline, but no matter where we stopped the results were the same, to the point that the bottom of the boat was full of sea bass. At one point my back was to the open ocean, and Peter yelled at me to turn around. I saw the enormous tail fluke of a humpback whale disappearing under the water. Peter had seen it rise to the surface and start to submerge again. It was a glorious day for me, and the only time I went fishing with my dad and my brother.

Another fishing trip became a lifetime memory, but in no way glorious. Peter invited me to come along with him and one of his best friends, Hank, to go out to Nitinat Lake to fish for salmon. Of course, I jumped at the chance. Once again, Peter had set up a campsite ahead of time, and we had only to get the boat and us there, and Hank would be waiting. As we got closer Peter pulled over and said that he was going to unload the boat into the lake. Apparently, the gravel roads were extremely potholed and rough, and he thought it would be too hard on the boat to bounce it the rest of the way. He said that he knew the road and that he would drive the pickup to the campsite and that he wanted me to run the boat up the lake to meet him. I had never really operated a powerboat before and was pretty nervous. He showed me the controls and gave me basic instructions and watched me pull away. It did not take long for me to get a feel for it, and it became quite fun. However, I started to worry about whether I might not be able to see the campground, and inadvertently go past it. I had no idea of the distance I needed to travel, nor any way of judging how far I had already gone, and the sun was going down and the light waning. I started to get apprehensive and stopped enjoying myself, similar to my experience skydiving before I knew my chute had opened successfully. Fortunately, the campground was obvious when I came around a corner of the lake as I saw trailers, tents, and pickups parked along the shoreline, along with Peter waiting for me.

The next morning, we were up and ready to go by dawn. Standing on shore next to Peter's boat, I was asked to put on a bright-orange survival suit. This caused immediate concern; why the need for a survival suit was the immediate question in my mind. Peter explained that taking a boat through "the Gap" out to the open ocean was treacherous, and that people had died in the attempt. It took an experienced captain to safely make it through. "The Gap," or Nitinat Narrows, allowed the Pacific Ocean to come through a narrow opening and flow into Nitinat Lake; the force and unpredictability of the waves and currents making it daunting. Peter was experienced and capable and as I put on the survival suit, I had little trepidation. What made this outing even more interesting was the unknown past the Gap. Nitinat Lake was quite placid, but the open ocean beyond was obscured by the waves crashing through the narrows. The ocean beyond could be calm or calamitous; you only found out by escaping the lake and popping out the other side. For someone like me who got violently seasick in rough water, I was tossing the dice hoping for the water to land in my favour. Not on this day, sadly.

Peter circled three times before making his attempt, aborting each time when he did not think he could make it. On the fourth attempt he gunned the outboard motor and we hurtled toward the waves, the bow crashing down against each wave with a jarring effect on all of us. He climbed and plummeted successive waves, until finally we were safely out into the ocean beyond the Gap. To my dismay, the water had a rough chop, and I knew it was going to be a tough time for me. Peter piloted the boat northward following the coastline at high speed to get to his favourite fishing spot. While the boat was travelling at high speed and planing, I was totally fine. However, as soon as he cut the motor to get his downriggers and gear ready, and his hooks baited with herring, the boat started to vigorously bob and rock about, and within a minute I was feeling queasy.

Once the lines were ready, he started the boat in motion again slowly at a trolling speed, gradually letting line out on two rods he had set up moments earlier. Only minutes later both lines had strikes simultaneously, and I found myself winding the line of the rod on the port side, with Hank bringing in his salmon on the starboard side, with Ron running the boat to assist us. I found myself standing with my left leg and knee braced against the side of the boat to help keep my balance while the boat rocked wildly, all the while trying to bring my salmon in as well. As my salmon came close to the boat, I yelled to Peter, who temporarily abandoned the controls to net my salmon and fling it into the boat. A moment later Hank's was also in the boat. Within minutes of our fishing expedition, we had landed two twenty-five-pound spring salmon. Fishing was good; Larry was not. As soon as I knew my salmon was safely in the boat, I dropped to my knees and was violently sick over the side, retching my guts out. Not a pretty sight. As I had caught my salmon, and because I was so sick, I completely lost interest in fishing more. I had brought with me a ginger ale in preparation for this outcome and sipped it slowly, while lying in the bottom of the boat, head hanging and stomach heaving. Peter and Hank ignored me as best they could, rebaiting the lines and throwing them over, looking for more strikes.

After about forty-five minutes of trolling with no further strikes, and with me retching, moaning, and pallid, they decided to take me back to shore so they could return and continue fishing on their own. I was immensely grateful; wanting only to either end my misery or to be put overboard. It mattered little to me at the time. When we arrived at the opening to the Gap, we found about a dozen other boats in the immediate vicinity. Peter surveyed the opening and determined that the conditions were too dangerous to make the attempt to return to Nitinat Lake. I was horrified to learn that I had to endure more for an undetermined amount of time. With each wave our boat would drop so far that all we could see was ocean water all around us, and then rise again to see the other dozen boats, only to drop again to see nothing again but water. This went on, moment by moment, wave by successive wave, for about forty-five minutes, until finally Peter felt it was safe enough to traverse the Gap.

Moments later we were docked by the shoreline, and I staggered out of the boat, only wanting to lay down somewhere and close my eyes. Peter gave me water and insisted I take sandwiches. Foolishly I refused, saying I could not imagine eating anything, and although he warned me that I would be hungry later, I sent them away. Once they were gone, I stumbled into the forest a short way from the path, unzipped my survival suit to leave it hanging down from my waist. I sat on the ground using a large hemlock tree to rest against and closed my eyes. It was now about 8:00 a.m. Peter and Hank would return triumphantly with three more salmon, five in total, about 3:30 in the afternoon.

The Gap was also a crossing-over point for the world-famous West Coast Trail. To traverse the trail from end to end, hikers needed to cross the Gap by boat. Within feet of where I was huddled in hiding, was a bell hanging from a tree. Hikers would ring the bell, and in time one of the members of the Ditidaht First Nation would come out of a hut to meet them. They would board a small aluminum boat, and for a fee, be transported to the other side to continue their journey. I would hear hikers talking as they approached the bell and slumped further to avoid being detected in the bushes.

After resting and recuperating for nearly four hours, I finally started to feel more normal. I also realized that I was starving. I had lost all of my breakfast in my ordeal on the boat, my stomach seemed completely empty. To my dismay, I recognized my foolishness in refusing to take sandwiches when Peter offered them. It was now noon, and I had no idea when they would be back. When I could not stand it any longer, I got slowly to my feet and leaned against the tree trunk to stabilize myself. I zipped up my survival suit and stepped onto the trail, watching three hikers step forward and ring the bell. I waited to see what would happen next, and after time saw the door of the hut open and out stepped the band member to ferry them across the narrows. He was wearing a black top hat, a jacket with tails, and sweatpants. When he returned and secured his boat against the dock, I stepped forward to talk to him. Once he was close enough to me, I recognized him as one of the kids who had travelled on the school bus with me to Lake Cowichan years earlier. We chatted for a bit, and he went back to wait for the bell to ring again.

I decided to stay near the bell, standing boldly in my bright-orange survival suit. When the next group of hikers came out of the forest and rang the bell, they saw me standing there and struck up a conversation. I asked how their trip had been so far, if it had met their expectations, and what had been highlights for them. Naturally, the conversation turned to me, and I was asked what I was doing out here in the middle of nowhere, wearing a bright-orange survival suit. Just what I had waited for! I spun my tail of adventure and woe, culminating with my recovery sitting in the forest near the trail. If I did not overtly ask for food, my tale of woe coupled with my growling stomach triggered compassion. They offered me snacks, and of course I politely refused. I was not overly convincing, and my stomach argued my case for me, and they pressed food into my hands. I thanked them profusely, and as soon as they had left to cross the Gap, I ravenously gobbled their gift.

Eventually Peter and Hank arrived with five spring salmon they had caught, and more important to me in the moment, a couple of sandwiches they had saved. I inhaled them in seconds and told Peter about the snacks the hikers had shared with me. Peter was aghast at me for taking food from them, explaining that the West Coast Trail is rugged and wild and takes eight to ten arduous days to complete. Only enough food for each hiker to complete the trip is allowed. Nothing extra. I had no idea of these restrictions at the time and was even more grateful for their generosity when I learned about it later. Devouring my sandwiches, we ended up spending an hour slowly drifting in the lake, netting crabs we could see scurrying across the lake floor. Peter never invited me to fish at Nitinat Lake again.

I was always ambitious. My entire life I craved acceptance and wanted to be valued and respected. Although only ten minutes older than my twin brother Don, I have always known I was the elder child in our family of five. I feel that in part, this has driven me to always look ahead for advancement and to improve my position, and with it also came a burden of responsibility. About twenty years ago I was sitting at a coffee shop in Toronto's Pearson International Airport, waiting for a return flight home from a business trip back to BC, talking with Don. We were forty-three years old at the time, and I asked him if at any time while growing up he had thought of one of us as being the "oldest." He quickly replied, "No," and I confessed that I had always thought of myself as the oldest and was exhausted from feeling responsible for the family. Although our parents had never told me: "Larry, you are the oldest, you have to look out for your brothers and sisters," I just "knew it" from the centre of my being. He released me by saying, "No one ever asked you to carry that burden; let it go."

To me, promotions and career advancements were acknowledgements of my value and worth, and also provided pay raises so that I could provide better for my family. So, when I started as a manager trainee with Sears at their retail store in Nanaimo, my objective was to move up in the ranks. Advancement would affirm for me that I was capable and had excelled and would provide salary increases. Starting out with no money working at CJRV in Port Alberni, using cardboard boxes disguised with fabric as furniture, living in rental apartments; my advancement at Sears allowed us to buy furniture, a microwave, a portable dishwasher, and our first home.

I came to realize that the opportunities for advancement in the retail store were extremely limited. From a trainee I would become a division manager and then shuffle around different divisions hoping to become a group manager at the store. A group manager would oversee a combination of divisions—for example, major appliances, furniture and carpeting, and paint. However, in a smaller store like ours in Nanaimo, there were only three of these positions. From there, a group manager had an opportunity of becoming the operating manager or store manager. After working as a division manager for seven years, I understood I might never advance further, and if I did, it could take years waiting for someone else to be promoted, be fired, or die. At every performance review I said I was "mobile" and eager to advance, not really giving thought to what that might entail. The store manager at that time had been there for years and essentially retired on the job; it was highly unlikely advancement would happen under his watch. When he finally did retire, I suddenly had an advantage; Roger, the new store manager, knew no one at the store, and impressions could be made.

At this time, I had been manager of custom draperies and bedding for almost three years. I knew every aspect of my business backwards and forwards. I was on top of my inventory positions, I knew my sales and gross profits numbers; in fact, I answered every question that Roger asked when he toured my area with the group manager. Afterwards my group manager told me I had impressed the heck out of Roger. I had become an expert in every aspect of my business, including how to install custom draperies, curtain rods, and all types of blinds. Roger was fixing up their new home as he had transferred from Winnipeg to Nanaimo, and he asked me to come over to his home one afternoon to help him install new vertical blinds, which I gladly did.

Soon after Roger called me into his office, closed the door and asked me to sit down. He said I had impressed him with my work and professionalism, and he had put my name forward for a promotion. I said I was flattered and thanked him and asked him what he proposed. He said the new job would be at the Sears head office in Toronto! With that offer, my life changed forever.

It was the spring of 1987, and I had worked at the Nanaimo store for seven years. In that time, I had two boys, my oldest now six and my youngest about nine months, and I had been married for nine years. Going to Toronto had never been on my radar, and I was taken aback. At home I told my wife, and she was unhappy about the prospect of Toronto. I assured her that I needed to interview for the job, and they may not like me or offer me the position. I was trapped because Roger had lobbied for me and because I had stated on every performance review during my seven years that I was "mobile" and wanted advancement. How could I turn down an offer now? I told Roger that I would go for the interview, and in hindsight these decades later, I confess that I was not honest with my family. I knew that if I interviewed, that I would get the job.

So, I flew into Toronto for the very first time in April 1987. From the air everything looked brown, flat, and dead. There seemed to be kilometres of warehouses near the airport as we were landing. The only joy of the trip was reuniting with Don, as my twin had moved there years earlier. Don picked me up early in the morning as I had taken the "red eye" flight from Vancouver to be there. On Monday morning I found myself on Jarvis Street in downtown Toronto at the Canadian headquarters of Sears. The head office was unremarkable, my interview went well, and before I knew it, I was back in Nanaimo with my family and friends waiting to hear what would happen next. Within a week, on a Friday afternoon, Roger called me into the office to tell me that I had been offered the job. He counselled me to go home and come back on Monday morning with my reply. From that point, I did absolutely everything wrong.

Where I got my ideas of the proper way to act (how to be a man) I can only speculate on; mostly I think from observation rather than preparation. I do not remember Dad sitting down and telling me what was required of me; rather, I listened and watched him and his friends. I remember my future father-in-law, Al, walking me around the streets in Penticton one summer evening after his daughter (my future ex-wife) had lost her temper and started yelling at me at their home. He told me, "You have made your bed, and now you have to lie in it." What I heard him say was that as difficult as I thought things were at home, I had made a commitment and had to make it work; in life you needed to "see things through" or "tough it out."

Couples rarely lived together in the 1960s and 1970s without getting married. "Shacking up" was a derogatory term. If you "knocked up" a girl, you married her. You did not "give up without a fight." You had to be "your own man" and "stand on your own two feet." On top of everything the world expected something from me.

As it turned out we were presented with a serendipitous gift of good timing. On the weekend that we needed to decide about my promotion and the family's transfer to Toronto, my in-laws showed up in Nanaimo. We should have jumped at this opportunity to get free time to talk and find our way; instead, we squandered our time and we visited with them and spent almost no time discussing the elephant in the room. By Sunday night we had not come to a mutual agreement. On Monday morning my wife said,

"It is your decision; do what you want." So, full of trepidation, and with a knot in my stomach, I sat in Roger's office and accepted the transfer.

We could have still made the next four years work if we both had embraced the move as an adventure. Neither of us had ever lived outside of BC and probably would never have done so in any other circumstance. On the inside my gut was telling me I had made a mistake, while I was exuding bravado on the outside. It felt like I had jumped into a river, and it was sweeping me away by currents I could not control.

Life in the Fast Lane

Album Cut:
"I'm In A Hurry (And Don't Know Why)"
Alabama
***American Pride*, released 1992**

APRIL TO JULY WAS A blur. I was working out of Toronto and flying home every couple of weeks for a couple of days and then back to Toronto. Our first home purchased in Nanaimo for $50,000 went up for sale, and we started the home-buying process in Ontario. I was really of little help to my family for those three months; instead, I was desperately trying to keep my head above water living out of the Delta Chelsea Hotel off Yonge Street, trying to get a handle on a new job, new people, and a new way of life. It was terribly lonely and disheartening.

A moment of excitement came one afternoon when I was walking back to the hotel after work; it was like a scene in an action movie. I heard a large crash behind me and turned to look, and saw a car flying through the air, upside down, heading straight at me. I clutched my briefcase and ran as fast as I could away from the flying car and heard it crash on the ground behind me. I ran another twenty feet and turned for a second look; the car was still heading in my direction, but this time it was skidding across the pavement on its roof, all four tires spinning in the air. It finally came to a rest up and over the curb onto the sidewalk, mere steps from me. My first aid training kicked in, and I ran to the driver's side window and saw a man suspended upside down. Both driver and passenger side windows were open, so I reached in around his body and turned the ignition switch off and then asked him if he was okay. He said he thought so, and I recognized that shock was setting in. Before I could ask him another question and evaluate him properly, an idiot reached in from the driver side window and unfastened his seatbelt, dropping him on his head onto the roof of the car. I was appalled and asked the driver again if he was okay, and again he said he thought so. He was trying to move out of the vehicle, so I assisted him to get out and stand up. By this time emergency crews had arrived on the scene, and they took over. The passerby who had reached in and dropped him on his head had disappeared. I hope he thought twice about what he did and the peril he put that driver in. I found out later that both cars were heading north on Yonge Street at a high speed when one tried to pass the other, clipping him and sending his car airborne. Fortunately, no one was injured, and life in the big city continued on without a pause.

In Toronto, the housing market was hot, and property prices were climbing rapidly, with multiple offers on the same property. In Nanaimo, my house was listed for $55,000, and I was trying to find a townhouse for under $125,000. This scared the heck out of me. The only way I could make this work financially was that as part of the transfer I was given a three-year, interest-free second mortgage by the company. On the recommendation of someone at work, I engaged over the phone with a realtor to find housing options so that my wife could come out and we could find a home we would both be okay with. I had not met the realtor in person, and in those days, no one had cellphones. I arranged to meet him on a Saturday morning in front of Union Station, which was a recognizable landmark. He told me he would be driving a grey Volvo, so I got there early and stood outside waiting for him.

Springtime in April in Toronto was totally unlike spring in Nanaimo. The air was brisk, and I stood there shivering and moving my feet to keep warm, glancing at my watch every few minutes. He did not arrive on time; after he was late by about thirty minutes, I started to panic, thinking we had missed each other. I was afraid to leave my spot and go into Union Station to find a pay phone to call him, but eventually I had no other choice. His office told me that he had arrived, waited for me for only a couple of minutes, and turned around, heading back to Mississauga. I was angry. I told her to tell him to turn around and come back to pick me up. I gathered from her that he had pulled up extremely near to where I was standing but sat in his car with the heater on, keeping himself toasty, and had not bothered to get out and walk up the street to find me.

When he finally picked me up, he could see I was annoyed, so he bought me a coffee, and we headed out toward Mississauga. He said he had three properties to show me, which also shocked me, as I had told him on the phone that I had only the weekend to look, and if we found something suitable, I needed to arrange for my wife to fly out to make any deal. I would have thought he would have been prepared to show me a dozen places. Two of the places I walked into and then walked straight out of. The third and final place was only okay. He drove me back to his office and insisted on writing up an offer; he said properties were selling quickly (true) and that this was the best place I would find anywhere at my price point (untrue). I told him that I would sign an offer subject to my wife's approval with a closing date of midnight, six days later on Friday. He was unhappy about the subject, but it was a deal breaker, and I told him so. I also clearly stated that I was not really keen on the place, and he would have to line up at least a dozen other places for my wife and me to do a proper comparison. He took me back to my hotel, and I called home.

Sears was incredibly good in all aspects of their transfer; they had my wife flown out on a plane the next morning at their expense, and we had a carefree day together. That night I called the realtor again and told him that we were looking forward to seeing all of the properties he had arranged for us to see. This time he picked both of us up at our hotel, and we headed back out toward Mississauga. This was my wife's first time to Toronto, and she felt as out of place as I had months earlier. He took us to the same two properties that I had dismissed before and one other equally bad, and then took us to the one I had put the offer on. My wife was less impressed than I was, but again he drove us to his office and brought out papers to close the deal. I told him, "No way," and gave him hell for not showing us more properties. It was obvious he cared more about making a sale, and less about our needs and situation.

Remember the "subject to my wife's approval" holding the property until Friday? He did. Pressure then came for us to release the subject so that he could sell the house to someone else. I told him, "No way," again. I said because he had not done his job for us, we had no idea whether this was the best opportunity for our money, and we were going to look around to make that determination for ourselves. He very unhappily drove us back to the hotel.

Vicky had been referred to me by a co-worker and showed us a night-and-day difference as a realtor and as a person. She really did take an interest in us as people. She also drove a late-model Fiat that we squeezed into, and this time we looked to the east of Toronto, literally spending an entire day looking at dozens of places. We liked the look of Ajax, about an hour's commute from downtown Toronto. It bordered on Lake Ontario and was quiet and had a nice feel to it. However, the market was hot, and the first place we put an offer on was lost in a bidding war at the last minute. It was now Thursday evening, and my wife was scheduled to return on Saturday morning to BC. Every night we got a call from the Mississauga realtor asking us to release the property; every day we told him, no, we were still looking. So, the pressure was on to find a home for the family in one day; Vicky took the challenge, and we looked at a score of homes, prepared to put in an offer with subject to clear that evening at midnight. She came through, finding an older but well-kept townhouse community about a kilometre from the lake. The deal finalized at midnight, and we were relieved and exhausted. I called the other realtor to tell him he could keep his property.

Two aspects of our move have indelibly stuck with me for the past thirty-five years. My parents, my sisters, and my brother Peter had come to Nanaimo to see us off. As we were leaving, Peter came over to me crying and telling me he was losing both his brothers. Peter the tough, strong, logger wept at my departure. On the other end of our move, in Ajax, it was not any happier. On the day we moved into our townhouse I remember my wife sitting on the stairs to the second level, crying her eyes out because she did not want to be there. Boxes left by the movers and piled everywhere around us were silent witnesses to the despair in the room.

It was hard for me to tell her I did not want to be there either. Over the three months I had been on my own I had come to hate my job, but my father-in-law's voice from years earlier was in my ear, saying, "You've made your bed; now you must sleep in it." It became my cross to bear. We set to making the place ours; we replaced all of the carpets, painted and wallpapered the entire interior, and bought furniture with part of the relocation money. Fortunately, about four doors down the row in our complex, my wife found a new friend. Wanda had a baby and was expecting a second; with our younger son Josh being eleven months old, they hit it off quickly. Having a friend steps away was a blessing for us.

My new job was as a catalogue merchandiser for product lines that included bathroom fixtures, air conditioners, hot water tanks, and toilet seats. Truly glamorous. There were five members on the team: Matt, a nice young guy who was the lead, and Katie, Lawrence, Chad, and me as merchandisers. The first couple of Monday mornings I remember coming in and sticking my head in each cubicle to say good morning, asking each of them about their weekends. Chad finally blurted out, "You are very West Coastish." I grasped the Toronto reality; people came to work, headed to their cubicles, kept their heads down, and left to go home at the end of the day. It was not the friendly, relaxed mentality of the West Coast. When I told people I came from Nanaimo, they had no idea where it was, so I got a large map of Vancouver Island and pinned it inside my cubicle. Not only was this a way to show people where I was from, but it also gave me something to hang onto. I missed my family and friends and felt alienated. Lawrence, an older guy, did his best to make me comfortable. Katie was lovely and showed me around the city, including The Danforth—the Greek section—and I had souvlaki for the first time.

I was there for less than a week when all five of us were brought into Rochelle's office. She was the manager overseeing our team, and I quickly saw her leadership style in action. She berated my four co-workers, lambasting them for issues that I did not understand at the time, wrapping up by calling them a "bunch of wimps." I wondered whether she chose her leadership style to advance in a male-dominated office environment.

The job of catalogue merchandiser was to project sales of a particular product in a specific catalogue, order sufficient quantities, distribute it to warehouses across Canada, and track demand and supply. Adjustments would be made if sales were slower than projected (plans were developed to liquidate excess inventory) or better (then we had to scurry for more product). This work was done in concert with buyers and marketing managers. Buyers would make contracts for merchandise with suppliers in Canada and around the world. Marketing managers would take photographs of merchandise and create the catalogue page layouts. In a well-run group, merchandisers, buyers, and marketing managers would work collaboratively. This was not the reality in all cases.

Depending on the scope of a buyer, he or she might have multiple assistant buyers. I found a number who were good to work with, and we worked effectively together; then there was J.R. He was an assistant buyer who sourced towel bars, bathroom accessories, and shower doors. He was always smartly dressed and groomed, confident, articulate, and urbane; I came to understand he was also conniving and underhanded. Instead of working collaboratively to solve an inventory problem, he would blame me, saying I had not done my job. After this happened openly in a group discussion with my boss and the national manager in attendance, I went to him and suggested in the future we should communicate better so we could isolate and handle problems before our weekly discussions with the national manager; he told me he agreed. The next Wednesday I went to his office and asked if there were any inventory or sourcing problems we should discuss before our Friday meeting; I told him there was nothing that I could see that would be an issue. He said not to worry; he did not believe there would be any problems, and he had not had the time to check yet. On Friday morning at our next meeting, he stood up and highlighted inventory problems and said it was my fault again; I could feel the knife sliding in between my ribs. I stood up and told the group, including my boss, it was the last national meeting I would attend. Firmly, I told them that these meetings were not about identifying potential problems and working together to solve them, but instead were inquisitions. So, while waiting for my family to move out to Toronto, I was fighting to keep myself alive in a challenging environment, trying to get a handle on the mechanics of my job, and working endless hours in the evenings and on weekends to try to keep up. Eating hotel food and getting little exercise, I also put on about twenty pounds over those three months.

To compound my troubles, I was the only merchandiser working without an assistant. To alleviate this, my boss informed me one morning that someone to be assigned as my assistant would start on the next Monday. I was pumped, hoping this would reduce the work I took home and lessen my stress.

I had been sitting at my desk on Monday morning for only minutes when Barb was brought in and introduced to me. She sat in a chair across from my desk in my tiny cubicle, and for the next couple of minutes I welcomed her and told her how much I was looking forward to collaborating with her. It quickly dawned on me that she was unresponsive to my welcome. She sat there unmoving, arms-crossed, stony-faced and quiet. I finally stopped and asked her if there was a problem. She told me emphatically that she did not want to be working with me, that she felt that she had been "demoted" in being moved to our area. I was flabbergasted. Instantly I brought my supervisor in and explained the situation. It was brought to Barb's attention that she was expected to do her job and work with me. And so, the nightmare began.

Later on, I found out that she had been an assistant on another floor and "taken over" her area, bullying everyone around her—even the management group. Instead of disciplining her, they had moved her to be my assistant. She missed almost every Monday due to migraines, she was slow at her job, and I was always behind schedule; as a result, I was being pressured by my boss. It went on day after day, with Barb getting more morose and difficult. When I confronted her, she openly admitted she was sabotaging me. Finally, I had to involve personnel, and she was given a ninety-day period to improve her performance; after the ninety -days, she was given another thirty -days to improve or be fired. Just before the completion of the thirty-day period, when I thought I was about to finally be rid of her (she had continued to get worse, not better), she was given a performance review by the office manager. All assistants worked in a pool under an office manager, who reviewed their performance. Tragically, I had no input. Barb received a glowing annual review, with a ranking even higher than mine. So, even though the thirty-day final warning was about to expire and I wanted to fire her, personnel now had a dilemma. So, she had to start the process all over again with another ninety-day warning period. Just before she was about to be let go for the second time, the office manager moved her to a different team. This was not the first time she had been saved. I could not believe she had been made someone else's problem again. Maybe they felt sorry for her because she was a single parent. Maybe she had charmed the office manager. In any event, management's decision was disappointing, but I was relieved to be rid of her.

A brief time later, soon after my ultimatum at the national meeting, I was told that I was being transferred to another floor to the menswear group.

It was a night-and-day difference. I still did not like my job, but everyone there worked really well together. During my first week in the menswear department, a couple of my co-workers asked me if I could keep my new boss busy for a couple of minutes before lunch. They told me it was his birthday, and they were going to go around the floor and gather everyone together to come over and sing "Happy Birthday" outside his door. I certainly did not mind; wanting to be seen as a team player in my new area, I readily agreed. I knocked on his door, poked my head inside, and asked him if he had a moment; he assured me he did and asked me to come in. We exchanged small talk for a minute because I had met him only days before. I was forced to spin stories when no one had come to the door as quickly as I hoped. So, I told him I was having back problems and was going to need physiotherapy and I might have to leave work early a couple of days a week. He said that would be okay as long as I talked with him ahead of time.

I then started to babble about what kinds of treatments I'd tried over the years and mentioned that I had never tried acupuncture. There was still no group at the door singing "Happy Birthday," and it slowly dawned on me that I had been pranked. I excused myself for a second, stood up, and opened his door to see my co-workers heading out with their coats on, laughing. I turned back into the room, smiled at my boss, and told him I had "been had." I apologized for wasting his time and told him I was not going to take any time off work. I did have a back problem but had not planned on treatment that would interfere with my work. Fortunately, he was a good guy and laughed it off; I knew that my co-workers would never be able to fool me again.

In the meantime, I had met Maurice on the commuter train heading into work one morning. We sat across from each other on a morning commute and recognized we both wore Sears lapel pins on our suit jackets. Breaking into conversation, we found commonality: he also had a young family, we both lived in Ajax, and he had also been transferred by Sears to Toronto. Maurice and his family had come from Montreal, and although he had prepared better for the transfer than I had, they also wanted to go back to their home province. A couple of months later Maurice bought an eleven-passenger commuter van and invited me along to be his backup driver. This was one of the best things that happened to me; now I had a friend as well. Maurice and I, with nine women heading to Sears every day, were a riot. All with different personalities, all were genuinely nice people. We were all about the same age, and all had kids except Kathleen. Maurice worked in the Sears credit card department, and Kathleen was his assistant. We would have crazy conversations every day, and the bus was filled with laughter. As with all city commuters, the buzz was in the morning (possibly caffeine-fuelled), and sleep was caught up on during the drive home in the afternoon.

As one of the riders was pregnant and expecting their first baby, the conversation in the back eventually turned to boys and the question of circumcision. The riders in the back each talked about whether their kids had been circumcised, and then naturally whether their husbands were or not. Maurice and I did not say anything, trying to avoid the conversation, when Jane yelled from the back, "What about you two? Are you guys circumcised?" Maurice and I looked at each other and grinned, and Maurice yelled back that it was too private to talk about in the van. They all hooted and told us we were all safe in the van together, so Maurice eventually relented and said, yes, he had been circumcised, forcing me to confess that I had not. The rule of thumb seemed to be that if the father was circumcised, then the baby was. I related to them that my brother Peter had been born in a Catholic hospital in northern Alberta while my dad was away in Iran, and the nuns had insisted that he be circumcised against my mom's wishes. Imagine how desperate my mom must have been with the hospital forcing her into a decision she did not want, with no one to defend her position.

Maurice and his family had become good friends with us, but they also wanted to go home—in their case, back to Quebec. After about three years he took a transfer to Ottawa, but moved to Gatineau, Quebec, across the river from Ottawa. We stayed connected, and about a year later, during the summer before we packed up and headed back to BC, we did a car trip with the kids to visit them and see the sights of Ottawa. Our timing was good, as the very next day was the Gatineau Hot Air Balloon Festival (Festival de montgolfières de Gatineau), held in the large Parc de la Baie less than a fifteen-minute drive from downtown Ottawa. The evening before, Maurice and I stood on his front porch during an impressive thunderstorm. The sky came alive at every minute, with spectacular lightning and booming thunder. We stood watching the rain pour down and the lightning flash for more than half an hour. Thunderstorms in southern Ontario and Quebec were impressive and unlike anything I had ever seen before. The next morning the weather cleared, and we went to the park. There was a buzz and a hum of activity; crews unpacking balloons on the ground, balloons half-inflated with crews scurrying around them, balloons just lifting off the ground, and balloons in the sky already fading off into the distance. The colours were amazing and the shapes astounding. There were the "normal" round shapes; there were balloons shaped like elephants, hammers, houses, and people, towering above us. It was fun and memorable. Years later, when I was back in BC living in Langley, I went up in a hot air balloon myself. It was an interesting experience. We drifted silently and easily through the air, high above the quiet farms and Langley Township below. The basket of the balloon was confining; six people, including the pilot, stood around the inside edge of the basket, with the intense heat from the flames keeping the balloon afloat. Our package included wine, cheese, and crackers when we touched down two hours later. Sadly, a couple of years later the operator's balloon caught fire, he was badly burned, and one of his passengers died. Risks in life abound even in seemingly benign experiences.

Back at the office, although I had gotten a handle on my job, I liked it even less. After the first six months I had understood I was on the wrong career path and was heading in a direction opposite to what I really wanted. I had hoped that by leaving Nanaimo I would find an opportunity to work in personnel at the head office, where I had none at the retail store level. To my dismay, this career path was to move from catalogue merchandiser to assistant buyer to buyer, to national manager. I set up a meeting with the national personnel manager to determine how I could make the transition, asking him whether there were any internal courses or training opportunities I could take to help me go in the right direction. Robert was a really good guy—professional, understanding, and honest. He told me there was no program at Sears that I could take but encouraged me to look at the colleges in the area. So, I enrolled in a two-year diploma program titled “Effective Supervision” at Durham College in Oshawa.

Now I was getting up at 5:30 in the morning to exercise and study before commuting to Toronto and back. Upon arriving home at 5:00 p.m., I would take over from our babysitter until my wife got home from her part-time job at a local grocery store. We would all have dinner together, and after they went to bed I would do paperwork to keep up at work and study some more if I could manage it. As well, I attended classes in Oshawa once a week. My day would repeat, Monday to Friday, over and over and over again.

I went through an annual performance review with my boss. Each year I would get excellent evaluations, and each year I would say in writing that I wanted to move to personnel. I was getting frustrated; even after graduating from Durham College I saw no movement. To make matters worse, I had coffee with a clothing buyer one day, and she told me that she was being transferred into personnel without having requested it. Finally, after three years of unhappiness and disappointment, I decided it was time to give Sears an ultimatum. After seven years in retail management in Nanaimo and three at the head office in Toronto—ten years in total—I finally put my interests forward in the bluntest way possible. I told them that I had received excellent performance reviews for ten years, that I had asked to be in personnel every year, and that I had taken the promotion and moved my family to Toronto for that end. I reminded them that I had graduated from Durham College in a program they had endorsed that would be beneficial in my quest. I told them if they did not transfer me into personnel, they should at least tell me honestly why they thought I was not suitable. Then I went home and put up my home for sale.

It was now late February, just past my thirty-third birthday, and we decided that we would sell our home and move back to BC at the end of school in June if I did not get a move into personnel. A week after my ultimatum, my manager sat me down and congratulated me on my promotion to the national training department. Although it was not exactly what I had been thinking about, I was relieved and happy.

This was great news for me, but not so much for my wife, who was desperate to move back to BC. We decided to keep our house on the market, and I would stay one year to get experience in the training department. It was an excellent choice. I was for the first time in ten years getting leadership training. My seven years in retail management had given me tremendous firsthand knowledge and experience but no formal training. I now took time management, leadership, and negotiation courses. I took over the orientation training for all new management moving into the head office. I taught time management and leadership courses. Everything was perfect. I was with a wonderful team and enjoying myself for the first time in three years in Toronto—that is, until I was tasked with putting together a training program for catalogue merchandisers.

I had so hated the job and disliked the people that the last thing I wanted was to be involved with catalogue merchandisers again. However, my boss explained to me that I was easily the best person to do this project. So, I ended up developing an entire course curriculum for merchandisers and facilitated the first classes. I eventually took great satisfaction in the course.

A "falling out of the sky" event impacted my life again. I arrived at work one Monday morning, and my boss Ellen was waiting for me as I walked through the door. She asked me to turn around, go home, and pack a bag, as she was sending me to Montreal for a training session the next morning. I found out that Stacey who was supposed to be heading to Montreal to conduct a two-day training session, was staying home to assist her brother. He had done his very first parachute jump the day before, and a gust of wind had kicked his feet out from under him as his feet were touching the ground, breaking his lower back. There are always stories of people dying from skydiving, but you rarely hear of the broken legs and backs.

I had never been to Montreal before and rushed home with excitement. By the time I had my bag packed and had arrived at Pearson International, Sears had completed the exchange of tickets from Stacey to me. This trip was typical of the myriad of business trips I would later make—interchanging one airport for another in a different city, arriving by taxi at one more hotel, doing a flurry of business over two or three days, and then heading home. On my first trip to Montreal, I saw nothing more than the insides of airports, taxis, hotels, and conference rooms. One of the things I disliked most about business travel was how solitary it was. I hated eating alone and would often order room service rather than sit by myself in a restaurant. Sometimes I would spot another business traveller on their own and ask them if they would like company over a meal. I met genuinely nice people over the years doing this. I knew I would have no chance to look around Montreal, so I asked the concierge about restaurants within walking distance that they might recommend. I left my room and ended up sharing the elevator ride to the lobby with a person also in town on business. He had been to Montreal before and knew his way around. He told me he was also heading out for dinner and asked if I would like to join him, which I gladly accepted. We ended up having a great dinner and a cold beer at a good Mexican restaurant. And that was the highlight of my first time in Montreal.

I was finally in a groove at work. My heart was in my job, and I was happy. However, things were not better at home. My wife still wanted to move back home to BC, and I had promised her we would move back after I had one year under my belt in the national training department. I never made a full year. On Halloween Day in 1990, Sears offered a severance package they called a VIP (Voluntary Incentive Plan) to every single employee of Sears in Eastern Canada—from top executives to warehouse employees to head office employees. It was a big push to reduce payroll in specific areas, disguised as a blanket staff reduction. In other words, they wanted to selectively eliminate staff in specific areas. Our offer letter stated that we had one month to accept or decline the offer, and then it would take effect as of December 31, 1990. Overall, thirteen of the thirty-nine national training department staff accepted the offer, including the national manager, my immediate boss Ellen, and myself. The company had not wanted to lose anyone in our department. Employees in other areas were sat down and told that they should seriously consider the offer; when they indicated their plan was to stay, they were asked again to consider the offer very seriously. In other words, they were expendable, and this would be their best option on the way out the door. I later found out from a former colleague, who had stayed at the head office, that one of the marketing managers in the menswear department that I had worked with had been squeezed out of his job, and as a consequence he subsequently took his life. Ross was a nice and kind man, and news of his death was a shock.

For our family, it was the way out we had been looking for. A severance package would provide funds to pay for the move back to BC and provide a continuing income for months. So, we jumped on the opportunity. At the same time, it was bittersweet for me, as I had finally found my niche after eleven years of effort, and now circumstances moved me on after only nine months.

The Long Way Home

Album Cut:
"Take the Long Way Home"
Supertramp
***Breakfast In America*, released 1979**

I HAVE ALWAYS LOOKED FOR the positive in every experience in my life, no matter how bleak. Partly because I am an eternal optimist, and partly because to do otherwise would acknowledge total failure. Life and work had been far more challenging than I could have imagined. As a result, I had grown stronger professionally in Toronto, while personally the family foundation had been unalterably shaken. After nearly four years living in Ontario, it was time to head home.

We shipped everything we had not sold or given away to BC for storage, and our bags were packed, and we were ready to depart. Unlike our arrival, there were no tears shed upon leaving Toronto in the rear-view mirror. The only disappointment was leaving Don, as I knew it would be a long time before I would come back to see him. In almost every way possible it was a relief to end our chapter in Toronto; the city had not been kind to us. However, accepting the severance package meant leaving a job and all of the associated benefits, like medical and dental and a pension plan. It meant uncertainty again for the family, with the two biggest questions: where to go and what to do next?

It was clear that we should land somewhere near family. With David now nine years old and Josh four, and with the prospect of choosing a new career, our choice was split between moving back to Vancouver Island or to Penticton. My family and my friends were on the Island, and her parents and family were in the Okanagan Valley. I had no idea of what I would do next for work, or where I might find that work. Vancouver Island had the challenge of requiring a ferry to come and go, which would be expensive, while the Okanagan was five hours distant to the larger Vancouver market. We decided to land in Penticton, BC and take our chances there. The ferry and the fact that my wife wanted to be closer to her parents were the main determining factors in our choice.

However, we decided to head straight to Vancouver Island first to visit my parents. Mom and Dad had come out to Toronto only once, I had not seen them in two years, and I knew that once we moved to Penticton it would be a long time before we were able to see them again. We put my wife and younger son Josh on a plane at Pearson International and they flew to Vancouver, arriving five hours later. On Boxing Day, December 26, 1990, David and I piled into our car and started our seven-day trek across the United States on our way to Vancouver. We had decided to go across the US rather than Canada on a recommendation and trip planning through the Ontario Automobile Association. They pointed out that if we had problems along the way, there were far more towns and places for help across the northern US than across the barren expanses of Canada. Armed with a Game Boy and snacks, we headed from Mississauga to Windsor and crossed the bridge into Detroit. We skirted around the edges of the large American cities, sliding past Detroit, turning around the bottom of Lake Michigan past Chicago, and glided into Wisconsin.

The morning we drove through Wisconsin was breathtaking. Pastoral farmland, with big red barns and farmhouses snugly blanketed with a new covering of snow. The sun shone brightly, the air was crisp, and we sailed through the state on well-ploughed roads. David saw little of the landscape; at nine years old, he was far more interested in playing with his new Game Boy. Our time passing through Wisconsin proved to be the most picturesque and peaceful. I knew leaving Ontario and driving across the continent in wintertime would have its risks. We hit our first challenge travelling through North Dakota. I always listen to local radio stations wherever I travel. I like to get a feel for the area and also track local weather and road conditions. The forecast for North Dakota sounded daunting with forecasts that the temperature would plummet throughout the day and evening.

Although my plan was to be on the road after breakfast each day, about 8:00 a.m., and stop about 4:00 p.m., I decided I would find a town to take refuge in earlier in the afternoon that day. I wanted to find a hardware store to buy a heavy-duty electrical cord to protect my motor from freezing. All cars sold in Ontario came with block heaters and most motels across the northern states had electrical plug-ins. That day we secured a room at a motel about three in the afternoon, with the temperature already at a bleak minus thirty degrees Fahrenheit. We quickly unloaded our gear and dropped it off in our room. With directions to a hardware store for the electrical cord, our noses also found us a burger joint. The burgers were poor but filled our tummies. Returning to our room an hour later, I quickly plugged the block heater into the car, and we found refuge in the motel room. That night the temperature was forecast to drop to a bone-chilling minus sixty degrees Fahrenheit; I have never been anywhere colder in my life since. I got little sleep, worrying about the car and what the roads would be like early in the morning. Upon loading our bags back in the car the next morning, I found I had left behind a gift; a bottle of white wine from a friend that had frozen solid in the back seat. I had no idea that alcohol could freeze until then.

We scurried through North Dakota and found ourselves crossing the expanse of Montana. The landscape seemed bleak, fairly flat with scrub, drifting snow, and blustery winds. It was so windy in Montana it was hard to stand outside and fuel my gas tank. I remember bringing David into the gas station so he could use the washroom and get himself a snack. After being on the road for days I tried to get him to choose something healthy; heck, this lonely outpost even had a basket of bananas on the counter. But after ten minutes of indecision, I let him choose a bag of chips and off we went. When our trip was finally over and I had time to thoroughly clean my car, I discovered a mountain of potato chip crumbs and debris on David's side of the car! Apart from listening to local radio stations, I also kept my eye out for historical sites and points of interest. We drove past a sign indicating the location of "Custer's Last Stand" approaching soon, and I reluctantly drove past without stopping. It was too cold and bleak, and nary a tour guide was in sight in any case.

So far, our journey had been a fun and unique experience with my son. Every night we phoned home, talking with David's mom, and giving the family a rundown of that day's adventures. But it was exhausting for me. I spent hours behind the wheel, sometimes with hands gripped tightly while navigating winter roads, and I was physically weary, and wanted to be reunited with my family. By the time we approached Idaho, the end of our journey was tantalizingly close. As we got close to Coeur d'Alene, Idaho, the weather changed on us again. Enormous snowflakes started hitting my windshield, and the road was quickly vanishing under a blanket of white. Even though it was early in the afternoon it was again time to stop and take refuge. Entering the town, I quickly spotted a motel, and by the time I had checked in and returned to the car to get our luggage there were already a couple of inches on the car; the snowflakes seemed as big as my hand. We barricaded ourselves and I was able to get a pizza delivered before the roads became totally impassable. Another sleepless night hoping the snowfall would stop and road maintenance crews would have cleared the roads before we headed out in the morning.

Unlike most mornings, we took the time for a large breakfast at a nearby café. Coffee and hot chocolate helped wash down pancakes, eggs, and bacon. Fortified, we bundled our belongings into the car and headed out on the highway. The snow had stopped early in the morning, and the snowploughs had done their job. The forecast looked promising, so we broke across the Washington State line, hoping to hit Seattle, about five hours away, without incident. Everything went well until we climbed high into the Cascade Mountain Range to reach the summit of the Snoqualmie Pass in Washington State at an elevation of 3,015 feet (919 metres). Just as we were reaching the peak, the snow started again. I kept my fingers crossed and kept going. As we started our descent, the road took a markedly downward slope, and the windshield wipers kept removing snowflakes with each swipe. Within minutes the snow turned to rain, and for a moment I was relieved, thinking the worst was behind us; but in a split second I realized freezing rain was hitting the windshield. Before I could think, chaos erupted all around me. Luckily, I did not panic and hit the brakes; without saying a word, not wanting to frighten David, I took my foot off the gas and prayed. In front of me a pickup truck had piled into the back end of tractor trailer unit; I saw the big rig operator jump from his cab and try to reach the pickup truck on the higher slope behind. The driver's door of the pickup was wide open, and I caught a quick look at the driver sitting behind the steering wheel. I gently manoeuvred around both vehicles; my only chance of survival now was to glide down the road without sliding off or colliding with anyone else. All around me I saw cars, trucks, and buses sliding sideways off the road. I glanced quickly in my rear-view mirror and saw a Jeep pull out to move around me and saw him vanish in an instant. Dozens of vehicles in a split second spun into disaster. We had an angel with us, finally coming to a silent rest at a level part of the road without a scratch. People were running about trying to assist each other, and there did not seem to be anyone in serious jeopardy, so after sitting with David for about a half an hour, I got out and walked down the road a bit. The freezing rain had stopped, and the temperature had risen just enough to remove the black ice. I saw other cars who had stopped safely in front of me start moving down the hill, and I decided to follow them. From that point on, driving lower and lower from the summit, the temperature continued to incrementally warm, and by the time we hit the bottom it was pouring rain. For as far as I could see ahead of me was a continuous line of big rigs stopped by their drivers to quickly put chains on their wheels before attempting the pass. It did not do them much good as the state troopers closed the pass behind us.

When we finally hit the border crossing back into Canada, a border guard questioned me first and then nine-year-old David. Fortunately, someone had advised us to have a letter from David's mom as to why we were travelling alone together. As child abductions by parents did happen, we were held by the border guard until he was satisfied that everything was okay. We finally were able to cross the border, took the BC Ferry from Tsawwassen to Victoria, and finally drove into Lake Cowichan at about 8:00 p.m., our adventure complete and our family reunited.

I was confident that my resumé would help me land a new job quickly; after all I had seven years of retail management experience in Nanaimo and close to four years' experience in a head office with one of the largest businesses in Canada under my belt. Once in Penticton, we moved into my in-laws' house, and I started sending resumes from their basement. Their home had always been welcoming, and my kids loved it. It was a tidy home, built by my father-in-law on property that his parents had given to them as a wedding present from their family. He built it as he could afford to, never having to take out a mortgage. We had a tiny bedroom on the main floor, and the boys shared a small room in the basement. My mother-in-law was one of the sweetest people you could ever meet, and she doted on her grandsons and us. My father-in-law was brusque and loud and always willing to give his opinion on any topic, but he had a decent heart.

I found out quickly two things: there were no jobs in Penticton matching my level of retail experience, and middle management jobs were scarce anywhere. Interviewing in dozens of places turned up few results. One application resulted in an interview for a management position with the BC Liquor Control Board in Vancouver, a five-hour drive away. Fate or bad luck found me with a terrible bout of flu the day of the interview, and I remember driving to Vancouver shivering and sick, stopping at a couple of gas stations along the way to get hot water to make NeoCitran cold medication. I arrived in time for the interview, but found a large part revolved around a written essay on my proposal for the board on how to move business forward. My head was not clear, I felt lousy, and I bombed the interview.

Back in Penticton, my family was content, glad to be back in BC. It was nice to be away from the bustle of Toronto and the demands of commuting and working long hours. However, I was still living in my father-in-law's house with limited privacy and freedom of movement. He was not a natural with kids by any means, and he would get cross when they were in the way. I truly needed to find another career and move the family back to a normal life in a new home. However, a career had to wait, as the priority became finding any employment, and what came up first was well below my pay grade but had the positive benefit of getting me in top physical shape.

A new business had started up in Penticton selling bottled water and installing water purifying systems. The owner hired me to deliver bottled water and set up new water coolers in homes and businesses in the local market. I would load dozens of five-gallon bottles into a van as well as water coolers, and then deliver them, carrying two bottles at a time weighing in total eighty-five pounds. Doing this eight hours a day for five days a week for six months, I got incredibly fit and strong—a real benefit after doing desk work for years. Even though it was not inspiring, and the money was not great, it was enough to consider purchasing our own home again. We decided to stay in Penticton rather than moving to a larger community with more opportunity. I got a bank to approve a mortgage based on a letter from my employer that I would be there for the long term. We found a perfect place to raise our kids and it was in our price range because it had been a rental and needed considerable updating.

My father-in-law and I tore out all the carpets, painted the entire interior, and updated all light fixtures. About three weeks later we happily moved into our new home. The very next morning I went in to work to begin my water deliveries and my boss fired me as I walked in the door. Apparently, he had hired someone else with mechanical abilities to not only deliver the water, but to also assist with the installation of purification systems. I can still see myself walking down the driveway to our new home, anxious about telling Kelley that I had no job.

In hindsight he had done me a favour. By signing the letter of reference for the bank, it had helped us get a home of our own. By firing me he had forced me to quickly shift from temporary job to a new career again. I was at a loss for a couple of weeks and then a light bulb turned on in my head. I thought of getting into the financial industry. I am not sure why, but I contacted my life insurance agent and spoke with him. After interviewing with two companies, I joined Imperial Life Insurance as a sales representative. The office had Walter, a crusty, sixty-five-year-old insurance veteran, and Carl, who was closer to my age and had been in the business for about fifteen years. Although the income was one hundred percent commission-sales-based, there was an office, a secretary, and computers at their office, and the location was more convenient for me being situated in Penticton, saving me an hour-long commute to Kelowna each day.

It was a hard way to make a living and a challenging career choice. Shortly after I started with them, Imperial Life changed their business model and took away the office, the secretary, and all support, and we now had to provide our own. This probably would have been a suitable time to walk away and get a job with a bank, but Carl persuaded me to stay. I spent the next five years working my tail off working at my craft and taking courses to improve my knowledge and skills. Although times were lean working on commission, it was not unlike any other entrepreneurial endeavour; the reality is that it takes time and effort to get any business off the ground. In the meantime, my wife had a job as a cashier at Safeway and fortunately made union wages plus benefits, so our family made out well enough between the two of us.

I immersed myself in the community, joining the local Kiwanis Club, my professional association, and Penticton Minor Baseball as a coach and later a director. It was rewarding on both personal and professional levels. From not knowing a single person when we arrived in Penticton, I was greatly expanding my network.

A couple of events over the next few years stood out, one being a near-miss with a tractor trailer unit in downtown Penticton. It was about 8:00 a.m., and I was on my way to a meeting. The sky was blue, the air was warm and fresh, and I was listening to the radio as I pulled up to a red light at an intersection. Seconds after I had come to a stop, a big rig pulled up in the lane to my right—a straight through lane. All I could see out of my passenger side windows was his enormous tires. In a couple of minutes, the light changed from red to green, and I took my foot off the brake pedal and was just starting to accelerate, when to my dismay I realized the big rig beside me in the straight through lane was turning left in front of me! I had to hit my brakes, and I laid on my horn for all of my might hoping he would stop. Instead, he kept turning, and the next thing I saw was his tires running over the front end of my Honda Civic. I could hear glass breaking and metal being crushed by the impact, and I released my seatbelt so I could escape out the driver's door if necessary. He made a complete turn in front of me, taking off the front end of my car, with my horn blaring, and he did not seem to notice a thing. When he finally completed his turn out of the intersection, he pulled off to the curb. People rushed over to assist me, and luckily the driver directly behind me offered to be a witness.

As it turned out, it became another life lesson in fear and cowardice. I could have been severely injured or possibly even killed. Police arrived on the scene and took my statement, and I watched the RCMP constable go over and talk with the truck driver and write something on his pad and hand it to the driver. It appeared that the driver had received a ticket for causing the accident. A tow truck came and hauled my car away, and I went to my meeting. Days later I was called by my insurance company and told that I would have to prove my claim. I found out that the truck driver had lied to the insurance company and told them that I had collided with him, not the reverse. It seemed he was so afraid about losing his job that he lied and tried to put the blame on to me instead. One of the first things I did was to contact the RCMP, as I had seen the officer pass a paper to the truck driver, and I wanted to confirm that he had in fact been charged with being at fault. Shockingly, I found that the RCMP constable had only given the trucker a warning at the scene. I explained to the officer that the trucker was lying to both the insurer and his boss, and that although I was the victim, he was forcing me to defend myself. I insisted that the officer charge him with causing the accident and rescind his warning notice. He agreed and coupled with witness statements from the scene, the insurer found him accountable for the accident. What people are willing to do to protect themselves has always amazed me.

Although I joined the Penticton Kiwanis Club to meet people in town and to network for business, I understood going in that I had to have a genuine interest in the organization and their goals, or it would be senseless. Over time, club members got to know and trust me, and business did come, even though there were a four other insurance and financial professionals already there. One day one of the older gents asked me to meet with him to go over his insurance. I said I would be happy to do that, but out of curiosity I asked him: "Why me?" He said he preferred not to share his personal and financial information with the other club members that he knew well.

The club primarily impacted the seniors' community in Penticton, building new residences for them. After a year as a member, I became a director and approached the club about diversifying and also doing something for youth in the city. I had wonderful memories of living in camp and the Christmas parties put on by the community. I suggested that we could create and put on a children's Christmas show in Penticton, free of charge so that families who had little means could have a fun experience for their kids and grandchildren. Kiwanis directors gave the event the green light to proceed, and I took the project on.

I determined that I wanted every child to come away with a Christmas stocking filled with goodies. I approached one of the supermarkets who generously provided candy canes and mandarin oranges, while a national retailer provided toys. I approached McDonalds as well, to get coupons, which sparked a terrific partnership. The local managers were excited and offered to not only provide coupons, but they would bring in Ronald McDonald to do a magic show. Our first year was appreciated by the community, but we only filled half of the auditorium. Word got around, though, and we also ramped up the newspaper and radio coverage, and consequently every year afterwards we would have lineups and filled the five-hundred-seat auditorium. Admittance was by donation, with proceeds going to Ronald McDonald House and the Kiwanis Club Children's Charities. We secured local entertainers: judo and gymnastic displays by local kids, musicians, and bands, but Ronald McDonald was always the star (with the exception of Santa, who would sit and individually talk with each child and give them their stocking). One year while waiting backstage with Ronald, I asked him where he came from, and without hesitation he said, "Apple Pie Lane." I organized the event and emceed the show for four years, and it was a truly rewarding experience. One of my prized possessions is a plastic plate with a picture of Ronald, Grimace, and the HamBurgler on the front, and on the back, an autograph saying, "Merry Christmas, Your Pal, Ronald McDonald."

Professionally I was not happy with how my career was progressing. After four years of effort, I was starting to break even financially; but there came a point when I realized that I was not doing what I was meant to do. I believed in the value of the work I was doing, but I also recognized that although I was a strong leader and had excellent business sense, I was not an entrepreneur. So, I shifted my efforts into finding a management role in the financial industry that would offer a good salary and benefits.

I was a member of a professional association for the financial planning sector in Canada and heard through contacts that they were creating a four-person marketing team, and I was happily hired as a marketing representative for the Pacific region (BC). I flew to their head office in Toronto and interviewed for the position. The vice-president for the project told me the project would have at least a three-year trial run. Based on this promise, I accepted the position, as did three other individuals in other regions across Canada. This would now provide me a decent salary and full benefits, so I relinquished my clients to my business partner and made the transition. It also allowed me to work from home and stay in Penticton, so it seemed to be absolutely perfect. I travelled all over BC interacting with insurance companies and financial firms with the goal of signing them up to our association. I met dozens of really good people and added to my range of contacts in the industry. What none of the four of us was aware of was things were rapidly changing at head office. The vice-president who had spearheaded this new project had been transferred by the company to another area of responsibility, and a new VP was appointed. She reviewed the program, decided it was not viable and decided to cancel it outright. I understood her decision because over the six months in the role I had come to a similar conclusion. So, six months after starting, the team was dismantled, and the program ended. Thank goodness the former vice-president had given me a verbal promise of a three-year tenure, because that leveraged a six-month severance package for me. That money gave me breathing room financially to keep the family going and to look for a new opportunity.

Through my contacts in the industry, I called the head office of Investors Group in Winnipeg, Manitoba and spoke with Debra who ran their national insurance manager operation. We had spoken previously, so she was familiar with my credentials, and she offered me an opportunity to be an insurance manager with Investors Group; however, positions were available in only Vancouver and Edmonton.

We had been enjoying a happy life in Penticton, apart from the difficulties of my employment. The boys were in school, David now in grade eleven and Josh finishing grade seven. They had made friends and saw their grandparents regularly. We had made good friends and I had been playing ice hockey for five years and loved every minute of it. None of us were really keen on moving, especially since the extreme challenges that came years earlier from our move to Toronto. In hindsight, the one thing we never explored was having me go back to university to allow me to get set on a new career. I realized that in the insurance and financial advice industry I had chosen five years earlier, the only meaningful opportunities would come in a larger centre. This time a mutual decision was made by both Kelley and me to move to Vancouver.

We took a more cautious approach, though. It was now spring of 1998, and I decided I would commute to Vancouver for a couple of months to make sure the job was a good fit before uprooting the family. I would leave Penticton about 4:30 a.m. on Monday morning and drive for four and half hours to Vancouver to start at 9:00 a.m. at the office; on Friday I would leave about 4:00 p.m. and be home in Penticton about 9:00 p.m. Exhausting but uneventful trips, except one morning outside of Keremeos, about ninety minutes from home a deer catapulted into the roadway in front of me from the driver's side. It was still pitch-black, but fortunately he had to cross the opposite lane first, and I reacted instinctively, slamming on the brakes and turning the steering wheel hard to avoid a collision. Instead of me hitting him head on, he slammed into the side of the truck near the rear wheel on my side.

As I came to a stop, I looked in my rear-view mirror and saw him lying on the roadway, and as I got out of the truck, he shakily got up on his feet and walked away into the darkness. I always hoped the poor deer that had struck my truck had survived the impact, but I would never know.

I enjoyed my job as an insurance manager, the pay was exceptionally good, and the people in the office were pretty decent. Based on my positive experience and after further discussion, we sold our home in Penticton and moved to Langley in the Lower Mainland, where I commuted forty-five minutes into Vancouver each day. The move was hardest on the kids this time. David decided to stay in Penticton to finish grade twelve and graduate and moved back into the basement of Grandma and Grandpa's house, while Josh moved to Langley with us. He started grade eight in a brand-new school, which was fortunately only about a five-minute walk from our new home. Josh was always an easygoing child but was also introverted, so making new friends and finding his feet took him about two years. We kept encouraging him to bring friends from school home, to little avail. By the time he graduated four years later, he had finally settled in and made lifetime friends.

When It All Came Together

<u>Album Cut</u>:
"The Road Home"
Travis Tritt
***Country Club*, released 1990**

WHEN I WAS TWELVE YEARS old and dreamt of being a radio announcer, I had this mental image of myself wearing a white shirt and necktie, sitting in front of a microphone, wearing headphones in a radio studio in a skyscraper in a city somewhere. To be honest I am not sure where this image came from, and the reality was starkly different. By the time I made it into radio in the mid-1970s, white shirts and ties had been traded for T-shirts, jeans, long hair, and facial hair. The city and the skyscraper had transformed into the basement of a Sandman Hotel in Princeton, BC.

But one evening I found myself working at my office in a skyscraper in downtown Vancouver. I was in my business attire, white shirt and tie included, and as I swivelled in my chair and looked out over the lights of the city it struck me that I was living the scene I had imagined for myself when I was young. The image though was not connected to my short-lived career in radio, but to my much longer career in business. It was a profound moment for me, and I was moved; transported back to my younger self in the logging camp so far away. There was comfort in realizing that I had brought my dream to life, even though it was not to be in broadcasting. The juxtaposition between logging camp and city life focused me back to choices my dad had made, and which I had followed, choosing location of work out of financial necessity versus preference of lifestyle. The satisfaction of my success in the moment never outweighed my desire to return to the small-town life that was truly the fabric of my soul.

I was in the skyscraper office because of another significant life moment and choice. I had been happily working with Investors Group in Vancouver for three years. They had been exceptionally kind to me and stood by me when I was devastated by the sudden and heartbreaking loss of my mother to cancer. Diagnosed with brain cancer and given about six months, she had succumbed within six weeks at age sixty-five. I remember going into my office days later, on a Monday morning and being greeted by one of my advisors who was joyful at the birth of a daughter over the weekend. The death of my mom and the birth of his daughter starkly highlighted to me the balance of the universe.

While I was content at Investors Group, I was also open to possibilities, and one of those came to me unexpectedly. A couple of years earlier I had met Leoni at a business meeting; she was a rep for Metropolitan Life at the time. She was lovely, smart, and had wonderful energy. Over the years we became good friends as well as colleagues. I received a phone call one day and the party on the other end of the line introduced themselves as having met Leonie at a conference, who had in turn recommended me highly to them. I was asked whether I would be interested in a meeting to discuss a new career opportunity. I believe in the power of listening and learning, and accepted their invitation, soon after meeting with Mark, a VP with MemberCare Financial Services a brief time later.

His offer was intriguing, MemberCare Financial had operations across Canada except for BC, and they were looking at buying a province-wide network to get up and running quickly, and they needed someone to run the new operation. MemberCare was aligned with CUMIS Life and supplied insurance coverage through the credit union system across Canada. The BC acquisition would instantly create a network of eighteen credit unions throughout BC. As the new regional manager, I would get autonomy to run the BC operation, there would be an increase of $10,000 per year in salary, and I would have an assistant and use of a company car, an offer worthy of thoughtful consideration.

As I was happy with Investors' Group, I certainly wanted to be diligent in reviewing and investigating the opportunity before any decision to leave them. I spent three weeks talking to a variety of people associated with both CUMIS and with MemberCare, including making a trip to Calgary to speak with an individual working within one of their top credit unions. Everything was favourable, and I accepted their offer to start October 1. It was quite exciting, to say the least. I was keen to accept the challenge and eager to get started. Mark was based in their Calgary office and planned to be in Vancouver for my first day to supply an overview of the operation and supply a list of key contacts. When we sat down in my new office (a spacious corner office looking over the cruise ship terminal, and with a spectacular view of the North Shore mountains), I leaned forward and asked Mark, "So, how many credit unions are under contract . . . all eighteen?" To which Mark replied: "We have one credit union under contract." When I questioned him about the rest of the network he had hired me to run, Mark said not to worry, that deal had fallen through, but we could build our own network.

In a flash I saw the full-time assistant disappear, and the bonus vanish before my eyes. To say I was shocked would have been quite the understatement. He explained that the deal to buy the network had not materialized and the network had simply come undone. It meant moving quickly to re-engage with all of them before competitors swooped in to sign them to individual deals. As fortune had it, this seeming calamity ended well for me professionally overall. I knew that I could run a business operation; the challenge now was to build one from the ground up. Although I was not an entrepreneur at heart, I knew from my experience with Sears and Investors Group how to approach building the enterprise.

When I say the office was bare, it was not an understatement. There was furniture, but no pens, paper, files, or plants. I can take pride in saying that I started the operation from the ground up. I instantly started a relationship with the only credit union that had been persuaded to stay with us and through considerable effort and dedication over the next year I signed six more credit unions spread across the province in: Salmon Arm, Summerland, Penticton, Gibson's, and Vancouver. Credit unions were "member" (customer) focused and took pride in having relationships rather than a business-first approach. I really liked the people and working at this time was the happiest experience I enjoyed during my twenty-five-year career in the financial industry. It was especially fun to work with Ron at his credit union in the Fraser Valley. He was the wealth manager for a network of credit unions in Abbotsford and Chilliwack, with a team of nine advisors.

One late summer afternoon over a beer we discussed a new insurance sales campaign for his team. It was decided it would be based on a hockey theme. Three months would equate to three periods and points would be awarded individually. To kick this off, Ron invited me to present the plan to the team and invited insurance company and mutual fund reps to round out the training while they were all together for the day. Combined with assistants and support staff, there were about twenty-four people in the room. To surprise Ron, I decided not to fill him in on my presentation plans, and because we had worked together for months, he trusted me with his team. I should have considered more carefully about the beer.

Being universally mocked for being a Toronto Maple Leafs fan, I decided to walk into the room carrying my hockey bag emblazoned with the Maple Leafs emblem. I dropped it on the floor, opened it up, and, while talking, started putting on my elbow pads, Leafs jersey, and baseball hat—all to a chorus of boos and catcalls. I then pulled out twenty-four white towels and passed them around the room so they could wave them like Roger Nielson's' classic protest. Then I pulled out a can of Molson's Canadian beer, opened it up and took a swig. Ron's eyes almost popped out. I explained that beer and hockey always went together; and then passed one can of beer to everyone in the room, with the intention that they would be taken home as souvenirs and to be enjoyed later. Having been there all morning, I decided to leave after my presentation while the group listened to presentations from the insurance and mutual fund reps.

There were three things I did not consider when I passed out the beer: not everyone liked beer, one or two people liked beer too much, and beer ended up being consumed at the meeting. Ron chided me days later. One of his guys had an alcohol problem which I was unaware of, and he drank his can of beer right away and then polished off two other cans from people who did not like beer. He got buzzed. Ron calmly suggested that I not bring alcohol into a meeting again. On the plus side, my presentation became legendary, and the sales campaign was a success.

Nothing lasts forever, and when three years later MemberCare was bought by another firm based in Vancouver, my perfect job started dissolving before my eyes. I took pride in the network I built and valued the relationships I had developed, and I hoped that the new company would keep me in place and promote me to the new Vice President position; I certainly would be the obvious choice. But that is not how things work in the corporate world. Century put their own people in place, firing employees from the MemberCare family across Canada, and appointed Bob as VP in Vancouver relegating me to his subordinate. At the same time, they fired my counterpart in Alberta, and I was told I would be regional manager for BC and Alberta. This was taxing on me and my family. For the next year and a half, I flew into Edmonton or Calgary once a month and rented a car to drive from credit union to credit union over a three-day period and then flew home. In the meantime, Bob took over all the relationships I had built and made all the decisions. It was an extremely hard pill to swallow, and I did not take it well. It would have been the logical time to leave and find another opportunity; however, a combination of loyalty to my credit union partners, pride, and stubbornness kept me there. Initially they also wanted to keep me because of my relationships and insurance expertise as Bob was purely an investment guy. Soon after, a Senior VP from the insurance industry was hired to oversee Canadian operations, and Bob fell under his jurisdiction. I was no longer indispensable to Bob, and he began telling me how to do my job.

Arrogantly, the new senior VP decided our plan should be to go in and tell the credit unions that they did not know what they were doing. Instead, I should go in and "show them how to do it" by pressuring their members for insurance sales. I told Bob that this would not fly. The credit unions prided themselves on caring about their members and would not appreciate that approach; I made the decision to keep doing my job the way I had been for the past couple of years. Bad choice, Larry.

At the end of the second year under Century, all the regional managers were brought into a meeting in Vancouver to go over national results. A PowerPoint presentation highlighted my success; I was the only region in Canada to beat my goals; in other words, I had the best results in the country and normally would have been congratulated. But because I had rebuffed their approach and had done it my way, not a word was said, and no thanks or congratulations were offered; it was extremely uncomfortable. Unsurprisingly, two weeks after the national meeting, Century ended my contract.

I should have known better. It was a tough life lesson. No matter how "right" you are, when given direction by your organization there are only two practical alternatives. If you cannot reconcile your differences, you should leave. The alternative is to embrace the new reality; there really is no middle ground. Foolishly I had thought that by my proving that my way would work best, the company would adopt my methods. Instead, my life was unhappy, and I had been stressed to the max ever since the takeover. In the end, it was not worth me hanging on. It is said that learning life lessons the hard way is best, but it is always more painful.

So, Larry is back on the street with another severance package to bridge the gap. After hustling for a new position and interviewing around Vancouver for months, it became discouraging. It was difficult to be walking down the streets of Vancouver seeing people in business attire bustling around the office buildings, laughing, and drinking their Starbucks. I felt lost and out of place. I decided to use my "off time" productively and decided to take the Provincial Instructor Diploma Program (PIDP)—a six-course, university-level program that supplied one-quarter of the points toward a Bachelor of Education degree. It was also used by tradesmen and people with industry experience to allow them to teach at places like BCIT. In my classes were bakers, carpenters, plumbers, and artists. I fast-tracked myself by taking courses wherever they popped up next: Victoria, New Westminster, Burnaby, and Vancouver. I found myself taking two of the courses at BCIT, where I had sat in broadcasting courses thirty years earlier.

A perfect position finally popped up on my radar as a training manager with Enlighten Financial. It was now 2006, it had been thirteen years since I had started in the financial industry in Penticton, and I was now forty-nine years old. Based on my resumé, the job was perfect on paper. The operations manager, Ray, was smooth and personable, and Cathy, who came out from their head office in London, Ontario, was smart and nice. When the position was offered to me, I took it. It had been six months since leaving Century, my severance money was getting low, and I was discouraged. The only flaw was the money was substantially less that what I had made with MemberCare and Century. In fact, my last year with Century had been the most lucrative. I had maxed out my bonus and earned well into a six-figure income that final year. Enlighten Financial started me at a rate lower than I had started with years earlier with Investors Group, with no bonus potential. It felt good to be working again, but my spouse was very unhappy with the drop in income.

My experience with Enlighten Financial was mixed. The national leadership under the training department were top-notch and welcoming, as were my counterparts around the country. I enjoyed collaborating with new advisors and was happy to share my experience. But over the next two years, I had glimpses of how Ray really operated. At the beginning he was your best friend, but over time I started to hear him badmouth advisors and members of the management team when their shine started to wear off. With him you either had to be a top performer or you were nothing, and he would start a campaign to have you leave. I was in his good books while I was a training manager, and he made a grand announcement in the office, praising me when I graduated from the PIDP program.

Sales Managers had two primary goals: generate sales from investments and insurance through their teams and recruit new people as advisors. There were substantial bonuses for them and for Ray for new recruits. One of the biggest flaws in the whole industry in my mind was (and is) the 100 percent commission income platform, which has been the model for over one hundred years. Considerable commitment is needed to earn insurance and investment licences, and to keep fiduciary relationships with clients. I saw very smart people, good people, who were hired, struggled financially, and left within the first two years. The industry saw very few people survive over a five-year period. I always felt a decent base salary, plus a bonus incentive, would have been a much better model.

I knew how difficult it was to recruit people into the industry. Heck, I remember my own reservations about the stigma of being dubbed an "insurance salesman." Over the years I had been offered several job opportunities to be a sales manager with different firms but had turned them all away because I did not want to recruit. But pressure from home about my current salary caused me to apply for one of the sales managers positions with Ray. Their salary was higher, and they had bonus opportunities, with the potential for me to earn closer to my former Century income. I made the terrible mistake of accepting a sales manager position, and the nightmare started.

I was given a team of six advisors based in Coquitlam. I was fortunate that three of them were experienced, high producing advisors; good guys all. The three of them alone would make the sales goals for my team. They valued my experience, and we worked very well together. Given a full team of experienced advisors, would have been a better fit and I would have excelled. Two of the other advisors were good people, but both were struggling; one was a young person in his twenties. He just simply did not have what it took to be successful. The other was a young mother who was bright and energetic but was struggling to earn enough money to survive. As she was willing and a good study, we were able to work very closely, and she went onto a successful path. The sixth member of the team was an absolute disaster.

When I first started with the team, I arranged one-on-one meetings to introduce myself and to learn more about who they were, what their strengths and weaknesses were, and to try to work out a plan with them. When Jared came into see me, he was a mess. He wore a tracksuit, he desperately needed a haircut and a shave, and was unprofessional in his appearance and manner. This was disrespectful, and I was shocked that anyone would come in to meet with their new boss in this condition. I introduced myself and asked him what he was thinking, coming in to meet me in so unprofessional a manner. I told him to go home and to come back the next day prepared to have a proper discussion. I told him he was improperly dressed and that he should shave and get a haircut. I needed to come down hard to establish my position with him, but also out of respect for the rest of the team.

The following day he showed up in a suit, sporting a new haircut and clean shaven. Now was an opportunity to have a meaningful dialogue about his business; his records showed he had been struggling mightily. He was not receptive, brushing aside all concerns because he had this "big deal in the works" and it would solve all his problems. I knew this was a recipe for failure; big deals rarely came in without a tremendous amount of work and he did not appear to have that ethic. Trying to score a big deal rather than having one materialize through the normal routine of financial planning was counter to Enlighten's training. Advisors were mandated as part of their contract to earn their Certified Financial Advisor designation, one of the core tenets being they would help their clients holistically. I did not want an advisor who was only looking to score "big deals." This meant that I had work to do with him to change his course; the challenge being that he would have to be willing.

After weeks of effort, I believed it to be futile. He never changed his approach, missed team meetings, and was always smug. I came to believe that he felt he was untouchable, which was partly true in that Enlighten Financial hated relinquishing an advisor, because it was so difficult to replace them. It meant that poor performing, mediocre advisors, were kept simply to have a head count on the books. Sales managers would be accountable for the advisor's inferior performance, and their abilities came under question.

Months later, with no improvement in results, coupled with a lousy attendance and a lousy attitude, he left me no choice. I requested a formal performance review to shake him up or weed him out. I felt a sense of déjà vu from years earlier at Sears in Toronto with Barb. When he did not put in any effort, and his results stayed stagnant, I made the decision to end his employment. I brought him into my office on a Friday afternoon and told him his employment had ended. I at once confirmed this with my boss, and within minutes Ray was on the phone instructing me to have Jared and myself come into Vancouver to his office for a meeting.

At the meeting Ray did lambaste him for his lack of performance. He told him that I had the right to end his contract. He asked him to go away for the weekend and consider if he really wanted to work here and that it may not even be possible as it would be my decision. After he left Ray turned to me and asked me to give it careful consideration over the weekend, but that the decision would be mine. We shook hands and I left his office. Over the weekend I played everything over and over in my mind, giving it significant thought, but at the end of the day I knew the right thing to do was to end his contract. As promised, first thing on Monday morning I called Ray and told him my decision. He went crazy on me.

Ray ranted for five minutes about what a lousy decision I had made, that it was "one of the stupidest decisions any manager could make," and what a poor manager I was. When he finally paused for a breath, I reminded him that he had given me the authority to make the decision and in fact he had pointedly expressed this in front of the advisor. He ranted again that I should have "known what he really wanted" and that I "should have been smarter than that." He then told me that even though I had terminated the advisor, he was going to find another sales manager to transfer him to. While I was happy that Jared was no longer my problem, I was now out of favour with Ray.

I tried to continue with my work, but it became increasingly difficult. Pressure from Ray was intense. In the meantime, I was under the gun with my immediate boss to consider hiring someone who had been referred to him. The person was near retirement age and had been working for another insurance firm. I called him to have a conversation and to invite him in for an interview and it struck me that he sounded hesitant, but he finally agreed to come in for an interview. On the appointed day and time, he did not show up. I waited for about fifteen minutes past the agreed-upon time and phoned him. When he answered the phone, I questioned whether he had understood we were to meet that day, to which he replied, "Yes," but did not offer any plausible explanation. Although normally I would have dropped him as a candidate on the spot, I set up another interview date because of the referral from my boss. He arrived in a suit and tie and looked very presentable. The very first thing I asked him was why he missed our first appointment; I suggested it appeared he had simply "blown it off." He acknowledged that to be true. Not a good sign.

He seemed lacklustre during our interview and did not seem to be eager for the opportunity. After he left, I went in to let my boss know that I was not going to proceed further with him. However, my boss insisted that I continue with the process because I needed a new hire. I expressed concerns that if I hired him, I would be having to work through a termination process with him soon after. No matter: my boss made it perfectly clear that I was to hire him anyway.

True to my instincts he did not work out. I spent months trying to help him, but he resisted our training and processes and never produced any sales. So, on top of my other troubles with Ray I was now going through the process of another employee termination situation. Ray continued putting pressure on me, and then one day asked me to have breakfast with him. I was apprehensive but could not refuse. We met early one morning a couple of days later. He gave me two options: "revert back to a sales role" or leave the company. He insisted it would be better for me to go into sales. I told him that I was never in a sales role with Enlighten Financial, and in fact had not been an advisor for years, so "reverting to a sales role" had no meaning. Despite that, he gave me a week to decide which direction I wanted to go. It was the last straw. I had been seeing my family doctor for weeks about stress and I went to him and told him I could no longer work under the pressure I was being put under. He made the decision that it would be detrimental to my health to continue working in that environment, and I went on disability leave for the next six months. Being absent from Ray and his pressure, and with treatment and care from my doctor, I became healthy again, and was medically able to return to work in February 2010, shortly after my fifty-third birthday. I told my boss I would be returning, and he asked me to come in and meet him at 8:30 in the morning on Monday. When I arrived, he instructed that I wait in the lobby, and when he brought me into his office, I was handed a severance package in an envelope, and in a brief five minutes, we had parted ways. It was a relief to be gone as I had not wanted to face Ray's abuse again. My mistake had been in not listening to my gut; I should never have taken the sales manager's role. I had only done it because of pressure from home to earn more money. What I should have done was to continue as a training manager and start looking for other roles outside of Enlighten Financial that paid better.

I had now worked for seventeen years in the financial services industry. I had met wonderful people, had unique experiences I never would have had in any other industry, had made a higher income than the average Canadian, but had also been beat up enough to know I was done. I wanted a different career for the rest of my working life. Finally, the best thing that could have happened did in the summer of 2010.

From a Different Place

<u>Album Cut</u>:
"Rocky Mountain High"
John Denver
***Rocky Mountain High*, released 1972**

THANK GOODNESS FOR SEVERANCE PACKAGES. They supply the financial freedom to pause, regroup, and move down another path. This time I needed my heart and soul to be in tune with my career. It was like me looking across the valley of my life, my career like a lazy river meandering across the plain below me, flowing where there seemed to be the least resistance.

I half-heartedly went on interviews in the financial sector, but the whole effort was wasted. This time I needed a seismic shift, and so it came to me to look toward the not-for-profit sector. In the same heartbeat that I made this decision, I read a job posting with the Canadian Cancer Society in Vancouver. It sounded like it was perfect, and the job posting ended two days later, on a Monday.

I emailed a heartfelt letter and my resumé. In my letter I told them that it was ten years since I had lost my mom to brain cancer, and I would love the opportunity to help them fight this terrible disease. I said my mom would be proud of me as well. On Monday

I was asked to come in for an interview; I was relieved and incredibly pleased.

Through my lifetime of working, I had been extremely fortunate to have many good leaders. In my early years, my dad, Dave the shop foreman in Nitinat, and Gabe my boss at Western Mines. At Sears, Farley, Snowman, and Grounder, and in the financial industry Dave and Linda. I was about to meet one of the best, Betty.

My first meeting with Betty was at a coffee shop a couple of blocks away from the Canadian Cancer Society office. Over an hour, not one word was spoken about the Society, the job, or my resumé. We spent the hour simply talking about life. Her approach was refreshing. She felt the most important thing was to figure out what kind of person I was, and to decide whether I could fit well into her team. My letter had caught her attention, my resumé had intrigued her, but who I was as a person was what was most important to her.

A couple of days later I was invited in for an interview and some pre-work—three different scenarios to prepare a presentation about. Three potential donors with different circumstances, ages, and financial means. I had never worked for a charity, had no experience in their industry, but I did understand people and how to build plans with them. I knew there would be six people conducting the interview, so I came ready with six professionally bound proposals, printed in colour, and walked them through each scenario. I fielded questions, and then Toni walked me to the elevator and rode down with me to the lobby. She told me that I had blown everyone away, and that I would hear from her soon. I knew then that my life had changed for the better.

Later she admitted they had been prepared to make an offer to another candidate until they had received my letter. Kismet, karma, the universe listening when I finally opened up to it; whatever the explanation, it was clear to me that the entirety of my work and my life experiences had landed me finally in the right place.

The whole vibe was different. Fundraising for a large, charitable organization is still business, but it is unlike anything else. I was meeting with people who had charitable hearts, had contributed through their lives, and were receptive. It was simply a matter of helping them decide what was important to them and help them do something meaningful. There was no pressure, and there was a different pace and rhythm much different from the corporate world I had escaped from.

I had joined their planned giving team. We were tasked with securing donations through estates and wills, and because of my background and experience, gifts of life insurance as well. I found that my experience and knowledge in financial planning (including estate planning) was a perfect fit and was unique in the charitable environment; so, I made a name for myself quickly around Vancouver. What I also brought forward was an extensive network of financial, legal, and accounting professionals throughout Vancouver. This enhanced the planned giving team at the society. Typically, planned giving teams for all charitable organizations focused on gifts left through wills. So, staff at all the charities were focused on trying to secure only these types of gifts. A large problem was that people could change their wills at any time and the charity would never know that their gift was lost. I proposed that gifts of life insurance would be guaranteed for the charity, supplying more stability for the future. Betty embraced this approach, and the Society became the happy recipient of millions of dollars in insurance gifts. Having lost my mom years earlier to cancer, while working at the society I also lost my dad. Although he had suffered with chronic heart disease for years, at the end, lung cancer took him first. During my time at the Canadian Cancer Society, I always thought of my parents and hoped they were proud of what I was now doing.

Betty did not always get the best of my efforts. I never wavered from my commitment and never gave anything less than what was possible, but tragedy and illness struck me during my five years there. My marriage had been shaky since I had returned from Toronto; the damage done from the move was never overcome. Twenty years after returning, in the winter of 2011 it finally collapsed, and then two weeks later my dad died. It was a double body blow, and I was reeling. I did not want anyone to know about my marriage failure, and as people knew my father had died, they assumed I was absorbed in my grief at his loss. With Dad's loss, I never had the opportunity to grieve fully. As his executor I had to instantly step in to manage his estate, and I was desperately trying to keep my head above water while living in the basement of my home.

Two months later I had to share my situation with Betty. I owed it to her because she had been kind and patient with me, even though I was not on top of my work. I told her everything about my marriage collapse, and she listened quietly and then told me not to worry. She had worked for years before the society with a major trust company, and so she offered her help and guidance in working through probating my dad's estate. I could not have made it through this period without her support.

It was also time to tell my family. Losing Dad, I did not want to burden them with my personal trauma as well, but I could not put it off any longer. I called Don in Ontario, and he arranged to be away from his business and flew out from Toronto to help me move into my own condominium. Thank God for him. I went over to Vancouver Island to see my best friend Barry, and we had drinks, cooked beef curry, and then after about two hours I finally told him as well. Barry had stood with me and my two brothers at my wedding thirty-three years earlier. Although I rarely drank, we both went ahead and got drunk and then ate his delicious homemade beef curry at midnight.

My right hip had also been bothering me for a year and was getting progressively worse. My doctor had told me that I had minor osteoarthritis and would eventually need surgery, and I could tell I needed to see him again. I had been suffering terrible pain and had been limping noticeably for ages. He prescribed pain medication, made a referral to see a surgeon, and gave me an ultimatum. I had put on a huge amount of weight and had kept buying bigger and bigger suits and clothes. I was depressed and was at a loss. He had been recommending that I get exercise for a long time, and I had been telling him I was in too much pain. He suggested going to a pool, and I had dismissed the idea because I was too embarrassed to go to a public pool. He had been my doctor for about twelve years since stitching my chin from a softball injury. He looked me straight in the eyes in his office and said, "I hate to use this term, but I need to tell you that I have to consider you clinically obese." He went on to say that I had a choice: I could be a victim, or I could improve my life; it was my choice. I left his office shaken and sat in my truck outside his office and reflected on his words. He had finally got through to me after all these years. I decided it was time to change my life. I bought a food scale and started following the Canada Food Guide, checking my portion sizes, and balancing the types of food that were better for me. I also joined a small, private fitness centre minutes away from where I lived. In the evenings after work, I had their pool completely to myself and with a pool noodle "water jogged" for months, starting with only fifteen minutes and working up to forty-five-minute sessions. I found that once my hip had warmed up after about the first five minutes, it was the only time I experienced no pain. Over the next few months, I lost thirty pounds. I felt better physically and emotionally and looked much better. I had tried almost every diet you could think of throughout my life but had always put weight back on. This time I did not diet; I simply changed my lifestyle, and by continuing I have kept this weight off now for over a decade.

After my doctor's referral I waited three months to see the surgeon, who then told me I would have six months to wait for a surgery date. By now my pain was unbearable. Reluctantly I had started using a cane, but walking was torture. My doctor knew I did not have an addictive personality and took a chance on Oxycontin and an anti-inflammatory drug, and I was also taking Tylenol Arthritis for the pain. I had trouble sleeping and found myself dozing off at my desk and worse, while driving home in rush-hour traffic. I finally left work on a disability claim and had my surgery about one month later.

In the summer of 2012, about one and half years after my dad had died, I met the most wonderful woman. Louise accepted me for who I was, and joked that when she met me, she thought I had a "wooden leg" because I limped so badly. She took care of me through this most difficult period and was by my side through my surgery and recovery. We married a year and a half later in late July of 2015, when I was fifty-eight. In August, five years after starting with them, the Canadian Cancer Society abruptly shut down their planned giving department, and Betty and I found ourselves on the outside looking in. I received my last severance package, my full-time working career ended, and I happily picked up a guitar.

Thicker than Water

<u>Album Cut</u>:
"Highway Patrol Man"
Johnny Cash
***Johnny 99*, released 1983**

I HAVE ALWAYS HAD A keen sense of family; I know this not to be true for everyone, but for me it is essential. That is why family slights and disagreements linger with me and hurt my soul.

After Dad had two heart attacks, followed by heart surgery, my siblings and I gathered around my dad in his bed in the hospital. We were joking and kibitzing partly because we were anxious, and also because Dad always joked to deflect from conversations he did not want to have. A nurse walked into his room to check on him and listened to the family banter and heard Dad say something offhand about what he planned to do when he got home. She looked at him and said, "Paul, look around at your family. You had a second chance; not everyone gets a second chance. When you go home you take care of yourself, and no fooling around." She told us that it was nice to see a family who got along so well together; she did not see that every day.

For the most part she was right; growing up we got along comparatively well. I had a great-aunt Daisy, and her family was renowned for fist fights at weddings or most any family gathering. Crazy stories about one of the boys putting his hand on a wood block and daring his brother to cut his finger off, which he then did with a hatchet, or one of the other boys as an adult joining a motorcycle gang and pointing a shotgun at a man in a pickup to take him to a store to buy peanut butter. We were never like that. However, I cannot say that we are now close as adults, and I cannot pinpoint why exactly. Perhaps it is in part because we made life decisions that scattered us around the country. I seldom see my siblings, and when I do now, I seem to come away unsettled, my expectations never quite met, and with a lingering sense of being out of step with them. I feel a vague distance, handshakes vs. hugs. Rather than a "Glad to see you, Lar," there is more a sense of, "What took you so long?"

I cannot speak to anyone else's memories but my own, but while I have a general sense of a happy childhood with softball games, summer picnics with Mom's potato salad in a large Tupperware bowl, and living in camp, I have few specific memories about my siblings. Peter was the younger brother and naturally a pest; I am sure to get the attention of his older brothers. He had blond hair and blue eyes and always could tell a delightful story even as a small boy, so people always loved him. I remember much more about him later in life, through his marriage, workplace traumas, and cancer. Peter is a man who would jump in to help without a moment's hesitation and has been a wonderful uncle for my sons. He came to Vancouver and stayed for a week after my first hip replacement surgery to help Louise with my care. He is a great brother.

Eve is less than a year younger than Don and me, and from our childhood I remember an incident when she was three years old. Dad bundled her up in a blanket and put in the back seat of the family car to get stitches from splitting her forehead open. Mom always knitted new slippers for us, and when she would wax the hardwood floors, they would not only gleam, but would be as slippery as ice in our woollen slippers. We would run about six steps and then see how far we could slide. Eve slid headfirst into a doorknob, and that ended our sliding (for a while, anyway). Mom had to stay at home with her three boys, and so it was Dad and Eve off to the hospital on their own.

I was eight when Rose was born, so I remember my first look at her. Dad, Don, Eve, Peter, and me stood outside in the parking lot of the Duncan Regional Hospital, and Mom held Rose up in her arms in a third-floor window so we could see her. When she came home, we helped Mom by changing diapers and feeding Rose. When she was old enough to sit up, we would put her in a laundry basket in our wagon and pull her around the yard. I remember taking her to Youbou in my pickup truck so she could stay with a friend overnight when she was ten and I was eighteen. I reflect now that she was only a girl, ten years old, when I left home to attend BCIT, never to return. I never knew her as a teenager or a young woman. Perhaps she felt I had abandoned her all those years ago. For years now she has chosen to estrange herself from me; I have no answers as to why, and it upsets me to such a degree that I have learned to close that box in my mind whenever it starts to open. Occasionally, I hear how she is doing through my other siblings. I would welcome her if she came to my door. Perhaps one day.

Don and I have been close, as you would imagine identical twins would be, so it is natural that I have countless stories and memories about the two of us. From grade one onward, our elementary school teachers had trouble telling us apart. Our voices are identical, we have similar mannerisms, and even I cannot tell us apart in photographs from when we were very young. I found photos Mom had taken when we were babies, and she had simply written "Twin" on them. We were born weeks premature in February 1957, at close to four pounds each. We stayed in the hospital until we were at a healthier weight, with Don designated to go home first as I was anemic. However, even the nurses in the hospital in Campbell River mixed us up, and I had been sent home in error.

We went through school together from grades one to twelve. I strongly encourage anyone with twins to allow this continuity. Your twin is your ally with you every day, and it is like having your best friend with you continually. In the younger grades we occasionally swapped seats to confuse our teachers. Once people got to know us, though, our mannerisms gave us away. One day in grade twelve I strayed a minute or two behind Don at my locker, and when I got to our homeroom, I found my girlfriend Catherine sitting on Don's lap at his desk! This discovery startled me so much that I exclaimed loudly, "Catherine!" She looked at me and then turned her head to look into Don's face, and he gave her an apologetic grin. She instantly jumped off his lap; it was hard not to tease her for a while afterwards.

My earliest memory of Don was when we lived in Mahatta River. We were about four at the time, and I had wanted to hang by my hands from two rings suspended on chains from a bar that the older kids would swing from. I was much too short to reach them, so an older boy lifted me up so I could hang from them. It was only seconds before I had to let go, but the older boy had bent over to tie his shoelaces, and I yelled that I was going to fall. Don stepped below me to catch me, and when I dropped, I landed on top of him in the dirt, breaking my eyeglasses. It has always impressed me that he stepped up to help me without any hesitation, at his peril. He would step up for me in another moment of crisis, decades later when my first marriage failed.

I started at BCIT in September 1975, and Don came over to start a term at Simon Fraser University in January 1976. For my first term I had lived in a basement suite with a couple of other guys. The deal was to have a room and breakfast and dinner included. However, conditions were so terrible that we all bailed at Christmas, so when Don came over to start at Simon Fraser, we decided to share a place. I was thrilled to reunite with him. It would be the first time in our lives we would have a space for just the two of us.

Rental units were at a premium at that time. We paid a rental accommodation listing service thirty dollars for a monthly list to assist us in finding a place that would work within our budget. As we called phone numbers on the list, we found room after room already gone. We finally struck gold, finding the perfect basement suite. However, when we called, they said the space was for only a single person. I explained that we were twins (and like a single person) and that we were clean and quiet, so after gentle persuasion they agreed to have us come over to take a look. It was a family home on Venables Street in Burnaby, about a thirty-minute walk to BCIT and close to a bus route to Simon Fraser. It was really nice, a tiny kitchen with a small living room and one bedroom. The family brought us upstairs where we sat at the kitchen table with the entire family and talked about ourselves. Over a glass of their homemade wine, we satisfied their concerns and they agreed to rent us the place. It turned out so well, that the mom would occasionally bring down a bottle of their wine for us, and each week she brought us a homemade loaf of bread, pizza, or cake. We could not have found a better place.

One day Don decided that he would prefer to have a car to get around the city easier. I offered to go car shopping with him and suggested we could find time to look at cars one day that week. I came home late one afternoon after classes and found Don sitting forlornly at the kitchen table. He asked if I had seen the green Chevy Vega outside when I had come home. I said yes but had not looked at it closely. He told me he had bought it and he thought he had made a mistake, and he could also not get it into reverse gear. The car salesperson had used high pressure tactics to get him to purchase the vehicle, so I suggested that he could still return it to the lot and then we could go out and look for a car together as we had planned. Don said no, he had made the decision, so he had to stick with it (it would be years later that my father-in-law told me, "You've made your bed; now you have to lie in it"). This male ethos of responsibility, the epitome of the British "stiff upper lip," was engrained in generations of men like my brother and me by every male authority figure that intersected with us.

We went outside to look more carefully at the car. It was clean and looked good both inside and out and it had a standard transmission with a stickshift on the floor. I got in and started the motor; everything sounded good, so I looked at the diagram on the shifter and attempted to shift into reverse and was unsuccessful on my first attempt. I studied the shifter and noticed a chrome ring around the shifter directly below the knob; I used my fingers and lifted the ring upward and then easily shifted into reverse, took my foot off the brake, and stepped on the gas. The car quietly moved backward. Don would have figured the shifter out on his own if he had not been so upset about getting pressured into buying the car. He stuck with his Vega for years, putting a portion of his future retirement income into oil for the engine.

Unfortunately for him, we later discovered that Vegas were significantly flawed and became infamous for their flaws. Launched in 1970, *Motor Trend* magazine named it "Car of the Year for 1971." However, it suffered from poor design and corporate mismanagement. It had a rust problem, the gas tank could catch fire and explode, and the aluminum block overheated, causing it to burn oil. Don's Vega would have been fine, except that it guzzled oil, about a quart a week. But at least he now had wheels.

While living together in Burnaby we started having twin experiences. One day I hopped a transit bus and sat beside a nice-looking girl, who instantly started talking to me, thinking that I was Don. Neither of us had told any of our friends that we had a twin, so occasions like this became fun for us. Another time Don and I were in Vancouver and had gone into a McDonald's for a burger. As we were leaving, I paused for a second to zip up my jacket and stepped onto Granville Street a couple of steps behind him. Don was engaged in a discussion with one of the broadcasting students who thought he was me. This was the person that I would later rescue, stoned, from a sauna in the Yellowhead Inn in Prince George. He was a strange dude, and when I came up behind him and called him by name, he turned and shrieked. He literally looked back and forth between the two of us and started babbling. We had to take him back inside and buy him a coffee and calm him down; he most likely freaked because he was stoned.

So, I decided it was time to bring Don with me to BCIT and introduce him to my friends, as well as show him around the broadcasting studios. Our studios were on the second floor of the building and the first guy we saw was one of my best friends, Rod. He was sitting with his back to us, editing audio tapes he had recorded, I said: "Hey, Rod." He swivelled in his chair and saw us leaning on either side of the door frame. The look on his face was priceless and other friends came around to see what was going on, and we had a gas. When we decided to leave, I told Don I would meet him downstairs, and I said a final goodbye to Rod and then started down the stairs to meet Don. A girl turned at the first landing, heading up the stairs as I was going down, and she stopped dead in her tracks, looking over her shoulder down the stairs and back up at me, and asked, "How did you do that?" Obviously, she had bumped into Don going down the stairs ahead of me. I simply replied, "I am fast," and continued down the stairs.

Unfortunately, we only were able to live together for that single term as Don decided to enrol in the University of Victoria the next term, and we had to give up that wonderful basement suite. The following year I got a room in a student residence (without meals) and primarily lived off Cheez Whiz and bread, or Big Macs, or greasy cheeseburgers from the Villa bar, and copious amounts of beer (depending on the week). Fortunately, my friends Rod and John were married, and their wives would invite me over for a proper meal occasionally.

A few years later Don had become a hairdresser and moved to Ontario to work at a shop near Burlington. After about ten years, he returned for a brief period to Victoria and bought his own shop, only to close it about a year and a half later, returning to Ontario, but this time moving about two hours east of Toronto to a small community named Harrington. My favourite memory of Harrington was going out to see Don in February 2007 for our fiftieth birthday. I had flown out that weekend to Toronto for a business trip and was able to go to his home in Harrington before returning to Vancouver. No one in Harrington was aware that Don had an identical twin, and we thought it would be fun if I wandered around town with his husband Sean, popping into shops and pretending to be Don. There had been an article in the local newspaper about his upcoming fiftieth birthday, so everywhere I went, shop owners around town greeted me with a "Happy fiftieth, Don!" I would then introduce myself as his twin brother Larry. That evening there was a large gathering at their place. I decided it would be fun to answer the doorbell and was greeted by hugs and kisses from people who thought I was Don. It was a great party and really fun to be a twin again, if only for the moment.

Four years later he came to my rescue, taking a week away from his business and flying to Vancouver to help me through the trauma of the end of my first marriage of nearly thirty-three years. He was wonderful. His support, love, and generosity meant everything to me, and I will be eternally grateful.

Mom

<u>Album Cut</u>:
"Loves Me Like A Rock"
Paul Simon
***There Goes Rhymin' Simon*, released 1973**

IT WOULD BE SIMPLE TO say that my first great love would be my mother, May. Sadly, I never fully appreciated that fact until I was an adult and a father, and worse yet until after she died, and I could no longer see her or talk with her. Twenty-one years since her passing, I miss her and respect what she did to raise me more each day.

I distinctly remember talking with her on the phone; it was a Wednesday evening in the spring of 2000. Mom had turned sixty-five on January 1 and seemed to be fine. We spoke every few weeks on the phone, and I had not talked with her for a while. After we'd exchanged chitchat, I noticed that she seemed to be slurring her words a little. She had stopped drinking years earlier, so I asked if she felt all right, and she simply replied that she was okay, she was just "a little tired." I called Eve the next day, as she lived only minutes from Mom, and told her I was worried and asked her to see Mom. On Friday she called and said that Mom had gotten a little worse and she had taken her to the family doctor who thought she may have suffered a small stroke, and recommended a CAT scan, but it would take weeks. I told Eve that she should take Mom to the emergency room at the Duncan Regional Hospital, and they would have to deal with her right away. The next morning at about 5:30 a.m. Peter called and woke me to tell me to get on the next ferry to the Island. A doctor in the emergency ward had diagnosed Mom with brain cancer.

It was impossible to process. I threw a bag of clothes together, jumped in the car, and headed to Horseshoe Bay in West Vancouver to board the first ferry to Nanaimo. I was beside myself the whole way. Between moments of panic, despair overwhelmed me in thinking about Mom's diagnosis. When I arrived at the emergency room I found Eve, Rose, and Peter there; Don was in Ontario going through his own shock and disbelief. The doctor quickly took Peter and me into a small office and broke the worst possible news: Mom's cancer was terminal, she had too many tumours to treat and had only about six months to live. He explained that some of the tumours were larger and were pressing on parts of her brain, causing the slurring in her voice. The doctor, Peter, and I went to her bed in the emergency room, and with all of us gathered round her the doctor told her she had cancer and had only months to live. It was the only time before she died, six weeks later, that I heard her cry; a wail that came from her Irish roots and coursed through her like electricity. It was devastatingly heartbreaking for me.

Tragedy had already befallen our family, as my dad the week before had suffered a heart attack and was also in the hospital three floors above, waiting for heart bypass surgery. He had no idea what had happened to Mom or that she was in an emergency room bed. After composing herself, Mom asked an orderly to take her in a wheelchair up to see Dad. Nurses got Dad up into his own wheelchair and they reunited in a small waiting room. We left them alone, facing each other in their wheelchairs to talk. I can only imagine their conversation. The emergency room doctor released Mom shortly afterwards, and Dad came home days later following his heart surgery. We mobilized to provide support and care for them, with Peter and Eve taking on the lion's share, both living within minutes from their home. Six weeks later, on June 10 at 7:00 p.m., when the call came in from the hospital from Eve that Mom had passed away, Dad sat in his chair with his head slumped and his shoulders sagging, and said quietly, "I have lost my best friend."

During the few weeks past her diagnosis and prior to her death, Mom lost the sight in one eye and the use of her right hand. Her family quickly arrived from northern BC and Alberta, and siblings who had not visited Lake Cowichan for years found themselves in her living room. I can see Mom sitting in a chair by the window, light streaming in around her. She laughed and joked and enjoyed herself. I wondered later if the tumours had made her forget the doctor's prognosis, or if she was just being irrepressible Mom and was making the best of her situation.

I understand now that loss and grief are painfully unique experiences, that every person follows their path at different paces and depths. Until the moment Mom died, I never let myself acknowledge that she would. Intellectually, I understood perfectly what the doctors had said; emotionally, I was in total denial. My siblings accepted her fate more quickly and could not understand why I could not. Mom had been whisked to the hospital by ambulance a week earlier, and we were taking turns being with her at the hospital, two of us at a time. On the day she died, Don and I were set to change with Eve and Rose at 8:00 p.m. In the interim we were in Dad's living room, and there was a hockey game on the TV. Don was fidgeting and impatient but did not tell me what he wanted. So, when Eve called at 7:00 p.m., Don was devastated that he had not been with Mom when she passed away.

Once at the hospital, everyone else went into Mom's room to see her. I could not bear to go in. I felt coerced and pressured to walk into the room by a sibling, and my vision of Mom lying back in her hospital bed will never leave me. I hardly crossed the threshold into the room and backtracked quickly into the hall. After spending the time my siblings needed with Mom, the family decided to leave, and I refused. I was inconsolable. Peter's wife, my favourite sister-in-law Jan, volunteered to stay with me. I could not bear the thought of abandoning my mom and could not leave the hospital. I was adamant it was wrong to simply walk away from her while she was still in her hospital bed. Finally, I agreed to leave when an orderly took her from her room on a gurney. I insisted on accompanying her as long as I could, and Jan and I saw her off at a lower level where an orderly took her away from me forever. I collapsed against Jan in the elevator, sobbing inconsolably. We made our way to my car in the hospital parking lot, and Jan offered to drive. A man stepped out of the shadows of his vehicle in front of ours, asking for a booster jump as his car battery had died. On instinct I started to rummage in my trunk for jumper cables, not really comprehending what I was doing, when Jan came to my rescue. She told the man that I had just lost my mom and that she was sorry, but we could not help him. I sagged into the passenger seat, relieved. Jan had always been my favourite, and I loved her as a sister, but the bond I had with her deepened in a profound way after that night. I have healed from the loss of my mom but will never fully recover.

Josh

<u>Album Cut</u>:
"Born to be Wild"
Steppenwolf
***Steppenwolf*, released 1968**

JOSH WOULD BE THE ONE to make the long pilgrimage with me, to return Mom back to her family in Spirit River, Alberta. Shortly after Mom had passed, Dad wisely told us that he wanted us to bring Mom's ashes to Alberta so her family could bury her in her hometown, thousands of kilometres away. He said, "Once I am gone, your mom's family will be all that you have left." He felt it would force us to connect with them from time to time by travelling there to her graveside.

It was now mid-August, a couple of months since Mom had died, and the timing seemed right for our trip. There had been a memorial tea in Lake Cowichan within days of Mom's passing, so my siblings decided they would not make the journey with Josh and me.

We piled camping gear, including a tent, sleeping bags, and a cooler chest with drinks and food for our journey into the back of my pickup truck and started on our 1,200-kilometre drive. As we approached Abbotsford, about an hour from home, I said to

Josh, "We have to turn around and go home," and signalled to take the upcoming highway exit. Josh asked why, and I said, "I forgot something." He pressed me on what could be so important that we had to turn around, and I said that we had "left Grandma behind." I had gathered all of our gear and food, and yet the box with Mom's ashes was still in my bedroom closet.

An hour later I pulled back into our driveway, opened the garage doors, and ran inside to grab the box from the closet. On the way back I stopped and grabbed a couple of popsicles from the freezer in the garage and returned with the box and treats. Josh was shocked and asked me if Grandma had been in the freezer the whole time. I laughed and to his immense relief I told him about the closet. We both agreed that Mom would have had a great laugh about the whole affair.

Mid-route on our journey we spent a memorable night at Barkerville. Gold miners chasing fortune from the California goldfields found their way to the BC Interior in the mid-1800s, among them William "Billy" Barker, who had had little success to that point. Wandering down Williams Creek further than anyone else, Billy struck gold on August 17, 1862. The town that sprang up then has been preserved as both a Provincial and National Historic Site today. We decided to stay in a campsite adjacent to the town and then spent a day having fun. Barkerville is still one of the largest living museums in North America. Actors in period costumes wander through and work among over one hundred twenty-five buildings, including a saloon, restaurants, and a courthouse nestled in the forest. You can pan for gold, ride a stagecoach, or wander around at your leisure.

We arrived on a pleasant afternoon, late August sunshine still warming the air. After setting up our tent, we unloaded our camp stove and portable barbecue, and enjoyed hamburgers for dinner. Rather than cleaning up right away, we relaxed by tossing a small football back and forth and chatted casually about our trip. The sun dimmed, and I looked up to the sky, noticing that half the sky had disappeared behind rapidly approaching clouds. They were so ominous looking we immediately started packing our cooking paraphernalia and threw everything into the back of our truck, under the canopy as quickly as we could. It was fortunate that we had decided to set up our tent before making dinner. No sooner had we dived into the tent and zipped it up, the sky opened, and the rain poured incessantly for hours. Using our lantern, we played cards and tried to stay above water. In the midst of the storm, we heard someone call us from outside of our tent. Cautiously, so as to not let too much moisture in, I unzipped enough to see who could possibly be out in this weather. A camp ranger was in the process of going campsite to campsite collecting the camping fee. Dressed in rain apparel, with water pouring off his hat and drops falling from his nose, he patiently waited for payment. The cash we offered him went quickly into a plastic bag, he gave us a receipt, and then he was off to another campsite. I admired his dedication to his task. The next morning, we woke to silence. The pounding of rain on our tent had finally stopped. We scrambled out to take stock and found the clouds had disappeared and the prospect of an enjoyable day was looking bright.

We were damp and freezing. Barkerville is nestled 1,240 metres in the Cariboo Mountains, an hour drive east of Quesnel but at three times the elevation, and our summer clothing had not fared us well. I made an easy decision to abandon our campsite and head into the historic town for breakfast. We found a quaint restaurant that served hot chocolate, steaming coffee, and enormous buckwheat pancakes with bacon. It was one of the most satisfying meals ever. After spending a memorable day in Barkerville, our tent had dried, so we packed up and headed down the mountain to our next stop in Prince George. As luck had it, the sky opened up again, this time depositing so much hail that I had to pull over and watch. In moments hail had covered the road in a frosty, white blanket. It was a reminder that even in August, the mountains can give you a preview of the coming winter.

In Canada, Spirit River is the birthplace of my mother's family. My great-grandparents arriving from County Donegal, Ireland in 1912 had accepted the challenge of taming the wilderness to build a farm and a family. Under the Dominion Lands Policy, 160 acres cost only ten dollars, but the homesteader had to build a house, often of log or sod, and cultivate a specified area within three years. Horses were too expensive, and the absence of proper roads made the backbreaking work of removing rocks, boulders, trees, and stumps to develop arable farmland even more challenging. Many failed in their efforts and gave up their land. My great-grandparents stayed, and my grandparents continued farming for decades with the help of their sixteen children.

Her family lovingly and quietly laid Mom to rest at White Mountain, minutes outside of Spirit River. Kilometres down dusty gravel farm roads, the cemetery sits peacefully with alder trees bordering farmland on all sides. We all stood quietly with the minister alongside her grave, mourning the devastating loss of a sister, a mother, and a grandmother.

With the assistance of my Uncle Harry, we lowered her box gently into place, and as it rested on the bottom, I broke down completely, inconsolable. When I was able to finally stand up, he helped me to my feet, and I leaned against him for support. We had brought a cassette tape with one of Mom's favourite songs, "Whispering Pines." With a slight breeze rustling the leaves in the alders, and her family quietly standing together for support, we heard Johnny Horton's voice carry over the prairie; the lyrics touching our hearts:

My darling is gone, oh she's gone
And I need your sympathy
Whispering pines, send my baby back to me

I was so devastated that I could not drive, so Uncle Lindsay drove us back to the family farm and everyone sat around the tiny home, sharing stories and food, and solidifying a bond for generations to come. Josh was only fourteen, and I am sure that his experience was profound and memorable; he saw his dad at his most vulnerable and brought to his knees by grief, but he also experienced the love and strength of a family pulling together.

Josh was the "easy child." Born at 8:35 in the morning, on a quiet August day in 1986 at the Nanaimo Regional Hospital, he slept through the night within weeks. As a child, he was obedient, quiet, and happy. My dad had a habit of telling my brothers and me that at any given moment one of us was his favourite. It was all in jest, and none of us took him seriously; but, for the record, I would like to establish that I love my boys equally, but like them differently.

I cannot for the life of me remember what it was, but Josh did something unsafe one day, and I gave him a swat on his diapered bottom as a warning; he was heartbroken. I never spanked him again. When he was in grade two, he said something mean to me at home one afternoon, and he could see the hurt and disappointment in my expression. An hour later he came back with a handwritten note, saying he was sorry for hurting my feelings.

He did become a procrastinator, putting things aside to the last minute. In grade six he agreed to go into a French Immersion program, in part so he could take band. His interest was in playing the drums, but the band teacher selected another child and instead he became a trumpet player. He made us proud by continuing with his trumpet until he graduated, and then he never played another note.

Catherine

<u>Album Cut</u>:
"I Can Help"
Billy Swan
***I Can Help*, released 1974**

SOMETIMES IN LIFE YOU DO not appreciate what or who you have right in front of your eyes; it is tragic that youth and immaturity can blind us. Although I had crushes on girls through elementary and secondary school (Linda, Karen, and Jennifer stand out), I had only one girlfriend. Catherine was fun, had a wonderful laugh, a smile that could light up a room, was pretty, and I liked her family. Her home in Youbou was like my home in camp: small and welcoming. Catherine had three brothers, but no sisters. Her parents liked me, and my parents liked her. We were inseparable through grades eleven and twelve and went to our graduation together. I remember going to a house party with Catherine in Youbou one weekend in grade twelve. Catherine did not drink, but foolishly I had too many rum and cokes and got drunk very quickly. When friends decided to move the party to another house down the hill and across the street from where we were, I was too drunk to stand. Friends carried me, one guy holding my hands and one my feet. Because I felt like I was going to be sick, I asked them to put me down. So, there I am, lying on my back in the mud and in darkness, with rain pounding into me, trying not to be sick. After a couple of minutes, they picked me up and managed to get me to the next party. I remember lying there on a couch, saying over and over again, "I love you, Catherine. I love you, Catherine." Not even close to my finest moment, and yet, she was there for me.

She wanted to be a mother, raise a family, and stay on Vancouver Island, and I wanted to go to the city to BCIT and chase my dream of being a radio DJ. Rather than doing the sensible thing, talking with her, and making plans for our future, I stupidly saw no way around our problem and broke up with her at the end of the school year. Years later, while working at a logging camp, I met her future husband, and I was happy to find that he was a nice guy. Fifteen years ago, I connected with Catherine on the internet and found they were still happily married decades later, with children and grandchildren. I was incredibly happy for her and will always hold her in my heart.

Getting It Together (Fishing and Louise)

<u>Album Cut</u>:
"Crazy Love"
Van Morrison
***Moondance*, released 1970**

I DO NOT BELIEVE THERE is a man on the planet who is a "natural" husband; as the old saying goes, we are "works in progress." After the failure of my first marriage after almost thirty-three years, I was so broken and dejected that I could never see myself getting married again. I had just turned fifty-four years old and was a mess physically and emotionally. My dad had recently died, my doctor had told me I was clinically obese, the osteoarthritis in my right hip was tormenting me, and I had moved into a condominium on my own, finding myself solitary for the very first time in decades. Wholly unattractive, any way you looked at it.

When I decided to move out of the basement of our townhouse and leave my married life behind, it was one of the most difficult and painful experiences of my life. I remember signing a one-year lease on a condominium, going out to my car, sitting in the driver's seat, and crying my eyes out. The physical act of moving my belongings to my new place was only slightly less traumatic. Sleeping in the condominium, on my own for the first time since working in Western Mines when I was a teenager, was terrible. I had a radio by my bedside and tried to listen to music to fall asleep but found that half the songs were about breaking up. Gad.

It took my doctor telling me that it was my choice whether to change my life and situation. It was up to me whether I wanted to be a "victim or not"; in other words, to "get my act together." So, with considerable effort and consistency over months, including daily exercise and the Canada Food Guide, I brought my weight down by thirty pounds and gradually got better physically. Emotionally I was still struggling, but after I'd lived alone for about six months, my younger son Josh moved in with me for the next year. Don also came out for a week from Harrington at about the same time to help me by hanging pictures and hanging around. My life slowly began to have balance again, and I started to feel more normal. I could go to a movie or out for breakfast on my own without feeling weird.

About a year and a half after the implosion of my marriage, I realized I did not want to live my life alone, and the thought of dating came to me for the first time. Although not divorced, my ex and I had finalized a separation agreement and were legally unentwined. But at fifty-five it was a scary prospect to date after so many years. Although I had scoffed at online dating, I realized the computer might provide the fastest way to meet someone. After researching online platforms, I settled on Plenty of Fish. Using a tripod and camera before work one morning, I took a variety of pictures of myself, and with the help of my sons wrote up commentary. After posting my own profile, it was time to search for someone who struck my interest.

Pictures of women posing with motorcycles or with alcohol were immediately passed over. I put an age parameter of five years younger than me to five years older than me. It was an interesting experience, to say the least. Dates usually ended within the span of one cup of coffee, as it was readily apparent there was no fit. A couple went longer but fizzled. One lady was quite attractive, and I found her interesting, but I knew she was not my soulmate. It was apparent, however, that she was interested in a sexual relationship. I came to realize that I was not the kind of man who wanted casual sex, and never really had been. I could not see myself "playing the field," as friends encouraged me to do. So, I kept looking.

The picture that finally caught my attention was of an attractive woman posing at an ice arena, wearing a long winter coat and a colourful scarf, her long red hair flowing over her shoulders, with a warm smile and sparkling eyes. To be honest, I cannot remember a single word of her profile but will never forget her picture. Louise and I started talking on the phone; I loved the sound of her voice and quickly found that we had similar life philosophies and values. She grabbed my attention and made me laugh. When we decided to meet, she chose a nice burger place situated beside the Fraser River, midway between our homes. We agreed to meet for the first time on a Saturday evening at 7:00 p.m. Earlier that day a good friend had invited me to go with him to the LPGA event at the Vancouver Golf and Country Club. It was a historic day for golf and for me. I was able to watch New Zealander Lydia Ko play through. The next day she went on to win the tournament; a bespectacled, fifteen-year-old high school student, beating the field by three shots, making history by becoming the youngest winner of an LPGA tourney. She turned pro the next year, returned to win the tournament, and became a sensation on the circuit. Seven years later in 2019, she became only the seventeenth player to earn over ten million dollars in winnings.

At the restaurant, disaster almost struck. I had arrived early (I hate being late for anything) and told the host who greeted me that I was expecting to meet a nice lady for the first time and gave a brief description based on her picture. She seated me at a patio table in the sunshine with a frosty glass of ice water in front of me and where I could watch people arriving. I was a little nervous and kept looking at my watch. I started to worry that I had the time wrong, and when it was after 7:00 p.m. and she had not arrived, I started fidgeting a bit. I was about to get up out of my seat and talk with the host when I saw Louise approaching. She walked purposefully, had a ready smile, and was even prettier than her picture had shown, and I was instantly smitten. However, there was a slight frown that came with the smile. It seemed that when she arrived at the restaurant, she also explained to the host that she was meeting someone. Unfortunately, the host replied that there was no one there waiting! Apparently, there were multiple hosts, and we had each spoken with a different one. She told me later that she was about to leave but decided to walk out to the patio to take a look for herself. To say it was fortunate that she did so is an understatement. We have now been together nine years and married for six, and I am deeply grateful every day that she is in my life. What if she had simply left and gone home?

It was a great evening. Previously I had found that these first dates were as long as it took to drink a cup of coffee, and certainly less than an hour. Louise and I spent the whole evening getting to know each other. We talked for over an hour and then ordered dinner. After dessert we walked out along the pier and watched boats move by on the Fraser River under the stars of a warm evening. After about three hours, we reluctantly had to part. I walked Louise to her car, not sure how to end the evening. When I had dated three decades earlier, it was polite to not kiss a girl on the first date, and now in my fifties I did not know what was acceptable. Louise made it easy for me. She said, "Well, are you going to kiss me or not?" There was only one answer. Days later, we had our second date, visiting the planetarium and then sitting on a bench, watching a gorgeous sunset transforming the sky from pink to orange and then to red, slowly sinking into the ocean. I kissed her happily without having to be asked this time.

I knew Louise was the right person for me, and now I wanted to spend my free time with her. Our first date had been at the end of July, and now it was late August. I left on my annual camping trip with a friend to Kentucky Lake outside of Merritt. Kentucky is a gorgeous lake, two and a half kilometres long, with sparkling, turquoise waters, perfect for kayaking and fishing. I kayaked, and my friend Rich fished for trout. Rich and I had been friends for years, and he and his wife had also been friends with my ex-wife, so I hesitated before bringing Louise up. The campsite was rustic, and there was no cellphone service unless you backtracked to the main road three kilometres away. So, without explanation, I told Rich I was going to head up the road to make a call. Of course, I wanted to talk with Louise and let her know how much I missed her. After a couple of times leaving to make a call, I needed to let Rich know what I was doing. We sat by the campfire on the second morning drinking coffee, when I told him I had been dating and that I had fallen for Louise. Rich is a Newfoundlander, soft-spoken and easygoing, with a practical outlook, and he was happy for me. It felt good to tell someone, and he was someone I could trust.

When the trip was over and I got home, I stowed my tent and camping gear away for the year, had a shower to wash away the grime and smoke from camping, and went over to her place. It was a grand reunion.

By November I knew that I wanted to move closer to Louise, and I recognized my current rent was too high for my budget. I moved to a condominium in Richmond, signing a one-year lease, which gave me a fifteen-minute shorter drive to work, put me in closer proximity to Louise, and saved me about three hundred dollars per month in rent, which I needed to put away for my retirement. I had not come away particularly well financially from my separation. At the same time my arthritis in my right hip was getting unbearable, and after a surgeon's consult it was determined I would need hip replacement surgery. Fortunately, I had kept up with my exercise and new life plan and had dropped an additional ten pounds.

Apart from my increasing pain and lessening of mobility, everything was going great. Louise and I were spending more time with each other, and her wonderful Wheaten terrier Connor and I became pals. Early in our relationship, Connor would jump on the couch and sit between us, protecting Louise. Later he would sit beside me so Louise and I could cuddle, and we became soulmates too.

In July, a year after we met, my property owner gave me notice that he wanted to break our lease early so he could rent the condominium to family. It put me in an interesting position. I knew that if I insisted on staying that he would kick me out in November at the end of my one-year lease anyway. I was also keenly aware the surgeon had scheduled my hip surgery for January. I agreed to move out at the end of August in return for free rent for a month and a half, which helped me offset my moving costs. The question was where to move next. Again, Louise made my decision simpler by suggesting I move in with her, in part because she wanted to be there as support after my surgery and also because she knew we were going to stay together. This was a big step and a significant acknowledgement that our relationship had moved to a more serious level. There was a time when both of us had said we would never get married again, after the trauma of our respective marriages ending badly. Louise was fifty-five and I was fifty-six, and it seemed like we were teenagers. We held hands, laughed, had fun, and got to know each other more deeply every day. Two years later, when we were married, friends marvelled at how much we loved each other, and for years referred to us as "honeymooners." I have never laughed more nor had more fun than with Louise. We had date nights every week and would pick a spot to go and explore, whether Honey Doughnuts in Deep Cove, Fort Langley for a burger, or a "fall foliage" drive up to Manning Park. She is an amazing travelling companion, and we have had fabulous adventures travelling through the Maritime provinces in Canada, doing a bus tour in Ireland, taking a car trip through Switzerland, France, and Germany, spending a week in Mexico, and on weekend getaways among the islands near to us, including Bowen, Mayne, and San Juan.

I had always wanted to be on stage and imagined myself doing so as part of a rock band. As I could not sing or play a musical instrument, radio had filled that void. Life has a way of turning slowly, and at sixty years of age, I started playing the guitar. After four years of practice and persistence, I finally stood on a small stage in front of an audience of family and friends and played with a band. Three acoustic guitars and an electric Fender Telecaster guitar now hang on a wall in my office ("Studio A" as I refer to it), and I have fulfilled a lifetime dream, in no small part due to love, patience, and encouragement from Louise.

We often speculate what our lives would have been like if we had met in our twenties, but I have come to believe that we meet people at different stages of our lives for specific reasons. Although I am confident that we would have made a good life from our twenties on, this was the time when we were meant to meet. I have never been happier, laughed as much, or been so much in my groove.

Finally

<u>Album Cut</u>:
"Circle"
Harry Chapin
***Sniper and other Love Songs*, released 1972**

OUR FAMILY DOCTOR DIAGNOSED DAVID with a life-threatening disorder called ITP (Idiopathic Thrombocytopenic Purpura) when he was fourteen. ITP is a blood disorder characterized by a decrease in the number of platelets in the blood. We had noticed he had bruises all over his body and questioned him as to whether he had fallen or been in an altercation, and he told us emphatically, "No." A couple of days later we noticed more bruising, including on his ears, and that is when we took him to see our family doctor. One look at David and the doctor said, "Take him to the hospital immediately, and I will meet you there." His concern was that David's symptoms presented in a way that could have indicated lymphoma or leukemia. Unfortunately, at fourteen, David was hitting his more obnoxious teen years, when he argued and fought against most everything. The family doctor told him that if he did not go voluntarily, he would force him to go via ambulance, so David came with us. His body fought also, struggling to get the

ITP under control, and after two failed blood transfusions we had discussions about possible surgery to have his spleen removed. Fortunately, on the third transfusion, his body finally cooperated, and he quickly rebounded. What started then and continues to this day is a skepticism about doctors of any kind—"quacks," as he referred to them back then. David's had been an emergency caesarean birth; he even fought about leaving the womb peaceably. I heard him cry for the first time at 1:36 p.m. in 1981, and becoming a dad was one of the most profound and joyous moments of my life. I remember sitting on the floor in our living room with my back against the stereo cabinet in our apartment in Nanaimo on the day we brought him home from the hospital, and the enormity of being responsible for David almost overwhelmed me in the moment.

My dad was old-school European; you never went to the doctor "unless you were dying." Preventive medicine was not something he understood. Dad would insist that we attend school with colds, the flu, or other maladies unless we were too sick to get up. Unthinkable today.

At eighteen, during my first year at BCIT, I decided to donate blood for the first time. A couple of weeks later I received a letter from the Canadian Red Cross telling me that I had Hepatitis B and should see a doctor immediately, and that they would not allow me to donate again. To be honest, it scared the daylights out of me. I made an appointment with the campus doctor, and the decision was for me to have follow-up blood tests indefinitely from that point on. At about the same time, I had to have a physical exam to be able to do my parachute jump. The receptionist led me into an examining room at the campus clinic, told me to remove my clothes, and advised that the doctor would see me soon. Minutes later, a woman in a white coat came in, and I realized that she was the doctor about to perform the first physical of my life. Being eighteen and shy, I was both surprised and embarrassed. I must confess that she was thorough and did a complete review, including checking my testicles. I now knew what to expect in future physical exams (cough, please, Larry).

So, unlike my father, I embraced preventive medicine and health care. My family doctor has been taking care of me now for over twenty-five years and has referred me to specialists when I have needed them, including chiropractors, osteopaths, physiotherapists, psychologists, and mental health counsellors. All good by me.

Like countless others, I have been through emotional and mental trauma throughout my life, including workplace harassment, the breakdown of my first marriage followed two weeks later by my dad's passing away, and, most significantly, the sudden and tragic death of my mom. I am not ashamed to say that I have been clinically depressed and got better only through counselling and with the assistance of a support group. Although I am an eternal optimist by nature, episodic depression has still crushed me more than once. It is wonderfully gratifying to be whole, at peace, and content today.

My parents taught us early to be resilient and to take care of ourselves. My father was the strong (but loving) figure that I admired and emulated. He taught me to stand on my own two feet and be independent. It forced me to make decisions on my own, sometimes learning through failure. I became proud of the fact that life could knock me down and I could dust myself off and get back on my feet quickly. Full understanding that my success was not solely because of my own efforts, and that no one really does it on their own, came to me over years. In my enlightened position today, to describe myself as a "self-made man" would be unfair and rather arrogant. Throughout life, support comes from any combination of family, friends, clergy, and colleagues. Fortune has also blessed me with wonderful mentors along the way.

I have suffered migraine headaches my whole life, as did my mother before me, occasionally debilitating enough to require trips to emergency rooms where doctors gave me injections to ease my suffering. Over years I have practised a simple form of meditation, closing my eyes and focusing on my breathing—in and out, in and out—pushing external sounds and thoughts to the side. This has had the added benefit of slowing me down in general, helping me take life in longer, slower strides.

Over my life I have either modified or rejected ideas I previously felt strongly about. When I was younger, I was a proponent of capital punishment, and had written an editorial while at BCIT in which I said: "Hang 'em. Hang 'em high" (steely-eyed Clint Eastwood was my hero). Maturity and awareness of too many wrongfully convicted and incarcerated people have reversed my view. I believe that taking even one innocent life is the strongest argument for a total ban on executions and am proud that Canada banned the death penalty decades ago.

I have never understood why all people on Earth cannot recognize each other as equal. Colour does not mean a thing to me, sex and gender do not mean a thing to me, where you are from is irrelevant, and sexual orientation is of no consequence to me. To me we are all created equal as human beings, sharing our planet. My dad used to say that the prime minister is no better than any other man, because he also "puts his pants on, one leg at a time." Pierre Trudeau as a young justice minister said, "There's no place for the state in the bedrooms of the nation." Trudeau continued, "What's done in private between adults doesn't concern the *Criminal Code*." Equality and freedom for all.

I think back to the "politics" Mom faced within the thirty-five-family community of camp. Her generation has mostly passed on now, and with them all of the slights and differences that seemed so important in the moment. What are left are the fond memories of those who loved them all. That is really the key to life and love. If humanity could only grasp the reality described by the rock group Kansas—"Nothing lasts forever but the earth and sky"—then we would have the humility and focus to eliminate disparity, hate, suffering, and hunger; harmony and peace would be ours.

However, inequality does exist, and the world is not always fair. There should be laws ensuring employers treat women in the workforce fairly, providing equality in income and in opportunities. Pay should be based on the specific job, and on performance. Years ago, I heard a female speaker at a conference posit that one reason that women are at a disadvantage is because they have never been trained to ask for a raise in pay. From early on in my working life, I learned to effectively ask employers for wage increases, mostly with success. I came to understand what to focus on and how to present my position. The speaker indicated that women believed that their employer was paying them fairly, and that they would be given an increase when the company felt it was appropriate. Men would bang on the door and ask for more.

Human history from start to finish is sadly predictable. The driving forces of men are greed, position, and power. You have something I want; I will take it. To do so I will grab a stick to hit you with, sharpen it into a spear and throw it at you, make a bow to kill you from further away, trade the bow for a musket, the musket for a Gatling gun, the Gatling gun for a nuclear bomb. And on it goes. Men made the rules, men determined that women could not vote, or drive, or go out for a drink without male accompaniment. I have lived my life with a profound sense of fair play, and a sense of outrage against those who take advantage. I am convinced that rules keep us from anarchy, and that every qualification we make to justify our breaking them, leads us toward chaos. At the same time, I believe in the power of peaceful protest and the freedom to speak. Especially in the face of tyrants and despots and those who have the power to decide who eats and who starves, who gets medicine and who dies, and who stays at home and whom they march off to war.

Yet we men have had our shining examples too: Da Vinci, Gandhi, Vivaldi, Mandela, Rembrandt, King Jr., and Banting.

There are good men, decent men, good husbands, and fathers. One of my favourite film scenes is from the movie *Saving Private Ryan*." Ryan is now an old man, surrounded by his wife, children, and grandchildren at a cemetery in France. He falls to his knees at the headstone of a man who gave his life to save his, who had told young Ryan in his last words, "Earn this." Ryan asks his family (and himself), "Have I led a good life?" and, "Am I a good man?"

These words resonate with me, and hopefully the answer will be kind. My friends and family will be the ones to balance my missteps, failures, and times of bad behaviour against the goodness and love that I have shared. I believe that I have always been a good man, and to be a better man I know I must continually work at it, embrace innovative ideas, respect the perspectives of others, and evolve. I would be satisfied with an epitaph that read: "A good man, who always strived to be better."

I have come to understand that nature hates neutrality. Nothing stays the same; it either thrives or dies. If you do not water your plant, it dies. If you never call your friend, the relationship ends. I have despaired in the past about lost friends, people I cared deeply about who have vanished from my life. Now I understand that people come in and out of our lives at various times for different purposes, and sometimes leave forever. Charlotte was there with me at the hospital in Nanaimo when Kelley suffered a miscarriage. I had tried to be brave and not let my emotions show to calm my wife, but once she fell asleep, I went out into the hallway in the hospital, feeling broken, and there was Charlotte coming to support her best friend. I told her that Kelley was sleeping, and then I broke down, weeping on her shoulder, the emotions of the day and the loss crashing over me in a wave. Yet, we later moved to Toronto and lost touch with Charlotte and her husband, and I have not seen her in more than thirty years.

At sixty-four, I still feel young, although my body frequently disagrees with me. I now have seen friends my age pass away, including recently my best friend Davey. My parents' generation is quietly disappearing, and it draws me into thoughts of my own mortality. Not to say that I morbidly sit and fret daily about how little time I have left on planet Earth. But I do reflect on my life and legacy. It is so reassuring to know that I will live the rest of my life with someone I cherish beside me. I have had a good life and look forward to another twenty to thirty years with Louise, all things going favourably. I am the sum of all of my experiences, good and bad, and am content with who I am. I believe my mom and dad would be proud of me, and that is what matters the most.

What comes afterwards? Brooks and Dunn in their song "Believe" sing: "They tell me that there's more to life / Than just what I can see / I believe." Although my mom sent us to Sunday School in Lake Cowichan with our cousins when we were quite young, religion never stuck. I deeply respect those of faith and admire their strength. I have stood in Saint Martin's church in Colmar, France, drawn in by the sounds from within. It was built between 1235 and 1365, with foundations dating back to the year 1000; the centuries weighed on me. I watched in silence and listened in awe to the singing of the priest at the altar, his words in French meaningless to me, but the power of his voice resonating through the expanse of the church was overwhelming. For centuries someone like him had stood in that very same spot, singing, and worshipping with others, and it seemed like I was in that moment a part of history.

I struggle mightily with organized religion. Inquisitions and Crusades, Muslims vs. Jews, Protestants vs. Catholics, brother against brother. As religion expanded over history and gained wealth, enormous power created hierarchies led exclusively by men; millions were killed in the name of God. Although I have visited Notre Dame Cathedral in Paris and marvelled, I am more drawn into the unpretentious churches found along quiet roads in smaller communities. I have joined in the joy of marriage and the sadness of funerals in my best friend's Sikh temple. I have enjoyed the most striking feature: people coming together in support and love.

I do believe in God. Humanity has always clung to the notion of a place after death. Cave sketches articulate this as clearly as the words in any book of faith or song.

There is absolutely no affirmative way of knowing this for a fact. It is faith in what comes next that unites and strengthens us. It shows us a path, a way of life, that accentuates good over evil and always insists on choosing to do the right thing.

I believe.

Printed in Canada